Why Men Hurt Women and Other Reflections on Love, Violence and Masculinity

Why Men Hurt Women and Other Reflections on Love, Violence and Masculinity

Kopano Ratele

WITS UNIVERSITY PRESS

Published in South Africa by:
Wits University Press
1 Jan Smuts Avenue
Johannesburg 2001

www.witspress.co.za

First published 2022

http://dx.doi.org.10.18772/12022097632

978-1-77614-763-2 (Paperback)
978-1-77614-764-9 (Hardback)
978-1-77614-765-6 (Web PDF)
978-1-77614-766-3 (EPUB)

This publication is peer reviewed following international best practice standards for academic
and scholarly books.

The financial assistance of the National Institute for the Humanities and Social Sciences
(NIHSS) towards this publication is hereby acknowledged. Opinions expressed and those
arrived at are those of the author and should not necessarily be attributed to the NIHSS.

NATIONAL INSTITUTE
FOR THE HUMANITIES
AND SOCIAL SCIENCES

Project manager: Lisa Compton
Copyeditor: Karen Press
Proofreader: Alison Lockhart
Indexer: Sanet le Roux
Cover design: Hybrid Creative
Typeset in 11.5 point Crimson

Contents

Foreword

Raewyn Connell

This is a remarkable book: troubling, moving and inspiring. It's a linked set of short narratives and essays, across a surprising range of topics: from a kids' football game in the street to rape myths, to the militarisation of police services. All are connected to the three great themes of love, violence and masculinity, and their paradoxical relationship.

The book works at several levels. Kopano talks about the emotions and uncertainties of relationship, with stories from his own life and work. He thinks aloud about the practicalities of feminist work, anti-racism and men's engagement in ending men's violence. At the same time he speaks of capitalism, corruption and economic inequality, colonisation and racism, and the patriarchal structures that oppress women and girls – but also damage the lives of men and boys.

This is a South African book, by an important South African public intellectual. Kopano grew up, as many others did, in an 'unforgiving environment'. He speaks of what he knows: the toxic racism of the apartheid regime, the massive economic inequalities that persist decades later, the terrifying levels of rape and murder that make South Africa one of the most dangerous countries for women and for men too. This gives urgency to his arguments. This is a discussion from which people everywhere can learn, for there is no place on earth that has yet achieved gender equality and social peace. Masculinities that are organised around power are found in every part of the world.

Reading through *Why Men Hurt Women and Other Reflections on Love, Violence and Masculinity*, I kept finding moments of insight that would deserve a whole book each. There are too many to list, but the reader might look out for these: boys' and men's need for care, and difficulty in giving it; the need for education of the emotions; the paradox of finding violence and love in the same place; the importance and difficulty of discussions about sexual consent; whether it's possible to forgive perpetrators of violence and abuse; 'peace' missions that end up killing children; what fathers' love can do for boys, and why so many men don't offer it.

Kopano is a researcher as well as a teacher and activist. He knows the demographic facts, he knows the value of good data and clear thinking. He is rightly sceptical of the idea of 'toxic masculinity', though understanding how women's anger is expressed in that phrase. He knows how race and class divisions work. He does not think all men are simply perpetrators or all women are simply victims. He knows that men and women have agency and the capacity to act differently. He knows also that growing up in a violent, power-drenched and deeply unequal environment makes more anger and violence likely. He knows that such a situation is very hard to change, and thinks that even a limited reduction in levels of violence is worth having.

Yet he has a larger hope, too. Indeed, it's implicit in the title. It is not *necessary* that men should hurt women, though the way masculinities are currently formed makes it likely that many will. Kopano proposes that love in its broadest sense – love as practical care, and as a cultural force – is a crucial part of the answer. To quote his text: 'love appears to me to be the most vital force against violence'. A simple concept, but very far from naïve – as you will see when you read this book. This is a book that deals with tough themes of life and death, truth and passion, justice and injustice, past and future. We urgently need thinking, and action, like this.

Part 1 | Love

Love:

(verb) dearly love, have love (only) for, love to distraction, adore, be sweet on, cherish, relish, treasure, hold dear, prize, value, esteem, have a high regard for, appreciate, like, desire, fancy, have a fancy for, have eyes for, go for, care for, have a soft spot for, have a weakness for, have a fondness for, hold in affection, make much of, revere, admire, idolize, worship, take pleasure in, delight in, take an interest in, feel for, think the world of, have a kind heart, have a kindness for, sympathize with.

—John Daintith, Elizabeth Martin, Fran Alexander and John Wright, eds.,
Bloomsbury Thesaurus

On passionate love:

Love certainly involves attachment and caring. But is that all? What about the agony of jealousy and the ecstasy of being loved by another person?

—John D. DeLamater and Daniel J. Myers, *Social Psychology*

Understanding is love's other name. If you don't understand you can't love.

—Thich Nhat Hanh, *How to Love*

1 | Why do women love men?

I have known Carmine for 27 years. It is longer than half of my life. We are having coffee. It's a Saturday morning. The sun is shining. We are sitting on the *stoep* [veranda]. We will move into the house at some point.

Why do you love me, I ask her?

Let me count the ways, she says.

We laugh.

I love you because you laugh at my jokes. When I saw you for the first time in Pretoria I thought: what a cute young man. You were so handsome with your dreadlocks. And then you opened your mouth. You know I like men who have brains. I don't like men who can't think.

When you are young and trying to have a close relationship, you tend to ask this question more often. Not so much later, when the burning passion of the first days has dissipated. Maybe it has something to do with life stages. Younger people may be more disposed to probe the meaning of intimacy, which is entwined with the meaning of identity and its development. The tendency to ask why one is loved is possibly more pronounced among individuals who have been influenced by a certain conception of love. This belief about love is defined by a molecular attention to the life of feelings, more broadly to psychological elements of love (as opposed to giving privilege to material acts such as washing dishes for another person). Feelings are, in this worldview, considered to contain the truth of intimate relationships. It may be of interest to note that such a consuming preoccupation with the psychology of love, the fine details of emotion, intimacy as something to be searched for, in fact originates in bourgeois Western society. In his influential theory of psychosocial development, ego psychologist Erik Erikson, whose name is associated with the concept of identity crisis, contends that following the adolescent wrestling with identity and role confusion, love becomes the central crisis of young adulthood. During this stage of the 'eight ages of man', which begins during late teenage years and young adulthood, young men and women turn toward the search for intimacy, 'the capacity to commit [oneself] to concrete affiliations and partnerships and to develop the ethical strength to abide by such commitments even though they may call for significant compromises'. If there is a lack of intimacy, young people are likely to experience isolation and loneliness.[1]

Like many young people, I used to ask the question quite a bit in my teens and twenties. I have not asked it in years, hopefully because I have, to a happy extent, successfully resolved the question of intimacy. Perhaps I have become more trusting of love itself. Perhaps it is because I love myself more than I used to back then. It may also be because I am feeling more psychologically secure in who I am as a man. These are just possible interpretations of how one becomes oneself; they are attempts to make sense of this process in hindsight, and cannot be taken for certainties.

When people are getting to know each other, the question of why one is loved arises more often than when they are used to one another – though there are always exceptions, of course. And, as I have said, the effort to understand ourselves and the person close to us – which is what this questioning is centrally about – by scrutinising what they might mean when they say they love us, in order to develop intimacy, is a very particular way of thinking about love. Though this view of love may originally have developed in the West, it is now part of our world, popularised in our society by, among other means, novels, films, glossy magazines and television series. This way of loving, *talking* about feelings, is more than encouraged. Even more importantly, individuals have to *reveal the self* by talking about it, rather than, for instance, showing it by taking practical care of a loved family member. The self is the response to the question, who are you?[2]

I am asking her to help me think.

She says, You get me.

I did not always get you, I respond.

I know. But as you say, 51 per cent is acceptable. You get me 51 per cent of the time. That's more than the time you don't get me.

Every person wants to be understood. I totally believe that. We want to be around people who get us.

I did not get her, it is true. Not at first. Not for a long time. I think that contributed to some of the relationship problems during that time. *Some* of them, because most of the problems were really me not wanting to commit. I used to say that I don't see the point of commitment to one person.

Philosophising about a long-term love is better done when you do not have one. Love is a complicated affair. It is many things. It changes. We change how we think of love. How we love. Whom we love and what we love about them. And as how and what we think of love changes, we too are changed.

People can and do get hurt in love relationships. When one person wants one thing and the other person wants another, there are only so many options available. You agree to live with the tension. One or both of you has to change. Or you go your separate ways. Sometimes it is because we love that we have to leave, let go.

In my head, she was this proper young woman in her blue outfit with big polka dots when we met. She had a fringe. She had not been involved in student politics. I found this unacceptable. I would find out much later that her brother was a dedicated trade unionist. She also could not speak any African language. Still, I thought we could have fun and have an early celebration of the new democratic dispensation just around the corner.

She did not want to have sex immediately. This was not going to work.

Ja, when you asked me what I thought about premarital sex, I thought, yes, cute, but what kind of pervert is this one?

I remember that. We had been in a workshop. We were supposed to role-play as interviewer and interviewee. When it was my turn to interview her, I asked her for her thoughts about premarital sex. Smooth.

It is not so much our age as the newness of a relationship that prompts us to want to find out what makes the other person love us. You are getting to know each other. Maybe, if you are perceptibly dissimilar, you are also surprised that this person loves you. Yet you don't always know what exactly it is they feel when they say 'I love you'. It can be confusing.

When I read back to her what I have written so that she can approve or change it, she says, It's not about the length of time that you know me. Isn't that true?

It's a private joke we share. Not a joke joke. We discuss this every time a year passes or we have to wish a friend happy anniversary. She rarely forgets people's anniversaries.

The quality of a marriage cannot be measured, in my assessment, simply by how long it has endured. What if for half of that time one of the partners has been abusing the other? What if one person believes he or she deserves more of a say in the home because they earn more? Or if, because he has paid *mahadi*,[3] a man harbours the sentiment that he can have sex with the woman whenever he wants it even if she does not feel like it? It is the quality, not the length, of the marriage that is all-important, though the word 'quality' is not really the right one – it is an ungainly way of speaking of the glue that holds the relationship together. You short-change yourself if you confuse being loved with being married. Love is more than a marriage-like or close filial relationship. Sometimes there is no love in marriage, or between child and parent. Indeed, in respect of marriage, understanding love as a form of passion is a relatively recent development and reason why humans marry each other. Bringing families together, having children, affording protection and making peace between tribes are some of the time-honoured reasons why people have joined in matrimony.

The discursive and bodily ensemble of acts, sensations, affects, connections and effects that we call love may or may not be found in a close relationship. While cultural in its stamp, love can be interpreted in so many different ways by different individuals and is often hard to articulate. And so, along with its recognisability, or its perceived deficiency or absence, in a family or other intimate sort of relationship, love may be an embodied narrative that manifests itself in fleeting encounters. Such encounters need not be sexual; they may occur in the course of political protests, in the workplace, in religious gatherings, in social clubs, or even in school classrooms. The discourse of love can be used to speak of sexual attraction or compatibility, prayer to God or the ancestors, or attraction to the material and physical assets of another person. It can refer to shared interests. It can indicate friendship. Support. Companionship. Understanding. So many other feelings, ideas, sensations, signs and practices.

She says, Ja, whatever. But of course not. Not when there is abuse.

We are having breakfast. Scones, two kinds of jam, strawberry and apricot, butter, margarine, Gouda cheese and tea.

I say, I like to think about humans and their relations with each other, and with other animals and the planet. But this book is about race, among other things. Could you say something about what we spoke about earlier and race – the relationship between love and race, that is?

It's quiet for a while.

I'm thinking, she says.

You're taking a long time to think. What are you thinking about?

I'm thinking about the connections.

Yes, please. Make clearer the connections between race and love, and violence and masculinity. These are four of the big issues whose links to each other I would like you to help me think about.

Maybe my pool of who to fall in love with wasn't that big.

We laugh out loud.

Ja, thank you very much. Thank you. You thought, 'in this sample of one, you are the best'.

We laugh some more.

The sample was rather small.

Thank you, I say again. I was the best of the worst.

I've only dated black men.

I think she implies that she cannot compare me with anyone else.

I ask, Why?

I don't know. I'm wondering now. I didn't have any white friends.

You have white friends now. Close acquaintances.

Who?

Cathy is white.

I wasn't going to date her husband.

Why not her?

I think I'm heterosexual.

But you have not had a thing with a woman? How can you rule out love with women?

I mean, I'm now with you. I guess I'm stuck.

We laugh some more.

When she speaks of being stuck, I am reminded of a friend of ours who identifies as bisexual but has been in a heterosexual marriage for decades. It seems to be working all right. I say, I must have a conversation with her about loving and marriage to a man. We have been speaking about knowing white people at this point.

What about white people when you started dating or looking for love? I ask.

I didn't know a lot of white people back then. I knew some white people. I think two of them were gay. Or three of them were gay. Four of them. No, I think the fourth one was not white.

As Jimmy Manyi might have said, the Western Cape was overpopulated with gay white people.[4]

So black men were your pool. What about your time at university? There were many black men around. I think that university was 99.9 per cent black.

She simply says, Ja.

She goes on to tell me about the men she knew while she was temping at a stationery shop.

There was a white man who used to come into the shop.

You liked him.

Mm. He used to buy me flowers and things.

That sounds like a dangerous one, I say. Or deluded. Or crazy. Like the guy in the old TV ad who brings flowers to the woman behind the counter at the car hire company because she does her job with a smile.

In fact, he is a well-known gynaecologist.

Oh, my goodness.

He used to come into the store all the time.

You know there is an important question here, I respond. Because you grew up around people who look a certain way, you are likely to find your partner among those people.

Exactly.

I say, When you realise that this may be because of the structure of the society in which you grew up, you can step back and ask, Am I attracted to this person because of where and how I grew up, or would I choose them even if I had not grown up with people like them?

She says, That is the funny thing, actually. How do you know someone? You think you know someone because they grew up similarly to you.

Mm.

So, I mean, we did not grow up similarly at all, she says about her and me. So you were a whole new kettle of fish.

Yup.

I never did date someone from our area, she goes on. The one person I dated was from Joburg, also a different kettle of fish. Joburg boys. Cape Town boys. But there was still, culturally, a similarity. I also knew where he was from, you know what I mean. I could identify. I knew, I recognised. You think you know where they come from. And you make certain assumptions. And choices on the basis of that. But there was another black man that I liked. He was my first – ah, not in the Biko or expanded definition of black. I can't tell you the story because you're going to put it in your book.

I say, Ja. I told you this.

So I won't tell you the story, she says.

This is not research, I say. It is a conversation that I will put in the book.

I'm not going to tell you about that story, she says again.

Okay, I say. You're hiding stuff from me, which is good.

I think I told you the story before, she says.

No, I don't remember it. I repressed it. Some stuff you don't want to know.

She says, He had a girlfriend. She is talking about the boy from Johannesburg. But he was very nice, she adds. As if boys from over there are suspect, I think.

The next question, I go on. You didn't know me. Because I am from somewhere else. I look nice. I might have been a *skelm* [scoundrel]. Potential murderer. Abuser. And by the way, it is not just physical abuse. I could have been one of those who put others down, telling you your hips are too big, or your bum is too small, you know? Or your colour is not the right one, I want you to be a little brighter or a little darker. And you had that unibrow thing going on there. Remember it?

And I had a fringe, she adds.

Yes, that fringe. Like some sort of early Michael Jackson.

You did use to say I had a Michael Jackson fringe.

I laugh.

And I still stuck around, I say.

You see, *that* is abuse. Write that in your book.

So, what are you saying about assessing the probabilities that I would not murder you? It really sounds ghoulish.

She replies, You draw on various things you look at, you're hoping that he's not a murderer. And I had very little to work with because, as you know, you were working on a 'share on a need-to-know basis'.

Yeah, I think I was. I was not very good at opening up in my twenties. Actually, I was terrible. Vulnerability and shame about how I grew up were locked in deep down. That could have turned out much worse than it did.

We get interrupted by the doorbell ringing. Someone asking for food or money. It's Siya. He usually comes around twice a week. We buy additional groceries for him. Today she prepares the food for him. One of us does this whenever he comes around. He likes cross-country running. He lives on his own in Philippi.[5] We've known him for years, since he was in primary school.

After some discussion about other things while she's preparing the food for the young man, our conversation resumes.

You were saying? I prompt her.

She says, I don't remember what I was saying. I was saying you need to know what you like, too. What your values are. What is non-negotiable for you.

I remind her of what she said earlier. You said you have to check the person in action with other people. You must know their parents, and their friends. I asked what if their parents are dead. You said, ja, but you must find out how they act when they are around other people. But you actually never fully know. That is what you said. I said I agreed. You can never fully know a person. You can only know the person's history up until yesterday, until a moment ago. They may have been good yesterday. The person may be funny, but when somebody makes a joke about them they turn violent. Or they are courageous in war but when you, as their partner, are in pain they cannot handle it. They fall apart. Even with a single quality, it might be expressed differently under different circumstances.

I ask, But you don't think I can hurt you, do you? That I can kill you?

I don't know. You *never* know. She stresses the words, dragging out 'never'. Maybe there are circumstances we haven't tested you under.

But the probabilities? I ask.

The probability is low, she responds. But there is always –

Ja, I know, I say.

There is always a chance, she says.

It may sound very strange. However, it is my view that talking like this, about almost everything, is the best guarantee, if there can ever be a guarantee, that there will be no murder in such a relationship.

I can hurt you emotionally, yes, I say. Not kill you.

I don't know, she says.

I don't feel that I'm capable of killing you.

You never know with perpetrators, she says.

You never actually know, I say. But why is that? I mean, is it the length of time –

I think I meant that even with the length of time you can never fully know what another person is capable of.

I would be shocked if you killed me.

She is referencing a private joke we heard about how Jamaican people talk of 'people waking up dead'.

I laugh.

You'd wake up dead.

We both laugh.

I would also be shocked if you killed me, I say. But hey, under duress, under extreme conditions, like if I was about to throw myself and your son off the bridge, you would shoot me.

Mm, she says. I probably would.

Is this macabre? It sounds like it when I read it afterward. You had to be in the kitchen while this was going on. I do not think an old married couple or even radical young lovers who love comedy speak about killing each other in this way.

So – what is your answer to the final question? I say.

What?

Why do black women love black men? What's your answer?

She says, I don't know. She is still preparing the package of food. I don't know, she repeats. I'm not sure. I like black men because that was the pool I could draw from, you know.

Mm.

For me, I do think it's about who I find attractive, she continues. So was it about race? she asks herself, as much as me. I don't know if I – if I could have fallen in love with a white man, she answers her own question.

It *was* about race then, I say.

I said I don't know if it was about race, she says.

And yet –

Because I did not have white friends, or people who were white that I interacted with. Or very few. Like I said, three of them were gay.

I ask her, Were they people who did not want to have sex with straight women?

No, I don't know, she answers.

It happens, you know. Maybe they were bisexual.

I wouldn't know, she says.

Like David.

Mm. I don't know.

She knows what I am referring to. He is a character in a television show that we watched together. He had sex with a woman, but I don't think he was a committed bisexual. Maybe he was not even bisexual at all.

But – but I could have fallen in love, and I did think at one point I was, with people who looked like me.

Ja.

Yes, with people who look a little bit like me, a little bit different.

I laugh. 'I can push it thus far', I put the words in her mouth. (More laughter from me.)

I can hear birds twittering outside in the trees and a dog barking some way off. A fly is buzzing around the kitchen, interrupting our banter.

Now and then we have to try and dodge it or swat it away. The boy is playing Fortnite in the TV room.

I ask her directly about race. The conversation takes in the boy in the TV room and who his friends are, the contrast between the way he is growing up and the way we, his parents, grew up. We talk about friends of ours who used to worry about their children bringing Paul instead of Mandla home, about friends who married across the colour line, about justice and freedom.

She says then, It is also about – and maybe this is in hindsight – but when I speak about values as well, it's also about values and race. So it is also about, you know, about equality and fairness. So I could possibly, if I had those friends, have fallen in love with a white man, who shared those kinds of values, who thought that racial segregation, or any segregation on the basis of class or gender, you know, is unjust. You understand what I mean.

If you had friends like that you could have fallen in love? I seek to clarify.

I could have possibly fallen in love, she agrees.

She adds, if he was cute. And he had white dreadlocks – you know, based on those qualities or those beliefs around those particular things.

All right. You are touching on something that you can answer again, something important, something in what you said when you said, 'you were cute', when you said that, right? It's something about the body, about the skin –

She interrupts. Ja, ja. No, I was attracted to you –

That is, attracted to how people look.

Ja. Ja. No, first, I mean, you didn't speak yet, I was attracted to how you look, I was attracted to your –

The skin that covers the body, basically, I interrupt.

Ja. Mm.

And hair. The way I look. You did say this. So when you get to this thing about, if there was this white person about whose skin, the skin that covers him, you would say, 'I like this. I like your look'. Okay. Ja.

14

We go on to talk about the boy, about his friendships, about the society we would like for him, about whom he might fall in love with, about the potential lover's values and beliefs, and we worry about how the person would treat our boy. I think we worry that we are setting him up for awful pain by teaching him to be kind and egalitarian and generous and care for others and the world around him. We talk about a party given by a twenty-something young woman we used to babysit when she was small, and the people who were at the party. And about another young woman, in her late teens, whom we also babysat. And the twenty-something's younger brother. More worries. And laughter.

I think we are talking around the question of what we are raising or helping raise these children for. And what it is they are learning from us about caring for themselves and others. And how they might turn out, or are turning out. And whether in this society they and their peers are being raised to believe in the same things and hold the same values.

I'm going to wash the dishes now, I say.

We stop.

2 | A double movement outward toward others and inward into the self

It has been a while now since I began to think about boys, men and masculinity. During this time, I have undertaken studies and written a couple of things in this area of scholarly interest. I have also taught university classes on these topics. Alongside the research and writing, I have dedicated many days to talking with boys and men about being a boy and being a man in a society like ours, when compared to others. These conversations have taken place in person, virtually, and via traditional and social media; my aim in them has been to learn about their experiences but also to talk about what I have learned from my studies. In a society soaked in violence, it would be curious not to touch on violence when studying and discussing masculinity. Even if I can imagine myself specialising in another topic related to masculinity, say men's fashion, the magnitude, urgency and far-reaching consequences of violence are simply unignorable. That violence, I should underscore, comes in different forms. It is direct and indirect. It is against children, against women, against other men and against the self.

I have spoken with girls and women, too, perhaps more often than with boys and men – because women, in my assessment, are more interested in masculinity than men are. It makes sense: while men's violence is a problem for both women and men, women generally appear keener than men to dig down to the roots of violent masculinity, and all other forms of masculinity. The apparent lack of interest among men in wanting to understand men's violence may have two causes, of different weight. Some of us may be convinced that we know all there is to know about men's violence. Some of us may be resistant, consciously or not, to speaking about ourselves as men. And for some, these two causes are hard to disentangle from each other.

Besides the focus on violence, my contemplations about men and boys are equally concerned with love and lovelessness in their lives. It is intriguing to me that it took me much longer to turn to love than to violence in relation to masculinity. I have wondered why this was so: did I feel that love was an inappropriate subject, too soft, when placed alongside the hardness of violence? Was it because those of us who study violence and design anti-violence strategies do not recognise the role of love in undoing violence, and instead prefer to discuss dry policies, tougher policing and public health interventions? Was it simply because it is still relatively uncommon to find researchers in the field of masculinity who study love, and I was just following what the majority in the field were doing?

You will have noticed, from the way I began this book, that these meditations are as much about my life as a scholar, teacher and participant in public life as they are about me as a father, son, husband, friend and colleague. I shamelessly learn and draw from all of these parts of me, one part educating another, augmenting, releasing or questioning it at different moments. My reflections therefore emerge from my work, intersubjectively, as much as from internal conversations – the ongoing dialogue I have with myself. For example, it is to expected that I would be interested in a big new study on fatherhood, because of my scholarly work; but there are times when I am also exceedingly interested in the fact that my son is absorbed by the screen, playing Fortnite or watching YouTube videos. I spend a long time wondering whether whatever we as his parents do, however much love we show him, will prevail over the values he soaks up from the games and videos. I have worried about whether the attention we give to him will make a difference to the person he becomes; yet week after week I speak on radio shows about giving loving attention to boys and hope that this work will make a difference.

Stated another way, my concern with men's violence doesn't stop when the academic journal article about it is published, for example. The citations the article may receive are truly not as important as having a group of men I am working with make useful sense of, say, why they were so enraged by something that happened at a certain point in their rela-tionship that they got violent, yet they acted calmly when something sim-ilar occurred at another time. My ability to facilitate the group's efforts to wring out the meaning of such violent acts may come from my studies of practices and ideologies of masculinity, but it comes equally, if not more so, from my attempts at empathetic understanding. This empathy is not just for them; it is also a way of trying to love myself a little better than I used to at times in the past.

I do not stand outside of the room of men to whom I am addressing myself in this book. Of course, the discussion I am provoking might happen outside, while watching the children play, or around a braai, or over the radio. But I do not stand apart from what I study as if I am analysing hormones and atoms. I am implicated. Even as I refer to boys and men – boys at school, mosque, sports club, the playground, university, church, or with devices in their hands; men in these places and at work, at a tavern, in a car, at the football stadium, or listening to the radio – I am also talking to myself as I was at an earlier age, and to myself at the age I am now. I am *remembering* and *reflecting* and *projecting*. And in these inner and public dialogues, I bring to the conversation two parts of myself that are in conversation with each other as much as they are in con-versation with other men and boys and their different parts.

The first part of me in this conversation is myself as a man, a father and a partner who is wrestling with ideas of masculinity at a time when society is facing incredible violence perpetrated by men against women, children and other men, as well as men's self-harming and suicidal behaviours. It is not only our country that grapples with questions of masculinity and different forms of violence. And these questions do not suddenly surface but rather have a long history. In any event, an interest in masculinity as a social and psychological production, and my experience as a man who has struggled in his life and grappled as a citizen and partner with many of the issues I discuss, are what inform the conversation.

The second part of me is the critical psychologist and critical mascu-linity scholar and teacher, who also participates in social action. I spend many of my days thinking of men and boys. My reading, research and the-ories on the social and subjective lives of men and boys are as important for thinking about men and boys as is embodied, lived experience. I wish to be careful here, though, as I am not talking to academics only. There is a tendency for a certain moralising tone to leak out of our work as academics and researchers. I am aware of this in myself and in others. It is odd and unfortunate, especially when it is evident among critical scholars, teachers and activists on the political left, particularly those who are part of oppressed communities and groups, that this is found in our work. Therefore, I do not want to be seen as superior in any way, for I am definitely not. Like most people, when it comes to *living* as opposed to *thinking about living*, *being a man* as analytically distinct from *studying manhood*, I constantly grapple with the dynamic and contested ideas about what is and what makes a good father, good man or good relationship. I think this ongoing reflection and wrestling, not only with theory and research but also with actual living, makes one a more 'understanding' being, I hope, and thus a more 'loving' masculine subject, as well as a more caring teacher and activist scholar.

In asking about, and turning and turning around, the need for love among boys and men, I therefore do so also as a son, man, partner and father. And so, at different times in my life, very possibly like many boys and men, I have asked myself: do I love her, does he love me, can I live without them, why do I love this person, will they miss me when I am gone? Sometimes one says, I *need* you. Or I need him. Or her.

What is it that I need when I need this person, though? When we verbalise this love – the need one person has for another, an awareness that one cannot live without the other person, a longing for them – when we ask ourselves about whether we love the other person, or whether they love us, or why, what I think most of us as men might also want to ask ourselves is, can we be better at *understanding*, *giving* and *receiving* love? If the answer is affirmative for all of these, it seems to point to learning to be open. Men, that is, have to learn to see emotional vulnerability not as weakness but as a gateway to fullness. For some it will be relearning, a catch-up lesson. Others need more. It may seem trite, but certain ideas of masculinity direct attention away from the obvious fact that 'soft' emotions (not just 'hard' ones that are acceptable in men, like anger) are a natural part of being human, and so of being a man – unless the person has blocked off facets of that nature. We therefore need to (re-)educate ourselves about the fact that one's vulnerability as an *emotional being* – an animal with feelings – is a precondition for a different kind of intimacy.

Emotional vulnerability also suggests a different kind of courage. One starts to appreciate that to 'shamelessly' ask to be loved – or to be touched in certain ways – and to love fearlessly is to be open to being rebuffed. A *no* is always a possibility. A *no* is a check on one's ego. It is an important critical lesson that challenges your subjective view of yourself and your reputed male powers of attraction, money or status. Being acutely aware of this possibility that you can be rejected, of other people's natural right to say *no* – you will be turned down sometimes if you ask often enough – is to put yourself in an emotionally vulnerable position. And that is a courageous emotional act.

How, though, does this idea of wanting to better at understanding, at giving and receiving love, tie in with masculinity? When I link it to the fact of being a man, a father, a partner, that question becomes for me: could I see myself embracing this idea of loving masculinity, accepting it as the model of masculinity that I inhabit?

It turns out that the claim that boys and men need love attracts many questions. One of these is, 'Yes, of course, don't we all?' Another is, 'What do you mean by love?' And yet another is, 'Do men even understand love?' Concerning love, I came to realise that in the process of putting down these observations, speculations and ideas, my aim was to understand for myself more richly something of how I love and am loved. In wrestling with how men love and are loved, what love makes men do or not do,[1] and, of course, how love is related to violence, I wanted to understand love in my own life. I hope a similar desire for self-examination and understanding might emerge among some readers. More crucially, though, I hope that we may fathom the causes and consequences of violence perpetrated by men against those close to them.

A seemingly contradictory desire is evident in some of us to want to both 'strangle' and 'embrace' another person. Hence, I must ask a lot of questions about ourselves as men and about our emotional and social life. For example, do men deserve love when they hurt the people they claim to love? What makes a man hurt the person he swears he loves? What (if any) calculation does a woman make that this new man she has met will not abuse her, will not kill her? What story does she tell herself when she meets a man? How does she get over being scared of men? And if you listen to her story, what do you have to do as a man? Does that change how you feel about her and about your relationship? Asking questions is important in itself, of course. It is at the same time valuable because the questions help us wrestle with what it means to be a boy or a man who has felt a deficit of love in his life, in a society characterised by the absence of loving concern, lack of attentive communication with each other, or lack of mutual understanding.

At the same time, in reflecting on these and other questions, I hope to harness the neglected yet transformative power of love. Crucially, I mean love as the essence of *botho* (a conception of being human, which I discuss more fully in chapter 3), as a social force, as solidarity, as the core of wanting justice for others, allowing us to cross over the violent terrain on which we find ourselves. It is in reflecting on love in men's lives that we may be enabled to move from violent masculinity toward caring masculinity.[2] Without love, we also obviously cannot nurture a loving form of masculinity.[3] Our aim should be to nurture boys and men so that they can develop a nurturing masculinity.

The stories we tell about love, like the stories we are told, can be dangerous to our lives, if we do not subject them to critique. Many of us can get sucked in by an infantile notion of romance, which we tend to see in movies with a happy ending, even when the signs of danger are obvious. I know he can get angry, but he really loves me, a person might say to herself, ignoring what is right in front of her. Another might say, he is overprotective, minimising the jealous rage. Such love stories can be very seductive, but they can also be mortally dangerous. Yet stories we must tell. Humans tell stories.

It seems obvious, but all of us need to be loved and to love. Even critical thinkers, including feminist thinkers, need love. To seek love springs from the desire to be more than what we are at any given moment – it is a double movement outward toward others and inward toward the earliest place where we sought to be cared for. If that is so, to be without love is not only to be unconnected to others, but to be detached from the self's deepest need.

3 | Love needs

In 1943, the American humanist psychologist Abraham Harold Maslow published a number of papers on motivation. Two of these were 'Preface to Human Motivation' and 'A Theory of Human Motivation'.[1] While they are interlinked, it was the latter paper that went on to become one of the most influential theoretical framings of what motivates people.

Thousands of articles have been written about Maslow's theory.[2] Many psychologists and non-psychologists have been influenced by his ideas. Many critical appraisals, too, have been made of his work. No undergraduate psychology students, not only in South Africa but all around the world, can get through their studies without having learned about the ideas in Maslow's theoretical articles on human motivation.

Parenthetically, I am impressed by the hegemonic influence of Maslow's Euroamerican-centric theory, even though it is a perfect example of why there is a need to counter the dominance of such knowledge over us.[3] The appeal of Maslow's thought goes well beyond the discipline of psychology to influence many other fields, including business and management studies, social sciences and the humanities. The reach of his ideas on motivation is evident well beyond the United States of America. Right here, in a suburb of Cape Town, where the Khoi and San people used to live, we too know about Maslow's hierarchy of needs. So, even though I am a scholar of a critical bent, which means one who thinks placing ourselves in the flow of life around us and digging through our experiences is the privileged way to understand our loves and identities, I cannot but be impressed with the hegemony of Maslow's ideas.

It is probably the intuitive and optimistic nature of the humanist psychological ideas Maslow advanced that gave his theory its wide appeal.[4] The main proposition of the theory is that there are five needs that motivate humans: physiological needs, safety needs, love needs, esteem needs and self-actualisation needs (figure 3.1). Note that the needs to self-actualise, to be esteemed and to be loved, like the needs for protection, housing and water, motivate behaviour.

A key element of the theory is that 'human needs arrange themselves in hierarchies of pre-potency'.[5] Pre-potency indicates that the most pressing need, usually a lower one (like safety), will consume us until it is partially satisfied, whereas the less pressing need (like self-actualisation) is pushed back or relinquished by our consciousness. It is this element that has led to Maslow's framing of motivation being referred to as the theory of hierarchy of needs – otherwise known as self-actualisation theory.

The notion of a needs hierarchy also means that 'the appearance of one need usually rests on the prior satisfaction of another, more pre-potent

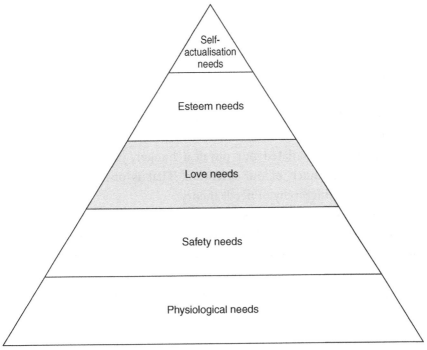

Figure 3.1 Maslow's hierarchy of needs

need . . . Also no need or drive can be treated as if it were isolated or discrete; every drive is related to the state of satisfaction or dissatisfaction of
other drives.'[6]

The first four needs outlined in the theory are referred to as deficiency
needs, while the fifth need, self-actualisation, is taken as a growth need.[7]
Deficiency needs are essentially health needs, as without their gratification
physical or psychological illness usually results. Growth needs are higher,
existential needs whose driver is the realisation of talents.

While the idea of a hierarchy of needs has become common knowledge, it is one of the specific needs described in the original paper that is
of paramount interest to me in relation to my concern with boys, men and
masculinity – namely, what Maslow gave the apt label of 'the love needs'. I
would like to quote him at some length:

> If both the physiological and the safety needs are fairly well gratified,
> then there will emerge the love and affection and belongingness needs . . .
> Now the person will feel keenly, as never before, the absence of friends,
> or a sweetheart, or a wife, or children. He will hunger for affectionate
> relations with people in general . . . namely, for a place in his group, and
> he will strive with great intensity to achieve this goal . . . In our society
> the thwarting of these needs is the most commonly found core in cases
> of maladjustment and more . . . severe psychopathology.[8]

When the need for oxygen has been met, the need for affection becomes
an insistent one.[9]

When we have satiated our physical hunger, psychical hunger for
belonging claims much of our attention. That is one deduction to be
derived from the hierarchy of needs theory.

A question that might be asked is, how certain can we be that the need
to ward off psychological suffering always waits until the need for protection from the elements and other animals has been taken care of? Or can
we confidently assert that providing a safe physical environment always
takes precedence over alleviating the mental pain that comes from being
unwanted? A generous interpretation of Maslow's theory is that the need
for shelter or sleep is more basic than the need to belong to others, but
this should not be interpreted to mean that the latter *only comes after* the

satiation of physiological drives. Love cannot be deferred for long, if at all. That is my contention, anyway. Infants need loving care as much as they need foods that will allow them to grow strong and healthy. Elderly people need relief from loneliness as urgently as they need medical attention, at least in certain moments. At every stage of their development, unless they are in some way drastically impaired, humans need psychosocial gratification.

It is a reasonable step, starting from Maslow's insight into basic human needs, to arrive at my first key proposal: *men in our society suffer from love-lessness*. Under this are interred various experiences and affects: feelings of being unlovable, of being unworthy of love, of being unloved, of a poorly gratified hunger for love, and of an inconsistently gratified need for love. What joins them together is that they are opposites, of one kind or another, of deep, consistent, nourishing, unconditional love. The love hunger in men is generally refused admittance into cultural consciousness. If men's needs for affection are noticed by the culture (including by men themselves), which appears to be rare, or confined to an earlier period of men's lives, the culture does not know how to process these love needs of adult men and assimilate them into its institutions.

Not all men suffer from being unloved or from a poorly sated need for love, of course not. And even those who have experienced periods in their lives when they have felt acutely unloved may have had moments when their love needs were met, however inadequately.

Men's psychical hole due to ungratified or inadequately satiated hunger for affection opens up during boyhood. There is a time in a boy's life, it seems to me, when he begins to be touched less (if he ever did receive adequate touch), spoken to in a more peremptory tone, and, as it were, left to his own emotional devices. The intimacy education, if there ever was any, seems to suddenly slow down and may even come to a halt.

The ungratified or poorly gratified love needs of men are largely veiled, minimised or displaced by conventional ideas of masculinity. The unrecognised hunger for love may be largely unconscious even in men themselves. As such, the association of effect (deleterious male behaviour) and cause (psychical wounds) may not be readily obvious.

It may be necessary to observe that given the nature of our society, it is some men more than others who suffer this great psychological hunger for affection. The men whose chronic love hunger is unappreciated, or dismissed, are the very ones in need of 'saving' from patriarchal masculinity ideology, particularly where this ideology intersects with racism and capitalism. Those who have grown up with conditional love, with poor evidence of love, if there was any love at all, often endure other forms of wretchedness.

To appreciate more fully what is perceived to be a deficiency of love in our private and social life – meaning the hunger for love in men and boys (but also the apparent disregard of the cultural and political uses of non-erotic love) – it is necessary to recognise how post-apartheid society is plagued by both direct and indirect violence.

Direct violence refers to visible, easy-to-count acts. Such violence is usually between people. Destruction of property is also included under direct violence. Sometimes cruelty against animals is covered under this type of violence. Mental cruelty, emotional abuse or psychologically violent behaviour is usually not included in police measures of violence. This omission may be founded on the belief that mental assaults are not as serious as violence that results in bloodshed or damage to a building. Of course, it may be that something like mental violence is too pervasive, not to mention elusive, to be effectively policed, and so psychological suffering is best left to individuals to manage. Examples of non-psychological direct violence include slapping another person, stabbing someone or setting fire to a building. Statistical rates of this kind of violence are disquieting; for example, those for rape, sexual assault, murder, attempted murder and grievous assault.[10]

While there are ongoing problems that affect the reliability of police data, and psychological violence is omitted from the picture, rape and sexual assault are known to be disproportionately committed against females, and murder or grave assaults are committed against males.[11] The protection offered by the state against even this form of readily recognisable violence is weak, patchy and, some would say, tends to favour the well-off and relatively safer areas more than the poor and those areas worst affected by the violence.

When we turn to indirect expressions of violence, a different scene is revealed, one not usually interpreted using the language of violence. That does not mean this violence is less tragic. Indirect violence may not straight away be seen as violence, but it can be as inhumane as direct violence. This type of violence is baked into the structure of society, becoming part of the common-sense idea of how the world works, an unremarkable part of the system. Hence it is also known as structural or systemic violence. As an example, when some schools in a country do not have toilets, although the state can afford to provide them, we talk of indirect violence against the children who attend such schools. Or where death from preventable causes is normalised, this indicates systemic violence because it is not accidental. Or in a country that can afford to feed all its people, and food is wasted or deliberately dumped while there is widespread hunger, this is structural violence. The extent of homelessness in a country is another example of this type of violence. Poor sanitation infrastructure or maintenance, inadequate educational facilities for the poor, electricity supply problems, and inadequate and unsafe public transport are other instances of this picture of violence. Let us not forget government maladministration, inefficiency and corruption: they may not immediately strike us as aspects of structural or systemic violence, but they must be recognised as expressions of a structural attitude, a systematic set of beliefs, held by those in charge of state bureaucracies regarding how (some) people can be (mis)treated. Finally, and most plainly, there is unemployment and economic inequality, which are largely racialised, and which on their own, but also because they are associated with other forms of violence, are grave and consequential cases of indirect violence.[12]

It is true, of course, that indirect as well as direct forms of violence have a long hateful history. That cruel history that began in 1652 with colonisation. That history of ours that endured through apartheid. And that history in whose wake we continue to live in the new republic. It is under these woeful but also rather unbelievable conditions for millions of us, where heterogeneous species of violence, visible and invisible, feed off each other, that we are to understand the hunger for love. It is under these conditions that we are supposed to claim the birthright to love and be loved, and what such a claim invites from the state, from different social groups, and from individuals.

I have suggested that we are not required to accept that there is a rigid hierarchy of needs in order to agree with the proposition that there is an unadmitted need for love and an apparent lovelessness in boys and men.

(A point that I shall return to several times is that precisely because this psychical hunger is unadmitted, it needs to be accentuated and allocated a place of prominence when working with boys and men toward achieving a more loving masculinity.) Neither is it necessary to regard the need for love as coming after the need for food and safety. We also need not regard the theoretical relationship between the individual's failure to find a place in the hearts of others and their psychosocial maladjustment as deterministic. Nor do we need to accept that without love, as defined in self-actualisation theory, every person will turn aggressive. I am comfortable with the basic claim that being loved and loving others appears to be a fundamental, positive human motivation, and therefore that the absence of love may have deleterious effects for the individual, for others close to them and for wider society.

It may be unnecessary to note that it is not only men and boys who may endure life with an unsated hunger for love. However, I feel compelled to do so, in case I am misread. Because it surfaced precisely this common need in a group other than the group I am concerned with in this book, I found a fine example of examination of the universal yen for love, affection and belonging. Using a feminist-phenomenological approach, the researchers went out looking for white, never-married, tertiary-educated, child-free South African women aged 30–40.[13] This group of women, because of all these desirable qualities and privileges they enjoy, may appear not to need love, specifically the love of men. I should highlight that these women identified themselves as heterosexual, even though some of them may not ever have been in a sexual relationship.

The first of two attractive features of the investigation is that these women were clear about what they valued. They told the researchers that they valued their independence. They liked the fact that they had careers. They enjoyed their freedom. And they treasured their autonomy from restrictive male partners. Yet all the women in the study 'believed that every human being needs and longs for a life partner' – although we may quibble about the notion of a 'life partner'.[14]

In light of this study of a group of white single women, a detour becomes inviting. The study signals something of great consequence about heterosexual relationships, and at the same time, something with implications for thinking about love and masculinity in a heteronormative, patriarchal environment. Stated directly, self-determining straight women may want men's love, yet not want their freedom restricted by men. They want what we can call *freeing love*. They want autonomy *in* love. Independence *and* interdependence.

When we understand that such women do not want to be controlled, yet want intimacy, we grasp not just a very important point about the power – positive power – that comes with being a single independent woman. This tension between freedom and intimacy also enables us to appreciate the character of close relationships between women and men in societies in which men *as a social group* rule women *as a social group*, and at the same time, where heterosexual desires are privileged over other possible desires (such as homosexual or pansexual desires). The tension is not essentially between domination and desire, for sadomasochism admits of such sexual expression. The tension arises when the object of desire refuses to be conquered. Since it is men who hold the power in such social environments, the strain crops up when women as sexual objects – in a psychoanalytic sense – who are expected to submit to heterosexual men do not want to be dominated. Because non-compliant women, women who do not want to submit themselves to men, are *not* what patriarchal men want. Women who seek freedom *and* closeness find themselves on the rack, torn between desire for autonomy and for belonging. Men who subscribe to patriarchal masculinity, because it offers them, in Raewyn Connell's words, 'specifically the benefits accruing to men from unequal shares of the products of social labour', are not tortured by the tension between sovereignty and interdependence.[15] Connell refers to these benefits as 'the patriarchal dividend'.

The question to ask is, can there be concordance between what men want, when it comes to relationships, and what independent women want, in such a society? In other words, do men like women who value their careers as much as they want to share their lives with a man? Put colloquially, are men afraid of strong women?[16]

As our society and the larger world change, with women demanding to be treated as equals in public and private life, it seems many men both fear *and* desire love between equals. A while ago British sociologist Anthony Giddens observed that many men cannot love women unless they dominate them: 'many men are not capable of loving others as equals, in circumstances of intimacy, but they are well able to offer love and care to those inferior in power'.[17] To contemplate men's love needs is thus to confront men's notions of power (but also their fear of embracing democratic relationships, since sexual equality is associated with loss of power). Any examination of love and violence in contemporary society that leaves out men's ambivalence toward women's autonomy, if not their fear of women who can live very well without men, therefore offers a false view.

We can now return to Maslow. Whereas there are overlaps between us about the fundamental human need for being close to others, there are some decisive differences between the essence of how he thought of love and how I conceive of it. While he also saw love as 'affectionate relations with people in general' (with which I partially concur, for love can take the form of *practical* solidarity as distinct from simply emotional connection), he appears to privilege love as something that happens between two people (which I cannot agree with). The foundation of how I regard love resides in what is referred to as *botho*. This idea can be understood as simply being human – in its most radical sense. The core of *botho* is that my very human existence makes no sense without your existence. Interdependence defines human society. I might even say, my happiness (or subjective well-being, or quality of life) is dependent on yours. And like love, *botho* is an elusive, culturally embedded, multidimensional concept.

The idea is that without our native need for each other, most obvious in the newborn's biological, existential need for nurturance, there is no chance of biological life as such, and therefore the development of our earliest interpersonal relations depends on the existence of others who care for us. This recognition of *botho* as a paradigmatic and social expression of love – indeed of any relationality – emerges from the recognition of our dependence on others. When a person recognises their need for belonging, which is to say the need to relate to or identify with others and thus *botho*, they are invited to treat others the way they want to be treated; to regard another person the way they would like that person to regard them. This will to interdependence defines humanness. It lies at the core of our connectedness to each other as humans.

If it is correct that the need for others and to be needed is the foundation of being human, then the passionate form of love between sexual mates merely intensifies *botho*. Similarly, if *botho* entails connectedness, the sometimes intricate bond between parent and child simply magnifies the essential *belonging with* others. Because love is essentially what enables us to unfold our humanness, it would do us good to nourish it, for then we are doing nothing more or less than realising our being human. We cannot then ignore love, as the affective-action aspect of *botho*, in the work we do of trying to lead boys and men toward better gender relations. This emotionally salient, liberating connectedness has a place in the work of changing the structure of society.

It is true that, beyond its survival significance, *botho* is a practice as well as a moral and ethical value. Because of its ideal nature, the notion that being human is defined by caring for others and being cared for by them is not always true to life. Of course, caring for others and loving them are not the same thing, but the two practices overlap. In Sesotho the distinction appears much clearer: care is the same as being concerned for others (*tsotello*), and the word for love (*lerato*) means the same as it does in English. One difference between the two is, in psychoanalytic language, the amount of libidinal energy that attaches itself to each of them.[18] And so, against the harsh facts of everyday life, of people's inhumanity to others, our *botho* is not always realised. Between the ideal and the material practice, we find evidence of hatred and exploitation, indifference and aggression, disconnection and isolation, even among individuals born into a culture within which the value of *botho* circulates. It is true, though, that for a value to lose its centrality within a culture does not imply that the value was never necessary or that it may not still be needed. It often simply means that other values have triumphed, that different values have displaced it, and reality may be ranged against the ideal.

A question we can now pose is this: how do men in our society, who have been brought up in the context of the frayed ideal of *botho*, a context pervaded by violence and an apparent lack of care for the suffering of others, experience this kind of hunger – the psychological hunger for affection? I would like to propose that men's deep love deficiency is in fact intensified because the cultural ideal of *botho* itself may have been weakened. If we admit that there is poorly satisfied love hunger among men, and if *botho* was the cornerstone of love in our society, in a time during which we witness high levels of men's violence, transforming masculinity would have to involve addressing their love deficiency and repairing the fabric of *botho*.

Nordic critical masculinity scholar and journalist Jørgen Lorentzen has sought to understand the discrepancy between the fact that for centuries men wrote about love, and yet seldom was love taken into account in critical studies on masculinities. 'Is there any love in men's lives? Is love anything that interests men, and is it in any way an important part of men's lives?' he asks.[19] In response he contends that 'looking at research on men and masculinities, the answer must be a clear *no*. If it is the case that researchers focus on the constitutive and essential elements of the objects they study, a review of the research on men and masculinities shows us that love is not at all an important part of heterosexual men's lives, since it is absent from the international studies in the area.'[20]

Delve into men's love and you will discern intense personal vulnerability in many. Most men learn to cordon off the vulnerability. At the same time, because of this ongoing defence against emotional vulnerability, further digging into their weakly satisfying love lives reveals complicity with the gendered social domination of women by men. Belief in a certain ruling form of masculinity means men do not want to show their vulnerabilities to women because that would supposedly *bring them down* to the level of the feminine. They do not want to be seen to be like women – hesitant, yielding, emotional, soft or whatever else is supposedly feminine. Hence, to probe men's love while keeping in mind men's violence reveals the dynamic interplay of male power and powerlessness, the structural and subjective meanings of masculine domination, and the fear of equality or subordination.

When a man wilfully hurts another person, power and its opposites (whether incompetence, weakness, failure, suffering, hurt or helplessness) are always in play, refracting through each other. Men's violence is always a reaction; a reassertion or deflection. Regardless of whether a person realises it, he uses violence to (re)assert power and to repel his sense of vulnerability, his own hurt and impotence, perhaps even a sense of hopelessness. More generally, power flows throughout love, now more easily recognisable, now less so, regardless of whether we are aware of it or not. Ultimately, power structures and animates all of our life of feelings.

I grew up with the discourse of *botho* around me; the hierarchy of needs theory I learnt about at university. Even if I had not come to know of Maslow, from the evidence of my own life, from observation of the lives of those with whom I have interacted throughout my life, and as a critically inclined psychologist, I recognise that the need for belonging, for human connection, is a powerful, enduring yet often under-appreciated hunger in our lives. We cannot wish away that basic human need. The hunger for others, for their affection and to be part of them, begins from the earliest moment in life. It is evolutionary in nature. It has protective and social reproduction functions. But it is when we carefully nourish it that we see how it enriches psychological and cultural life. What we nurture is likely to grow, just as what we starve is likely to wither. It seems self-evident. Why, then, is it not obvious that men are emotionally stunted because they are starved of a nourishing critical discourse of love and belonging *for* their lives? Where is the discourse of loving masculinities in defiance of the patriarchal order?

In its myriad manifestations, love is the sticky stuff that connects us to one another. If *botho* is important to us, connectedness to each other, to other animals and to the land is a defining element of our communities; at least that is what it was meant to be. Caring for others and the cosmos, and being cared for by them, were considered to be the beginning and the end of all human existence, at once the simplest yet also the most diffi-cult *human* question regarding how to live with others. The value of care is the social force that counters isolation and violence, and *the* primary socio-emotional foundation of a civil society.[21] This suggests that the *dim-inution* of *botho* is probably associated with increased violence.

In light of these propositions, I would like to put forward the second key idea regarding love and lovelessness: *lovelessness appears to lie at the root of some of the violence of men against women.* (The same holds for the vio-lence of men against other men, against children, and against themselves, given that alcohol and drug abuse can be taken as examples of forms of self-directed harm.) Lovelessness explains some, certainly not all, of the violence of men. Lovelessness does not justify violence. The experience and affect of lovelessness, I ought to stress, appear to be entombed within the experience and identity of being men (and women) in a patriarchal, racist and capitalist world – a nested relation we must constantly figure out if we are to understand ourselves and the effects of these systems. Consider, for instance, the fact that racism is an expression of the sys-temic denial of *botho* of black people. Without *botho* there can never be any kind of sustaining love. Hence, a man's feelings of lovelessness, of being unloved, or even of being unworthy of being loved – which is to say the feeling he might have that he is *not quite motho* (meaning not quite human) – must always been seen in relation to the influence of racist institutions, practices and ideas that shape and reshape his inner life and interactions. This implies that the continual necessity to probe why he feels the way he does is a lifelong activity.

Lovelessness, or ungratified love hunger, or feeling unworthy of being loved, usually develops early in our lives. In some cases, the satisfaction of our yearning for love in childhood is made conditional: 'I will show you love if you are a good child'; 'I give you this [a token of love], if you behave'. In other cases, the ones of especial interest to me, love's gratification, but more distinctly, utterances concerning love from parents or caregivers, are interlaced with harsh discipline or punishment: 'I am doing this because I love you'. In either instance, the satiation of affective needs becomes enmeshed with hurts, or terms and conditions, leading to a picture being drawn in our interiors of love coiled around hurting. This picture of a wounding love may loom large in our later relations with others. For some of us, because of the depth of this hurting affect, and given that our inner lives tend to be left largely unexamined, we live with love and pain scrambled together. It is when our ways of loving are scrutinised and carefully unscrambled from the punishment that may have attended how our need for love was gratified, if it was at all, that we are enabled to enjoy less-wounding love.

The hunger for love ought to be considered against the background of the governing economic structures and social policies, political and religious discourses, and cultural institutions and their norms within a society. That is, lovelessness is social fact, not only a psychical reality. Crucial as the quality of love is that we receive from the first moments of our lives throughout all of life, we must never minimise the role played by the structures, policies, discourses and institutions that govern, influence and mould our interiorities. Government structures and state policies are usually not expected to show us love, although we may chance upon the word 'care' in government documents. But how government structures treat us – for example, how the police treat us when we come to lay charges – influences our experience and affects our subjectivities. In other words, love (or at least a sense that others care) is best thought of not merely as a private condition that originates inside us, but as a series of internalisations shaped, experienced and expressed within the context of structures, policies, discourses, institutions and cultural norms.

In our society, the shortage of love shows itself in the childhood of many boys. It is a deficiency that begins at home, naturally, in acts of parental abandonment and child abuse, and in child-headed households. Ironically, the abandonment particularly of boys by their fathers is a significant factor in the unmet need for male love. The absence of adult men in the lives of young boys, specifically their biological fathers, is implicated in the relative dearth of models of engaged loving manhood in society.

We might ask, are girls not also abandoned by their fathers? Many girls also experience a deficiency of father-love. Girls need loving adult men as much as boys do. They need present, caring fathers to show them how to relate to men healthily and authentically, whether in platonic or sexual ways, in their own adult lives. However, while girls are also abandoned by their fathers, they have mothers and other adult women with whom they can readily *identify* and who can show them how to be women without men. In contrast, a boy who grows up without the presence of an involved, loving father does not have an adult male with whom he can readily identify.

What I am advancing is no radical idea. I perceive a deep and dense hurt at the heart of why some men hurt others. Violence against boys and men, which is another way of speaking of the life-pervading experience of boys and men being unloved and vulnerably loving others, is enmeshed with the violence of men. This bodily and psychic violence is not separate from the violence of patriarchy and racism and economic exploitation. There appears to be a widespread lack of adequate and appropriate care for, and care by, boys and men among us. In a phrase, boys and men have an unmet affective need to care and to be cared for.[22] They need others, although this need for belonging may be unconscious or unadmitted. Even if they may not always be consciously aware of it, or think that it is not as urgent as having a good job, or even if they have a leading role in public life (receiving a kind of 'love' from multitudes), they need to feel valued and to value others in private life, early on, in a consistent manner.

A lack of connection to others, and to what they really need, must be recognised by those who want men to change and by men themselves. Men cannot fully live with others – kin, friends, colleagues, followers, fellow social club members – if others do not empathise with them and if they cannot empathise with others. They need a shared sense of life with others, of interdependence, commonality. This is what I mean when I say they need love. Indeed, to want a leading role in public life, for example, cannot be entirely separated from a desire to be noticed, to receive recognition – a form of love. Similarly, we want to be gainfully employed so that we can take care of ourselves and others.

It should also be made unambiguous that my concern with the lack of care for and among boys and men of all ages – lack of loving and being loved, of understanding, passion, enduring friendships, presence, support, listening and solidarity – is not opposed to the concern of love and care needed by and among girls and women. Care for boys and care for girls are mutually reinforcing. The same holds when it comes to adult life. Care for one is care for the other; without that the likelihood of conflict in society, as in subjective life, will increase, when those who are uncared for become aware of and articulate their needs in one way or another. Both are necessary for the improvement of gender and sexual relations in our world.

I have suggested that the need for connection, belonging and care on the one hand, and the need for adequate food, water and shelter, on the other, often overlap. Giving food can be an act of practical and emotional care, of sharing, of solidarity with those who do not have. One of the things we can learn from placebo studies is precisely that people can feel better simply from being told that the medicine they receive will cure their ailments, even if it has no active properties. In other words, the simple attention of a medical expert can sometimes be the cure. Presence matters. The fact that someone is concerned for our well-being can be all that we need. And for there to be care, there must be people who have learned to care. It would benefit the world if those who are taught to care for us included boys and men, not just girls and women.

It is my understanding that without the feeling that others are concerned for us, that they care for us and we in turn care for them, that we are needed, the soul wilts. Our emotional garden requires continual tending, or else we slowly begin to die inside. Of course, it is not physical expiration to which I am referring. However, it can be seen as a kind of death, as a psychosocial wasting away. Its cause is the lack of something that makes life liveable, which is a connectedness to others. The result of protracted periods of living with the unmet need for love is not only loneliness. There are more insidious and far-reaching effects. The argument that lack of care can lead to psychosocial death, a point I wish to underscore in relation to the care hunger suffered by many a boy and young man in our society, is evidenced in these lines:

> The love need . . . is a deficit need. It is a hole which has to be filled . . . If this healing necessity is not available, severe pathology results; if it *is* available at the right time, in the right quantities and with proper style, then pathology is averted. Intermediate states of pathology and health follow upon intermediate states of thwarting or satiation. If the pathology is not too severe and if it is caught early enough, replacement therapy can cure . . . Love hunger is a deficiency disease exactly as is salt hunger or the avitaminoses.[23]

With respect to efforts to understand the development of boys into men, we should recognise that lovelessness and absence of care may be sources of aggression. This is another way of saying that those who experience a protracted ungratified hunger for love may internalise the lack of care for others as much as for themselves. Lack of concern breeds social pathology. It is to this possibility that we ought to attend, for we have done little of that work.

My decolonial and other critical friends may baulk at the fact that I have referenced a theory by an American psychologist, and question me as to whether this idea of a 'love need' is a colonial or Euroamerican-centric one. I think not. The most serious omission in Maslow's work, alongside its neglect of the cultural specificity of how love is thought of and practised, is the fact of power, of men's social relationships with women. However, to care for others and to be cared for oneself are anything but colonial. One might even say love humanises; which is to say it opposes, in its non-humiliating form, the oppressive power relations inaugurated by colonialism. Love, in its non-dehumanising expression, is justice up close and personal. Since a colonising masculinity is driven by the will to dominate, in public space and private life, a loving masculinity, when informed by gender justice, is non-colonising. It is not only a way of *being that cares*, but one that struggles for justice for other forms of life.

To my critical friends I would like to suggest, then, that it is not what we can call the 'coloniality of love' that should bother us so much. What we ought to devote ourselves to are matters such as how the need to be loved and to love manifests in *our* cultures; the structures in our society that enable or obstruct caring for each other; what love looks like in our subjective relations, given the laws and norms of our society; what factors hamper love from being realised *here*, and thus how we might go about actualising what we call decolonial love. By decolonial love, I mean the same thing as humanising love, just love. I mean love that builds, connects and understands instead of deforming, colonising. Love that heals. Frees. This is non-proprietary love.

This potential of love that heals and builds is what I would like us to nurture in boys and men, because I have seen what love can do even with all its elusiveness, agonies and dynamics. In dedicating ourselves to unleashing this potential, we would refuse to be subject to exploitative, apartheid and colonial patriarchal rules of love, even if, as I suspect, it may be a long while before we entirely leave them behind.

The fact is, there are too few love projects among boys and men in our societies. Hence, I cannot make any definitive conclusions about how boys and men think of, feel and 'do' love. But my meditations on the subject impel me to want to understand this need, even while I do not intend to be read as offering any certainties, if any can be offered with regard to love.

Another question that may be of interest is, do women and girls really experience love in the same way as men and boys? Perhaps there is a difference, perhaps not. If there is a difference, my suspicion is that it is not biological in nature. And if it is social and psychological, it means we can reduce or eliminate this difference – although that does not mean that changing social and psychological life is easier than changing biology. It may in fact be the case that some men who hurt women cannot be changed.

All these questions suggest that what we may need to do is to make an effort to understand the commonalities as well as the differences within and across societies, genders, age groups and cultures. I would be interested to see the dissimilarities and convergences in care practices among men raised in households that believed in physical discipline, and men who were raised where children were allowed to negotiate; or differences and similarities regarding love among men who enjoy guns, those who enjoy football and those who enjoy reading.

In sum, the lack of psychosocial, spiritual and culturally embedded care for boys and men, the lack of their connectedness to others, especially girls and women, but also to warm and supportive groups of other men, is deeply concerning. It is my reading that, along with structural, institutional and psychological factors, male disconnectedness and lack of adequate, appropriate and progressive care for men and boys may be behind men's impulse to injure others and themselves. The lack of care and caring is entangled in a number of social issues such as child abandonment, school dropout rates and alcohol abuse. To propose that boys and men need to be loved and to give love does not take away from the need for care and other needs felt by girls and women, including the need for safety and protection from male aggression in its various guises. Concern for boys and men is, in my view, interdependent with concern for the welfare of girls and women. It seems a self-evident truth that both girls and boys need non-violent love from all the adults in their lives – their fathers, grandfathers, uncles, male neighbours and male teachers – and not only from the adult women with whom they live and by whom they are raised.

4 | We can change how we love, but not without changing how we fight

'When you remove the conflict within yourself,' Vietnamese Thiền Buddhist monk and peace activist Thich Nhat Hanh said, 'you also remove the conflict between yourself and others.'[1] I am not exactly sure how removing conflict with others follows from removing conflict with the self. It is easy to imagine how experiencing inner conflict is related to conflict with others, such as when you are upset with your child for not doing their homework, and then become upset after your interaction with them, and then you ruminate on whether you could have spoken to them in a better way. Inner disharmony can make us suffer, of course. Some of the biggest fights of our lives are caused by what is going on inside, although it may not feel like that when you want to torture your supervisor. Knowing all that, I cannot quite figure out the detail of how the process of resolving internal discord actually leads to the resolution of disputes with others.

Regardless, it would seem that some of the very painful fights within the self arise from a sense of lovelessness. The feeling that you are not loved, or are insipidly loved, by those who are supposed to love you – the biological father who has abandoned you, for instance – can cause deep heartache. And this painful feeling can swirl around within the self for a long time. Many of us do manage to live with it; but then, seemingly out of the blue, on the taxi ride home from work or in the middle of prayer, the stinging grief unexpectedly slips through and we may not know why we are feeling mad or blue.

If indeed a person can live with unrecognised suffering generated by persistent hunger for love, the conflict within is not easy or quick to resolve. Externalising that conflict, or damping it down with alcohol or other mind-altering substances, may be a way to make ourselves feel better for a moment. None of these things seems to be the best way to sate the psychological need, though. Paradoxically, it could be that changing our thoughts about suffering and conflict, about who is the enemy and how best to fight them, could depend on expanding our conceptions of love. Capacious conceptions of love – understanding that hunger for love starts with defining love for ourselves, broadening our perception of love, having a view about how we want to love and be loved – in turn can help us endure feelings we may experience of being unloved.

To be without love is to *already* suffer. Love is one of the names humans attach to what relieves their existential suffering, the isolation always threatening to engulf the individual. Suffering is an inevitable part of being alive; there is no way to completely avoid it. Love lightens that unbearableness. To be without love is therefore to suffer without relief.

More prosaically, we suffer because of different things, some common, others less so. We endure suffering in different ways, too. With what certainty can we then say that three boys abandoned by their fathers have similar experiences of their condition? Who are we to assign unequal weights to the suffering of a woman whose son has stolen everything in the house because of his *whoonga*[2] addiction and the suffering of the addicted son himself? While some of us quantophiles are obsessed with measuring quality of life and unhappiness, it is worthwhile to be reminded that just because we can subject individuals to our instruments does not mean we fully grasp the suffering of one of them as more pitiful than that of another. That implies that even while I propose that men as a group hurt, and hurt others, from a deficiency of love, and that as a society we do not seem to understand their suffering and the connection of that pain to their personhood and to their violence, we cannot fully comprehend the individual man's subjective experience of mental pain, of being himself.

It has never been plain to me which is more engrossing: trying to intellectually snap love into place, or navigating in actual life love's promises, disappointments and compensations. While it is not totally ridiculous that quantitative psychological research, which I have done in the course of my education and which I continue to read and conduct, wants a phenomenon to be measurable, countable, if it is to be comprehended and its occurrence predicted, it is irrational to think we can compare two loves in any exact way. Love is frustratingly difficult to define. Even more maddening is to try to measure it.

All of that which holds for love applies to lovelessness. It is difficult to have one definition of lovelessness that will satisfy all people. And it may even be harder to measure.

All that being the case, it is useful to have some idea of the phenomena about which we are troubling ourselves. We should have a working idea of what it is we mean when we say we love another person (or ourselves) or are not loved (or badly loved). Even then, it is not my desire to dwell on the fine-grained details and debates involved in definitions of love, because it can take us far from where I would like us to go.

It is prudent to acknowledge that even if you think you have cognitively figured love out, maybe feel assured that you could speak at length about its true nature if you were asked to give a lecture on love, it is a problem of a different order when it comes to a real-life situation. It is not always advisable to take humans at their word because, while one may be well-read on the subject of love, it is in the nature of the mind that what and whom individuals love is not completely logically reasoned out, like a mathematical problem. Why we end up with the person we do has less to do with conscious methodical thought than with unconscious desires connected to 'the infantile fixation of tender feelings on the mother', the father of psychoanalysis wrote in one of his essays on the psychology of love.[3] How can you then be assured that it is love you are confronted with, and not something to do with her parents, when a girlfriend says to you, 'I loved you from the word go'? How can we ever be assured we are loved for who we are, that an act is a sign of true love and not misunderstanding or delusion? It is also true, though, that love appears in many forms, some of which you may not be able to endure or simply cannot relate to; in such cases, how do you reconcile the disharmony between action and word? How can this act be love?

Consider, then, the list below of five meanings and behaviours associated with the word love. I have made up the list, though not entirely out of the blue. Philosophers have said there are different kinds of love: for example, universal love (*agape*), brotherly love (*philia*), and the more common variety, romantic love or *eros*. The ancient Greeks gifted us that idea in their writings.[4] Psychologists, too, have defined different kinds of love relationship – namely, passionate, infatuated, empty, companionate and consummate love.[5] But you can find the items I have included in the list in most psychology textbooks that discuss love.

- Emotional care
- Sexual affection
- Companionship
- Solidarity
- Practical support

Now rank them from the one closest to your own meaning of love, to the least close. There is no right or wrong answer. That said, solidarity and practical support are more often than not seen as the wrong kind of love by many people in Western and westernised societies. At least, they are not readily associated with love. Nonetheless, supporting your children economically – particularly but not only among the impoverished, when you have to suffer indignities and humiliation to earn money to support your family – can be regarded as a supreme act of love. Political solidarity and support – shown by acts such as participating in protests, visiting those who have been arrested for their political beliefs, or writing letters to activate international support – probably carry more weight for those living in non-westernised communities and societies. In some of these societies, it is also not strange to express love for, or feeling close to, a leader as the highest form of love.

The truth is, these meanings and acts have different valences for different people. They also carry a different weight depending on your situatedness. A sick man or woman is more likely to need practical healthcare or companionship than passionate sex in their relationship. At a certain time in your life you may choose physical attraction over shared interests, but at another, you may choose emotional care. And at other times still, you may prefer love to mean practical support. All of this is to indicate that although the *need* for what we give the name 'love' to, for belonging, or connectedness, or devotion, or care, may arguably be universal, no universally agreed definition of love exists.

I have already introduced the idea of love as the embellishment and channelling of *botho*, the fact that we have to develop our thinking and feelings about how to be with others in the world we share. That is to say, this thinking and feelings that characterise *botho* do not come with a manual. They have to be developed by subjects.

The lack of a simple, universally agreed idea of love may be precisely because love is many things. This heterogeneousness of love is an idea we must hold on to. One might even say, just as food is whatever feeds and does not kill us while satiating our hunger, love is whatever feeds our souls while confirming that we matter to others. All the same, all we can say with confidence is that the meanings, sources, varieties, routes, possibilities and effects of love are variegated, time-bound, and culturally and historically embedded.

Take for a moment the example of how love is imagined and understood where I grew up, first in the small village of Maboloka, North West Province, and later, through my teenage years, in Katlehong, a relatively large urban area in Gauteng Province. There was – and still is – a practice called *ho fereha* in Sesotho, though most people use the term *ho shela*, from the isiZulu *ukushela*. A rough English equivalent used by many people is 'proposing love', which may be the worst ever translation. This is how it works: a man approaches a woman (it is a very heteronormative practice) to persuade her that he loves her, and that she should love him in return. Historically, the discursive persuasion involved a kind of praise singing or spoken-word poetry about the woman's abilities, ancestry, beauty or other physical, behavioural and cultural assets, as well as the man's own assets. The best outcome in this love game is to get a yes at first shot. But in most cases the man will have to return several times until the woman is persuaded that he is 'serious'. Love, in this worldview, is verbal performance, a language game in which the object of having his love accepted has to be argued for.

When I read for a postgraduate degree at university, at an institution that was then a predominantly white university, I would learn that *ho shela* was unknown among the majority of my fellow students. And even later, in my adult life, as I began to travel more widely in the United States and Europe, I learned that the practice was unknown among contemporary Americans and Europeans. Given the dominance of Western cultural ideas in our lives, many westernised Africans (that includes myself) also turn away from *ukushela*. You quickly learn that it is not acceptable to walk up to someone and unpack to her why you love her and why you deserve to be loved by her. Usually, among groups that do not *shela*, love is supposed to follow after a certain undetermined period of the practice of dating, going to the movies and restaurants, and other such activities in order to get to know each other. As a shorthand, let us call this a predominantly modern Western practice of *getting* to love. Since a Western practice of love dominates other ways of thinking about practising love in our society, like *ho shela*, when mentioning the word 'love' it is this predominant idea of love that is being referred to. However, what I am trying to do here is to draw attention to what can be gained from expanding the dominant conception and practice of love.

It is true that when most people in our society hear the word 'love', what comes to mind may be parental or sexual love. While many people will declare their love of God, that tends to be reserved for specific situations or when their understanding of love is being probed. There is also the love of one's work, which can be as absorbing as love of a sexual or parental kind, although it is regarded with ambivalence if a person says they love their work as much as their partner. Many people hate their work, so this may also not be what first comes to mind.

Perhaps it is unnecessary to point out that when the word 'love' is used, the associations many of us call up in our minds are not inborn. However, I must reiterate the fact that, just like justice, love is not genetically determined. There is a tendency when people hear that something is non-genetic to regard it as less real, important or urgent. However, to say something is socially determined does not mean it is less central to human existence. Humans are, if you will, *naturally social beings*. We live in groups. We need other humans – even when conflict is likely to arise at some point. Culture is as essential to our existence as biology. Without others to look after us, especially at the beginning of our lives, we would not survive. As a result, to say that love is a cultural fact does not imply that it is a trifling concern.

We might not come into the world knowing what love is, but we cannot live without it. We are taught how it feels, what it looks like, and what we are supposed to do about what we recognise as love. All of this implies that we need others to teach us. We think of love the way we do because of the beliefs, perceptions, feelings and acts of love (whatever forms these take) in the family into which we are born and the relationships we develop when we gain some autonomy and competence in social life. The family, peers and relationship partners in turn construct love from the cultural discourses and images that circulate in their family and social circles and from their life conditions. Vehicles that transport these discourses include religious institutions, radio stories, television soap operas, advertisements, magazines, books, newspapers, films and social media.

Several interesting consequences become visible as a result of the fact that we learn what love is from our families, other people and the cultural discourses to which we all are exposed. Some of the consequences are favourable, while others are not so favourable.

An unfavourable consequence is that because our parents loom large in our early life, they can implant distorted beliefs about and practices of love in us. But these beliefs and practices do not have be distorted to be unfavourable to us – it can simply be that they are *our parents'* beliefs and practices, not our own. When a child is raised in a family where punishment is paired with words of love, it can set down a pattern where in later life violence is associated with love. An example is when a parent hits a child and says, 'I am doing this because I love you'. The child could learn to think that this is what love does, developing the view that there is nothing curious about beating a person you love (or using verbally abusive words toward them). Another example is that of the many children who grow up in families where the idea of spending time playing with their parents is not recognised. That could have an impact on them later on in life: it could be as straightforward as not spending time playing with their own children when they become parents, even though the socio-emotional benefits of parents playing with their children may be clear from research; or over-compensating for a lack of playful interaction in their early years by being over-indulgent in parenting their children.[6]

Being taught what love is has a favourable consequence. Because we *learn* to love, we can change how we *think* of love. This is important. It is related to another point: we can change *how* we love. And we can change how we are loved. We are able to be deliberate in choosing *whom* we love.

I would like to say that if it is true that we can change our ideas about love and love actions, and that love can assume different forms, the change that will open young and older males toward healthy manhood emerges from being taught and learning to *love vulnerably*. Stated simply, to do love vulnerably requires, for those of us who have not had the benefit of these lessons, an education in intimacy. To be able to love without fearing that we are making ourselves vulnerable, we must learn to ask, learn to take rejection, learn to identify and name what happens inside us, learn to speak of what we like and do not like, learn to reflect on the self so that we may become more understanding of ourselves, and learn to talk. In this education we unearth ideas and practices of a different love. At the simplest, these lessons might entail asking, for instance, 'would you [add whatever it is you desire from another person]?' It goes without saying that a person also needs to learn that he may not get what he asks for and yet remain willing to be vulnerable. Or you might say, 'I do not like it when you do that', and so influence a change in behaviour in another person (although you must also expect resistance or a termination of the relationship). You could say, 'I enjoy that very much', and so increase the likelihood of whatever it is that you enjoy happening. I hope these examples are not considered to be proposals for self-help strategies. I am simply trying to exemplify how we might get to fold vulnerability into how we love as men.

Changing the patterns set in the family of origin is not easy, though. It also means transforming how a group of people considers love, and that is even harder than changing the way an individual understands love. But as every family is part of a culture – which is to say that, like any group, it absorbs cultural ideas of how to conceive of and do love – shifting prevalent cultural ideas about love usually takes time and may never happen in your lifetime. But it does not mean you do not have to try to do so.

As individuals, changing how we relate to others can sometimes result in the ending of relationships. Saying no to something when we have accepted or been silent about it for months or years can have undesirable consequences. Changing how we love or are loved may mean changing the self itself, and that can be painful. Yet it does not mean we have to endure a love we do not want, because we now know that we can change.

In the psychological literature, and particularly in textbooks, what tends to be discussed when love is mentioned is sexual love, also referred to as passionate or romantic love. (Parental love is not discussed in terms of the concept of love, and is instead included in discussions of attachment. It may also be obliquely referred to in discussions of developmental stages.) Even when we limit ourselves to sexual love, though, answers to many questions we may have about love are usually missing in psychology textbooks. In these books, for instance, there is an underlying assumption that individuals are largely free to choose to whom they give their love. Love following an arranged marriage is usually absent. The encumbrance of love by patriarchy is unexamined. In reading these textbooks, I find it worthwhile to keep in mind that most of the love being discussed is not just narrowly defined love but also very socially determined, and then go on to imagine the kind of love that exists outside the narrow spectrum being studied.

It is rare in the psychological literature to find discussions on whether it is possible to be clear about the difference between love and *responsibility for or to another*. In other words, while such responsibility appears to be taken for granted in discussions of parental love, it is usually neglected in discussions of adult sexual love (where there is no terminal or chronic illness).[7] Yet responsibility is a big part of love.

Love in relation to law and justice, such as in cases where unjust laws prohibit love between individuals of different races or castes, is also rarely to be found in the psychological literature on love. It is unusual to read about how an unjust ideological system shapes feelings of love.[8] Yet our interiorities, the ideas we have of love, are formed by ideology, the most effective of which is not even seen as ideology.

Turning to parent–child relationships, the task of raising offspring is not child's play. The small daily practices of parents leave deep impressions in children's hearts. (And these practices can communicate love or its inadequacy, even though sometimes preparing dinner for a child is just preparing dinner for a child, not a coded message of love; and even if the parent might put their heart into preparing a special meal, the child may not read anything special into it.) Discipline is one such practice. Data on child discipline from the 2016 *South Africa Demographic and Health Survey* show that 'about 4 in 10 women (41%) and 1 in 4 men (26%) with co-resident children physically disciplined their children with a hand or implement in the 12 months preceding the survey'.[9]

In regard to these data, we might wish to ask how parents square hitting their children with loving them. I do not mean to stereotype, pathologise or criminalise parents who use a hand to discipline their children. (We can also use an example of parents who prefer psychological discipline, since the tendency is to regard corporal punishment as what is wrong, yet not all violence is physical.) However, if parents regard using a hand on their children and loving them as non-contradictory, I surmise that such discipline is unlikely to be regarded as abuse by the children. Furthermore, parents may not know how to change a child's unwanted behaviour without using a hand, harsh word, shoe or rod.

Let me admit that *I* am not always very precise when I use the word 'love'. When I sign off a note 'with love', what exactly do I mean? I think we can see the same inexactitude when a person says, 'I love that car'; we are probably correct in assuming that they do not mean the same thing as when they say, 'I love my wife', but is this difference one of intensity or variety of love?

Let me also admit I have realised that my thinking on love has changed. So have my feelings on love and how I love. They may keep changing as I age. Even now, though, on one day I might feel as if I know just what I mean when I use the word 'love'. And then the next day, I realise that what I thought was love is only one type of love, and the many manifestations of even *that* type are too numerous to fully comprehend. Or when I use the word while talking to a lover, surely I intend something different from when I use it in talking to my spouse.

Grappling with the meanings of love for oneself is the point I am at pains to make. You do not have to take my idea of love as the last word. Instead, each of us has to reflect on love for ourselves if we are going to understand how the hunger for love, hunger that depends on a specific definition of love, is related to our suffering, and how that can spill out into violence. Finally, we have to give ourselves permission to change our thoughts and feelings about love.

5 | Love hunger shows itself in many acts, and violence may be one of them

In 2011, my collaborators and I began to probe love in a series of small studies.[1] Some of the questions for which we sought answers were these: How much weight do our histories carry in who we love? Is love a magical sort of process, something hard to explain, or can we predict who a person will love from looking at the people around them? Can we only love what we know, and what kind of people get to love those who appear very different from them? Do we only know what we love because we do not have other 'languages of love', do not possess different ways of speaking of loving? Do we love what, and who, is available to us, which means if we grew up differently, with different people, we could have loved differently?

While I still have many questions that I would like answers to, in these studies we could realistically pursue only a few of these questions. For example, in one study conducted with my 2011 master's degree intern, Candice Rule-Groenewald, we sought to understand why men and women love the people they do.[2] We posited that race was an important yet hidden variable in who people fall in love with. In another study, with my 2012 intern, Mandisa Malinga, we examined the place of love in young heterosexual men's lives.[3]

What this is meant to indicate is merely that I have had an interest in the question of love in men's lives for some time now, an interest strong enough to be investigated. Along the way, alongside the narratives of romantic love, I became interested in other kinds of love, in what we mean when we say we love, and in what we do when we (do) love. I wanted to witness love in action, such as how care is performed in feminist and traditional families, and not just to hear accounts of love, because these two, acts and accounts of love, do not always correspond.[4] Sometimes we are able to show love more than we can verbally express it. At other times we may be better at articulating love than at bodily practising it. There is much, then, to be gained, when trying to understand love, from observing people who are in close relationships and not only relying on interviews. There is much to be learned in witnessing the quality of silence between people, in seeing how they play, how they 'fight' (and how we fight is something that deserves a long meditation), in minding how they attend to each other, all of which may be glimpsed through hanging around them for a long period to see what their love is made of. From those early studies, my interest in love as much more than a subjective feeling has expanded in several directions.

It sounds obvious now, but when I started imagining what kinds of practices communicated love I was anxious that I was asking the wrong question and would soon run out of different varieties of articulation of love. I was mistaken, I can now happily say. Love and intimacy show themselves in so many ways. It is not only in passionate kisses and cuddling. Often it is someone preparing a meal for the family. Sometimes it is in how a couple hold hands. Doing the dishes can be an act of love. How two people look at one another, if you can capture that look. Sitting with a dead body. Writing a note. It is a hand in the groove of the back, raising money for charity, praying, a touch on the cheek, making a call, fixing the other person's tie, marching in a protest, or brushing off fluff from a dress. Making a gift is a common way to say one cares. Love can be as simple as how people talk with one another.

As time passed, I came to see that love is to be found in many other places my interlocutors and I had not looked into – because I was asking the wrong questions and my framing was influencing me to misperceive my object of thought. I did not appreciate that love is as simple as understanding, that it is present in different kinds of care work, solidarity-signifying acts, friendship, or making a sacrifice. And this implies that restricting ourselves to romantic relationships when we imagine love is imprisoning our own understanding.

Love shows itself in many acts. I have referred to the example of the ties between parents and children. That kind of love is non-sexual. Whereas some people may mainly recognise duty in the parent–child relationship, the essence of parenting is care (if not love). I am aware that parental love, according to Freud, is also sexual (in the expanded sense of the term, as he was wont to state). According to him, all love 'objects' are ultimately 'sexual objects' and the origins of our attachments are traceable to early relationships between child and parents.

In one of his major theoretical works, 'The Ego and the Id', which first appeared in April 1923, Freud wrote something of interest regarding boys:

> At a very early age the little boy develops an object cathexis[5] for his mother which originally relates to the mother's breast and is the prototype of an object-choice on the anaclitic model; the boy deals with his father by identifying himself with him. For a time these two relationships proceed side by side, until the boy's sexual wishes in regard to his mother become more intense and his father is perceived as an obstacle to them; from this the Oedipus complex originates.[6]

Freud may be the father of psychoanalysis, and he wrote a great many things and has many followers, and I read him myself, but we do not have to take any of his words as though they are gospel.

All the same, there are jobs and institutions which we can call *caring jobs and institutions* because they centrally involve care work. The care performed by people in these jobs and institutions cannot all be reduced to transactional acts. These aspects of the work can be regarded as doing the work for the love of it. An example of this can be observed in hospitals, which one can contrast with work people do in the field of finance. It is true that nurses, like stockbrokers, are paid to perform their duties. But there is always an excess in nursing that tilts toward work for the love of it and not only for money. And, from the perspective of patient care, it is well known that while expertise is fine, the simple fact of being cared for plays a part in the recovery of one's health.

Or consider teaching. I am not on top of the literature in this regard, so caution is necessary in reading what I say.[7] It is possible that the best teachers, meaning those who bring out the grit, creativity and meaning of education in students, are not necessarily those who have knowledge of content, but those who, with just enough content knowledge, exhibit love of learning and for their students. According to Daniel Liston, 'teaching occurs on affective and cognitive terrain; it is emotional and intellectual work'.[8] Writing about the need to infuse Black Consciousness into education, Mosibudi Mangena said that 'it is much harder to think of the teaching profession without love for children, their young pliable minds and the stimulating exercise of knowledge sharing'.[9] Surely, giving extra lessons to a student without expectation of monetary reward is very much an act of love.

Here is another example that indicates that love goes beyond close romantic relationships. Have you ever seen men weep at a sports game? This apparently simple and, for sports fans, understandable behaviour, where men can cry because their team has lost, suggests that our attachments are more complex than what happens between two people. We can be attached to others through shared support for a sports team, support that sometimes connects us with millions of others around the world who love the same team as we do.

If a kind of love is to be found in simply being heard, a friend who lends an ear when you are in need of someone to talk with is demonstrating one of the many faces of love. To be sure, friendship – for instance, between two women who care for one another in every way except sexually – can sometimes be fulfilling in a way that a relationship with a sexual partner can never be. That said, it is worth referring again to Freud, as he was adamant that the sexual was to be thought of in an extended way:

> Among the hypothetical concepts which enabled the doctor to deal with the analytic material, the first we mention is that of 'libido'. Libido means in psycho-analysis in the first instance the force (thought of as quantitatively variable and measurable) of the sexual instincts directed towards an object – 'sexual' in the extended sense required by analytic theory.[10]

Whether through libidinal force, evolutionary instinct or cultural imperative, humans express love and meet love needs in a range of familiar and creative ways. I have not mentioned revolutionary love, which is related to love for 'a cause' or 'the people'; patriotism or love for one's country; and love that an artist has for their work. One kind of love that many people of different faiths will recognise is the love of God. For some people, God's love surpasses all other forms of love. It is a kind of love that makes people give up everything else, including reason (which may explain how religious leaders can have so much power over their followers, a fact that can result in abuse, as we have observed all too often in our society.)

All these can be as strong as passionate *eros* and parent–child ties. Sometimes they can be even more consuming. All of them fulfil a strong human need to be connected to others, to care and be cared for, to live for something other than oneself. At the risk of becoming tiresome, what I would like is for us to broaden our view in imagining love, in order that we may integrate men's affection needs into our society and into our conception of masculinity. In this way, we can better see love and even harness its positive energy toward the goal of engendering gender justice.

In the love studies I have mentioned, there was one question I had not asked. It took me a while to arrive at it, to be sure. What if there is no love where we would normally expect to see it? What if the love is conditional? If being recognised carries in it something of what we give the name love, what happens if the people we hope will understand us continually misrecognise us? In other words, it took me a while to probe into ungratified or insufficiently assuaged hunger for love, into lovelessness. What fills the space of love? As soon as I asked the question of what if there is no love where there ought to be love, I glimpsed the links with not just a withering away of the self, but also rage and violence.

I have come to think that the feeling of conditional love, or being inadequately loved, or being unwanted, may be a potentially powerful motive underlying the lack of care for others. Lack of care comes from a festering rage. Am I not worthy of love? A result of feeling that the self is unloved, living with the sense of being unworthy of sustaining love, is that you can internalise the state of not caring when others are hurt, because you have internalised a sense of not being worthy of care. Such a state surely can lead a person to not opening themselves up to fully giving love to others, but rather hurting others so that their own hurt can be assuaged.

It seems that to be unloved, or to *experience* the self as unloved or unlovable, may be a breeding ground for different kinds of violence against others. But the feeling that you are unloved or unlovable can become so deeply buried in the psyche that you are not able to trace the real causes of your aggressive acts. The violence arising from feelings of lovelessness can be turned inward, against the self, and evidenced in risky sexual behaviour, alcohol abuse, self-harm and suicide. And, of course, to be unloved can be thought of as an instance of psychical violence.

That is to say, a deficiency of love can result in a variety of unfavourable consequences.

6 | Why there is no love in the *Plan*

In 2018, women and gender non-conforming persons embarked on a well-publicised series of protest actions, mainly under the #TotalShutDown banner, to bring attention to the high level of men's violence against women (or rather womxn)[1] and gender non-conforming persons. Marches were staged around the country. In Cape Town, for instance, marchers headed to parliament to deliver their list of 24 demands, while in Pretoria, another group of marchers led by the steering committee of #TotalShutDown went to the Union Buildings, where they called for President Cyril Ramaphosa to come out and receive the same list of demands, which he did.[2] Among the demands were that the president speak out strongly against gender-based violence against womxn (GBVAW), commit to establishing a process to address and reduce GBVAW, and hold a summit on GBVAW before 30 August 2018.

While it did not take place by the given date, the Presidential Summit on Gender-Based Violence and Femicide (GBVF) was held in November 2018. One of the outcomes of the summit was the establishment of the Interim Steering Committee on Gender-Based Violence and Femicide (ISCGBVF). The committee in turn was tasked with the development of the *Emergency Response Action Plan on Gender-Based Violence and Femicide*, which was published in 2020.[3] The committee also facilitated the development of the *National Strategic Plan on Gender-Based Violence and Femicide* in the same year.[4]

In light of the history of womxn's fears, hurts, frustration, anger, deaths and outcries against men's violence, the developments initiated by #TotalShutDown and the organic movement of womxn are both noteworthy and impressive. (At the same time, of course, these developments are linked to a history of women's campaigns that should be recognised. Women have been fighting for gender and racial justice for decades. It is not the history of women's struggles against male domination to which I am drawing attention, though.) The development of the *National Strategic Plan* was an undeniable milestone in women's fight against gender-based violence and femicide. As the *Plan* states, the presence of gender-based violence and femicide in our society is a crisis. This is no exaggeration. I cannot fully bring to mind what it is to be a woman aware of the magnitude of violence in our country. However, because of my awareness of the pervasiveness of violence, even I, in this man's body, can sense to some degree how unbearable it is to live with the knowledge that, because you are a woman, you may be harmed not just by strangers but by men close to you. Irrespective of the precautions they take, many women recognise that random violence lurks nearby. Imagine living with the sense of that danger. Imagine reading, on a weekly basis, that violence is so close as to be present in your relationship with your partner. What kind of life calculation does a person have to perform to live truly freely in such a society? Even in this man's body, I am cognisant of what life in a violent society can do to one's interiority. I have an enduring memory of an awareness that pervaded my interior during my youth: that white people could attack me for no reason and that I would die violently from attacks by other young males like me. One's life becomes soaked in a feeling of daily, low-hum psychosocial insecurity.

The *Plan* is a strategic document against violence. There is obviously a great deal of thinking and activism that has gone into it. However, even as the *Plan* recognises violence in intimate partnerships as the most common form of violence in the world, it contains no readily obvious thought of love, of the need for affection, of the desire for belonging. To some degree, the absence of love in a national strategic response to the crisis of GBVF is totally understandable. Why do we have to waste time on love when what we want is for men's violence to stop? And yet it seems much more close-up practical and analytical work is necessary to understand the roots of men's violence in love relationships, to understand what goes on in the mind and social life of a man who declares love for a woman and proceeds to harm her.

I have used love and care as if they mean one and the same thing. Let me try to correct that. The two do not always coincide. There are important distinctions to be held in mind between care and love.[5] While some might say care is a form of love, it can be argued that love is an intensified, denser, non-erotic and thus essentially human form of care. Some instances of care include eroticised or non-eroticised loving feelings, but the absence of such feelings does not nullify the caring nature of an act. You can receive practical care without being loved. While care is usually, though not always, practical, love can be nearly all affect. It is not unusual for love to involve, for instance, jealousy or possessiveness, qualities that care does not seem to invite.

So why do we need to think of love as a social force and in our work with men? How does one learn to love in a violent society like ours? What realistic counterweight can an ethos of care be in a community (or provincial or national) plan on gender-based violence and femicide? Should I even be entertaining thoughts on affection and belonging – because, indeed, it may sound as if to ask questions of love is to seek entertainment in a burning house?

Let me say it once again: I regard love as a vital social force as much as a fundamental personal need. Love can be a political philosophy, as we know from the Black Consciousness Movement, just as it can be an intersubjective connective tissue.[6] And power is the artery that runs from love as a subjective hunger to love as a cultural bond. As such, both love as a societal truss and love as an individual need cannot be fully conceptualised outside of power in its various shapes. Furthermore, because it is a societal force and not just an emotion felt by individuals, love is able to be exploited or approved by religions, families or states. It is well known that in some creeds and countries women have been expected or are enjoined to only desire men, or to be convinced that the best life partner is one from people of their own faith, or are encouraged to seek love from people of only their own colour. Ostracisation and sometimes even imprisonment are the consequences of defiance. In these examples, then, we already observe the interpenetration of violence and love, one being part of structural inhibitions, the other a force for resistance. To insist on love, especially where such love faces barriers, is to fight *already existing* institutional violence.

It would be injudicious for anyone to expect the *National Strategic Plan* to pay full attention to all the factors that contribute toward the crisis of men's violence, factors that stretch from the minute and momentary unfolding of interactions to macro factors, both contemporary and historical. These factors include the unavoidable intersubjective dynamics as well as economic inequality that bedevil the country, and the harsh social conditions in many communities as well as millions of households. They include each individual's own history as a child, how satisfactorily or badly they were cared for, as well as the colonial and apartheid history of gender that brought South Africa to this moment of crisis. And they include the contemporary heteropatriarchal conditions that frame gender and sexual relations. This is a lot.

But I am persuaded that we cannot understand ourselves and how we relate to others – violently or kindly, malignly or benevolently, indifferently or gratefully – if we do not consider love. And we need to do more than merely acknowledge it. We need to expand our thinking about love and its objects. Expanding our thinking about love also facilitates the expansion of possibilities for our subjective and social lives.

Yet, as I have observed, it is difficult to have a universal definition of love in all its various guises, and this might be seen as an obstacle to harnessing kindness in the fight against different forms of injustice. Perhaps this is one of the reasons why the term 'love' is not mentioned in the body of the *National Strategic Plan*. Perhaps it is also the reason why love is not considered in other government policies on, for instance, the environment (even if we may love nature) or education (even if the education of the young is informed by caring attitudes), let alone the criminal justice system.

It is simply almost impossible to define love once and for all, even when we confine ourselves to one type of love. But we need not confine ourselves to the predominant ways in which love has been thought of in Western psychological theory. We need to consider love as a cultural force, the core of *botho*, and use it to counter gender, economic, racial, sexual and environmental injustice. We need boys and adult men to love shamelessly, without fear that others will see them as weak because they care so artlessly. And we need to put love into our government policies and programmes.

It is not entirely true, though, that the *National Strategic Plan* does not mention love at all. It does cite the 'Love Not Hate' programme, a joint initiative of six lesbian, gay, bisexual, transgender or intersex (LGBTI) civil society organisations, focused on homophobic violence and hate crimes.[7] What the *National Strategic Plan* does not do is place love at the centre of fighting gender-based violence and femicide – maybe because love itself is assumed to be the problem; that is, violent love.

Love, as I have said, can be thought of as a particular form of caring and being cared for. A domestic worker does not love her employer's children, although she takes care of them. It may be for this reason that while love is not mentioned, the term 'care' is used in several places in the *Plan*, and is mentioned as one of its six pillars. In this regard, care is seen as a necessary component of 'services by the State and civil society' that victims and survivors of gender-based violence and their families require to recover and heal.[8] Care is also referred to in connection with the emotional, physical and financial care that falls on women, especially black women, and the unpaid care work that they perform.[9] And it is mentioned with respect to Thuthuzela Care Centres[10] and to the care needs of healthcare victims and survivors.[11]

Another reason for the absence of love *as* love in the *Plan* may be that it is unusual for the idea of love to be centred in work against violence. Working against violence does not usually entail working toward loving gender relations. The raison d'être of anti-violence projects is, of course, to end violence (an impossible goal) or to reduce it (which is more achievable, depending on the targets set).

Yet, since men's violence against those to whom they are close expresses lovelessness, love seems to bookend violence on either side. The beginning of (sexual) love promises a life untouched by wilful violence – or at least it should. The end of violence promises the beginning of not just peace but also love – or at least it should. Of course, to be denied love is to experience something akin to psychical violence.

But, as I have contended, love is both a subjective feeling and a social force. It satisfies personal needs but also bonds us to others within the social groups to which we belong (such as the shared idolisation of the Kaizer Chiefs Football Club among its fans), although in many such non-intimate cases love might not always be referred to as such. We minimise our need to be regarded with love – at least to be regarded as if we are loved, as if we matter – by social institutions, bosses and underlings, religious leaders,

God and the state, because we misperceive the power of love as a social good. A satisfying life implies more than a life free of violence. Typically, people expect not to be hurt by those close to them, emotionally or physically. It is not fatuous to expect not to be harmed, unless we live in a time of war or in a society riddled with conflict. We need love (or care, at least) from those who are close to us precisely because such closeness suggests intimacy, belonging. And we look for recognition, whether from intimates, acquaintances or strangers – which is to say, *first* to be treated with *botho*. For as I have said, love is an intensification of *botho*. Such recognition communicates to us our inherent value, even our love-worthiness.

There may also be a view that, in contrast to violence, which feminism has convinced us is a social issue, love must remain private. There may be a feeling that to talk about sexual love, we have to pry into people's homes, hearts or psyches; this is not necessary when it comes to violence, which we can march against. And yet one reason why many women and men who have been sexually violated in intimate relationships feel shame and never speak about their experiences is precisely because talking about violence in our close relationships can sometimes be an even more private matter than talking about love. At the same time, like violence, thinking of love as an element of *botho* makes it available as a cultural force. We can demand that the state show us love. We can march for love. We can write love into our policies.

All of this should not be read as a rejection of the *National Strategic Plan* because it ignores the hunger for love in men and boys. I cannot expect that the *Plan*, which has women and non-conforming individuals at its centre, should also devote resources to the effects of lovelessness in contributing to the perpetration of violence by men. While I see it as crucial to pay attention to the lack of caring attention to boys, so that we can guide them away from forms of masculinity configured around toughness, risk and violence, toward more compassionate and emotionally connected forms, we cannot expect women who want to end violence against women to do the work of loving boys for us. That task, of nurturing loving masculinities, must fall on those of us who are interested in the question of the making of boys, men and masculinity – whoever we are, be it parents, grandfathers, brothers or uncles; activists, non-governmental organisations (NGOs) or funders; teachers, community-based organisations or businesspeople;

researchers, faith-based organisations, unions, or other individuals and groups.

In my assessment, what we need to do in order to make masculinity anew is not only to repress violence but, at the same time, to bombard boys and men with the idea of vulnerable love. The repression of violence is seen in the same way that Michael Billig understood Freudian repression: as the keeping out of conscious awareness and cultural circulation 'that which is considered socially shameful'.[12] But the repression (and therefore reduction) of violence is not enough on its own when it comes to changing society. Love must be cultivated in the place of violence, if violence is to remain repressed. Violent men must be replaced with loving men. Relations between and among men and women will need to be radically transformed, with love, and new gender relations allowed to emerge. Only then, where generative, interdependent and mutually supportive masculinities and femininities sprout, will we begin to see a truly new society. (Of course, the elements of the unconscious can and do spill out, which is to say violence can never be completely eradicated from human affairs.)

Interventions geared toward building a more loving masculinity as the cultural ideal are, however, as far as I know, rare. A loving masculinity is a vulnerable masculinity, as I have already noted; a set of practices that involves among other things talking about feelings and changing nappies without fearing that one will be laughed at. As I have indicated, though, a loving masculinity can also be taken to indicate a caring masculinity.[13] A caring masculinity is characterised not just by practices of emotional, practical or solidary acts of love, but also by a sensitivity to vulnerability in others and in oneself. This implies thinking about the work to be done toward building loving masculinity as work whose objective is to engage men in more care work (if not to be more caring of and to themselves as such). From that perspective, where love is equated with care work, there are in fact many people around the world in the fields of studies of boys, men and masculinities who are already conducting interventions whose goal is (*love as performing*) *care work* and in which care work is seen as a vehicle of transforming masculinity.

7 | I love you, but I wish to hurt you

In 2017 I saw *Unbroken Silence*, an unpublished play by Phumeza Rashe-Matoti, who was then artist-in-residence at the Centre for Humanities Research at the University of the Western Cape. It stayed with me for some time afterward. What stuck in my head were the lines uttered by one of the characters in the play: 'My heart refuses to love and hurt at the same time, so I'm just gonna love you more even though you would kick and strangle me at 12 weeks pregnant.' These words were so memorable they would lead me to invite and collaborate with the playwright and actors in a subsequent staging of the play at the University of Cape Town in May 2018.

The truth is, I found the character in *Unbroken Silence* at once recognisable and objectionable, someone I knew too well and who frustrated me. This is then to say she was true to life, complicated. She reminded me once again of that question that had for a long time troubled me, but on which I had delayed reflecting at length. Maybe I had not had the courage up to the moment of my collaboration with the playwright and performers to ask it in writing. Why would a woman love a man who hurts her?

It took me a while, but a time arrived when I found a way to ask the question without being seen as accusatory, for I did not want to be misinterpreted. It could, of course, be a man, a non-binary, gender-fluid or trans individual who is the perpetrator or victim of the aggression. In no way do I blame victims of violence. This is very important to underscore: a person who loves another who kicks her in no way is asking for it, deserves it, or is to blame for the violence.

But a significant breakthrough happened for me. I came to see that what the character in the play was expressing was a mirror image of what some men might say: 'God knows I love you, but why do you make me hurt you so much?'

It is vital that I also underscore that I do not blame all men for the violence some men commit against women. Even though all men benefit from a system that subordinates women to men – that is to say, patriarchy – the rewards of patriarchal structures are differentiated among men. And there are women who benefit from patriarchy, including the threat of violence that constitutes its power, sometimes more than men, as a result of any number of variables: for instance, their class, sexuality, occupational status, beauty, nationality or race. I do not, then, wish to be read as saying all men hurt women, or that all women have is love.

I had been thinking about men who hurt women they love (that is, women these men say they love) for some time, alongside women who (say they) love men who hurt them. So when I heard that character in the play say the words I quoted at the start of this chapter, my memory dredged up a real-life character who says, 'I love you, but I will kill you if you keep doing that'. These two examples are not the same kinds of love, but what brought them together in my mind was that they may not make sense to some of us. How do we make sense of these loves?

What I would like to consider here is not so much why some women would want to love men who would beat them (which can be gleaned from studies of intimate partner violence and battered women).[1] Rather, I wish to delve into why some men wish to and do hurt women whom they (claim to) love.[2] My interest is in a certain play of emotions connected to wishing to hurt others (without altogether ignoring the feelings of the person who is being hurt and yet continues to love the abuser), and not in advancing explanations that snap into place too easily. I do not wish to present theoretical formulations about violence and masculinities. Instead, I want to probe men's affect, in order to learn to stay with the disturbing emotions that might offer a view into what enables some people, and not others, to integrate their memories of being hurt and not wish for retribution.

•

In trying to understand Rashe-Matoti's play and what she thought about men's violence against women, I would find occasion to put the question to her: given that she had written a play about it, what did she think would cause some women to love the men who hurt them? That interaction, and many others, contributed to the accumulation of notes I have made about men, women, love and violence that has resulted in my attempts in this book to unscramble the puzzle of love and violence. But what I could not get help with was the parallel question, which can be seen as the flip side: *why do men hurt those they claim to love?* With this question in mind, then, and considering it alongside the question of why women love men who violate them, I became increasingly persuaded of the need to consider the puzzle of why there is violence, or its threat, where one might expect only acts and words of love.

The issue of violence in close relationships, which researchers of violence and gender have grappled with from various angles, is an important concern for me. It is significant from my point of view as a masculinity scholar, but also as a man who came around to seeing *the work of the love* of women in my own life as a son, husband, co-parent, friend and colleague.

Several answers can be given to the question of why men hurt those close to them, surely. This may be due to the fact that the question overlaps with other questions, is intertwined with other facts about relationships. These include questions about parenting practices; issues of the embeddedness of love in restricting or enabling larger social relations, including laws and cultural mores; sexual desires and how we name them; racial identities and how they are supposed to bring us close together, yet do not necessarily offer protection; the institutions we have built around love and whether they are fit for purpose; and the institutions and new values we have failed to build and nurture, but which we seem to need. While all of these are worth pursuing, there is one important answer that I offer in the end.

An answer that has become common in contemporary life is conveyed in the discourse of *toxic masculinity*. The term has gained currency among women in our country, as it has among women in other parts of the world, when they try to explain men's violence, controlling behaviours, sexism and misogyny.[3] However, we must take care when using terms and their definitions. It is true that over a decade and a half ago South African masculinity scholar Robert Morrell signalled the issue of toxic masculinity in a study on fathers, when he asked 'how fatherhood can be conceived as part of [a] broader project to enhance the development of ... non-toxic-masculinities'.[4] However, it is not always clear what toxic masculinity refers to when it is used. Is it all bad things done by males? Does it refer to what bad males are, or to traits in men? Is it the same thing as patriarchal, or violent, or dominant masculinity? Does it indicate a form of ideology or attitude? Given the fact of female masculinity, which indicates that masculinity exists even without men, and which therefore implies that what is called toxic masculinity can be enacted by females and gender non-conforming people and not only by men, why are we wont to conflate masculinity with biological maleness? And why do we tend to organise against gender oppression and violence in binary gender terms (of male-born people and female-born people)? Female masculinity, which reaches beyond lesbian masculinity, beyond bodies and sexual orientation, signals that masculinity should not be used as a synonym for people with male genitalia or male-like bodies, or who look like they are men.[5] The simple fact is that in any society, masculinity is *shaped, constructed* and *practised* by possibly all the people and institutions in that society – at one or another point in time.

Some writers seem to understand dominant masculinity, traditional masculinity and toxic masculinity as the same thing, describing such masculinity as 'based on simplified norms and understandings of traditionally masculine characteristics such as violence, physical strength, suppression of emotion and devaluation of women'.[6] Toxic masculinity is then essentially a term to indicate censure of some men's behaviour. This implies that it has nothing to say about *structures* of power. And power is the key to any understanding of gender relations.

While it may offer a ready handle to speak of the reprehensible things men do, or the views they hold, toxic masculinity as a concept is inadequate when it comes to offering us a good grasp of masculinity itself. It also does not get us far in trying to understand the causes of men's violence.

It is also interesting that the term 'toxic masculinity' was coined within the mythopoetic men's movement.[7] In other words, 'good men' in subtly anti-feminist men's groups who believe in the subordination of women coined the term to dissociate themselves from 'bad men'. The term then took off outside these conservative men's groups, in wider public exchanges about masculinity around the world and in other exchanges relating to policy and therapy.

In my reading, toxic masculinity is another trope that typologises masculinity. That is, instead of offering analysis of what men do that hurts women and other men, and more importantly, *why* men hurt others, it places men in one of two categories: toxic and non-toxic. Neither masculinity as part of societal structures nor men's *agency* receives any attention in this typology. And, as contended by Andrea Waling, who offers one of the coherent analyses of 'toxic masculinity', the term 'emerged through *misinterpretations* of Connell's work on toxic practices of masculinity in peripheral fields, such as in health and criminology among others'.[8]

While some feminists have embraced the term, and attribute men's violence as well as many other unfavourable things men do to toxic masculinity, some researchers have maintained that it is ill-advised to 'adopt toxic masculinity as an analytical concept'. This is not only because the term individualises responsibility for gender inequalities to certain bad men, but also because, paradoxically, it perpetuates within- and cross-gender hierarchies.[9] The language of toxic masculinity therefore offers little true understanding and no strategy I know of to transform gender relations, or men. And it does not seem to have a plan for how to shift the nature of masculinity from toxicity toward its opposites, among which, I presume, will be non-violence, anti-racism, integrity, environmentalism, vulnerability, anti-sexism, kindness, *botho* and, of course, love. Furthermore, and worryingly, the discourse of toxic masculinity easily tips over into regarding all that is masculine as toxic.

It is worthwhile to recognise that while male violence is used to assert male control over females, it is also possible to have a society in which the domination of males is everywhere evident, yet the levels of direct violence are low. Call this soft domination. If men's violence against women emanates from the fact that social arrangements enable men to have social power over women, then the answer to the question of why men hurt those they love cannot simply be toxic masculinity. In fact, you may not need any toxic masculinity, just a society where men and women are allocated different positions. In such a society, the unspoken rule is that a woman must follow the rules set by men, and then they will not be hurt. It is when women refuse to follow these rules that violence ensues.

Rules point to an answer that has a much longer and more tested track record in explaining men's violence: *patriarchy*.[10] Very simply stated, patriarchy refers to the rule of families, communities and societies by fathers (or older men). Patriarchy is essentially about gender structures. Men, in patriarchal terms, have a right to rule over women because the world is ordered in that way. And patriarchal dominance is enforced through various of forms violence, overt and subtle.

While it offers a persuasive framework for analysing men's love in relation to power, simply uttering the word 'patriarchy' is not the same thing as unpacking why men hurt women. There are certainly complicated dynamics involved in why individuals hurt the people they say they love, and it seems to me that if we are to develop our understanding of this, we ought to slow down and probe these dynamics.

There is a set of related questions that I find at times I hold back from asking, because it can be misinterpreted, and which points to a different set of reasons why men hurt women. Namely, can there be affection in a place like this, where we have been through so much, with a historical trauma such as ours? Does not the saturation of our society in a history of violence, and its persistence in the democratic dispensation, mean that cruel treatment of each other will leak into our psyches and close relationships, even when we want to be loved and to love?

Stating that men hurt women they love because of patriarchy is not untrue. But it is not the complete picture, and more importantly, it does not show us how it is that some men resist this way of relating to women – that is, why not all men in patriarchal societies hurt women.

At the same time, contending that the upstream causes of men's violence against women are to be found in the historical and contemporary sociopolitical architecture of our society is also not untrue. But that, too, is not the whole story, as not all men, or their children, who endured the humiliations of apartheid are violent. There is an intricate relationship between patriarchal power and racist power. And both do not stop at the level of institutions. They get internalised. But there is also resistance.

The answer I wish to advance can be found in one word: *contradiction*. Contradiction is not unusual in psychological and social life, in affective life as well as within structures. An individual can oppose him- or herself. A social structure can contain contradictions. The capability to recognise contradictions in our psychologies and social conditions, and where necessary to live productively with them, is essential if we are to grasp love in a violent world. More vitally, this capacity is indispensable in understanding and living with ourselves and in this society.

I have said that mathematical reasoning may not be the best to use when we wish to understand love (or violence, or masculinity) as psychosocial phenomena. I said also that if we were to unwrap an individual's declarations of love, we might find what I call 'unlove', feelings that are opposed to what we regard as love, even loathing and a belief that one is unlovable. Similarly, in almost the same moment a person can be violent and feel tenderness toward the person against whom they are aggressing. What I see as abusive behaviour another person may see as loving concern; this indicates that there are conflicting ideas about love among people within one society, even one family. And contradiction is behind the fact that an adult male can feel like a man at one moment and less of man at another, which points to not only his internal contradiction but also the reality that masculinity itself may be inherently unstable.

Is this not psychologising the problem of men's violence against those they love? Yes, it can descend into psychological reductionism. That said, the history of the distribution of power in societies, which includes the social psychology of groups, is also the history of the internalisation of power. Men's and women's needs for closeness to, or segregationist attitudes toward, others happens within a terrain scripted by power. There is no subjective life outside of power. Power even follows us into our bedrooms. It is an element in a feeling life. It shapes our political acts as much as our intimate behaviour, what we do in our workplaces as much as in our homes.

It may be of consequence to state explicitly that I take violence to be related to power, the will to control, and frustration of this desire to control other people and events. That is to say, violence is not only related to inflicting suffering. Yet I appreciate that some men can feel so unlovable that they wish to hurt those who show them love, in order to communicate how unlovable they feel. For many of us, pausing to think critically about our power is not something that comes naturally. We feel, we react.

In spite of the propensity to portray violent men as strangers, in particular in popular images of rape, we know that many women will experience violence from their intimate partners and from other men they know. It may be unnecessary to say this, because there is already wide agreement with the sentiment. Nonetheless, to be *in a relationship* (as a Facebook status might indicate) can be far from saying one is *being loved* or *loving someone*.

It is the same with being married. It does not necessarily mean being valued. Whereas I do use the term 'intimate partner', that term, important as it is in studies of men's violence toward their girlfriends and spouses, does not quite capture the relationship I set out to understand. I want to know about a relationship where the word 'love' is said to be central.

We also know that too many women who are abused by their partners will not leave their abusers. There are many explanations for this phenomenon offered in the literature, including the need for financial support, feelings of psychosocial insecurity, low self-esteem, desire for respectability, cultural expectations, psychological dependency, and the hope that the abuser will change. And we should note that it is not only poor women who do not leave their abusers. Well-educated, financially secure women find it difficult to acknowledge and leave an abusive relationship. Gender scholars and feminists have been central voices in the work of making it clear that violence against women is a social problem and not a private matter. The hashtags #MeToo, #MenAreTrash and #TimeIsUp can be seen as iterations of the long-standing gender-critical and feminist efforts to give women a voice, to enable them to refuse to remain quiet about men's violence, abuse, gender discrimination and sexual harassment.

Needless to say, the work of conscientising women to revolt against male oppression, discrimination and harassment continues to be necessary. But, to belabour the point, given the question of why some men hurt the women they love, of even greater significance is the work of shifting the psychologies of men and boys, and undermining the structures that perpetuate patriarchal domination, even the apparently 'nice' kind of patriarchy.

8 | To love is to receive and to give

Chimamanda Ngozi Adichie said a childhood friend asked her for help regarding how to raise a baby girl as a feminist. The novelist said that, while at first she was hesitant and felt it was a huge request, she decided to write a letter in response to her friend's question. The letter, published as *Dear Ijeawele*, takes the form of 15 suggestions. This is what she says in the 13th suggestion:

> Teach her that to love is not only to give but also to take. This is important because we give girls subtle cues about their lives – we teach girls that a large component of their ability to love is the ability to sacrifice their selves. We do not teach this to boys. Teach her that to love she must give of herself emotionally but she must also expect to be given to.[1]

Who teaches girls and who teaches boys about love? We assume that it is parents. And we assume that fathers play a role in teaching boys love, which empirical reality proves to be highly improbable. Where love education happens, such education being scant, it is unlikely to be fathers who do it. According to the first *State of South Africa's Fathers* report, published in 2018, only 34 per cent of children lived with both their biological parents.[2] The report argues that 'the most telling point about the lives of South Africa's children is the significant number who live with neither of their parents. While Black children are the worst affected, even more staggering is that two in every three Black children do not live with their biological fathers.'[3] The question that arises from that fact is, what if parents, and fathers in particular, are not available to teach their children?

I have made it clear that boys need to be given love and need to be taught to give it to others. Maybe for some people love is not the most valuable thing in life, but surely it comes very close to being one of the things without which human life is very poor. If it is true that one of most important things humans can live for is being valued and valuing others – that is, if it is true that love nourishes life – I am in total agreement with Adichie when she asks, 'Why do we raise only one half of the world to value this?'[4] To be able to adeptly embrace love comes from being *taught* how to love others as well as yourself. It seems that others are forced to carry the labour of loving (or simply caring for) children and of teaching love to children, as a significant number of them grow up away from their biological parents. This love labour is taken on in those children's lives by grandparents, aunts, uncles, older siblings and the whole village. Even so, in all cases, but particularly where children grow up without parental love, the different state organs and government of the day must be persuaded to propagate a caring ethos; this is something that demands intensive activation, given the brutal past of colonialism and apartheid that has shaped families.

In parent–child relationships, it is normal that the parent does more of the loving work, especially when the child is an infant, and perhaps well past adolescence. In adult love relationships, some fairness, reciprocity, justice (in time spent doing the labour of love) might be expected. And yet it is well known that this is not the case. Unfairness is not unusual in close adult relations.

Many adult men simply never learn the reciprocity that ought to characterise love. It may have been assumed that they would pick it up during their boyhood. At the same time, while the girls and young women and aunts were talking about people and relationships, boys and young men were outside with the uncles and fathers working on the car or in the garden – if the fathers were around, that is, for in our society a significant percentage of men abandon their children. Conversations about relationships that girls and women have contain lessons about relationships, of course. They also convey education about emotional life. In contrast, when adulthood arrives, because they did not have as many such conversations, the men do not have as much of what I have referred to as intimacy education as do the women. Intimacy education is simply conscious life lessons about close relationships. With no such education, there is likely to be a mismatch between, in particular, heterosexual men and women. My larger contention about men's need for affection and its relationship to violence applies to all men. But since the majority of males tend to identify as heterosexual (instead of non-binary, trans, gay, gender-fluid, bisexual or other kinds of queer), and since the age of younger males gives them a chance of receiving relationship education during their lifetimes, heterosexual adult males' relationship education and emotional life may be in need of remedial intervention.

Maybe it is too late for adult men. However, we can still do something about educating boys and younger men about their interior lives, relationships and the importance of emotions for living a more fulfilling existence. Such an education will include not just experiencing joy, gratitude, love, caring for others as well as themselves, connections with others, empathy, compassion and understanding, but also learning how to face up to and cope with more negative, uncomfortable affects like shame and anger. That education does not necessarily mean sitting in a class or a workshop. We have to use the many tools at our disposal to cultivate this kind of understanding, and those tools include different kinds of literature, images, videos, films and art.

In my lived experience as a man and from my work as a person who writes about and works with boys and men, I have learned that teaching boys and men to give and receive love is not as easy as it sounds. What I have learned from boys, young men and older men I encounter as part of my work, I have learned by listening to what they are saying about their emotions. What I hear much more often is what they do not say, when we get to the topic of feelings. We hear about the incredibly hard circumstances under which these boys and men grew up, their respect for their mothers who were present in their lives, and in many cases about the absence of their fathers and their desire to be different men, all of which is filled with deep emotion.

What have I learned in my subjective life, in trying to teach one boy about expressing emotions? If I know anything, it is that it is a continual, full-time job. It has its daily frustrations, but also its surprises and satisfactions. And you have to be around, psychologically present if not physically so, to be a father. The teaching includes everything from how to use the toilet, make the bed, brush his teeth, be comfortable with tears as well as with joy, to doing homework, being grateful, making cards for friends, playing soccer or tennis, and learning to swim and ride a bike. And when you have taught him things like saying please and thank you, and telling others what hurts him or gives him joy, you have to contend with the fact that his peers, boys and girls, might not think saying please and thank you and expressing emotions are such cool things.

Later in this book I shall say something about this boy we are raising. I shall talk about how I have felt helpless knowing that, because of the kind of person he is becoming, he will be hurt. I have that feeling because, to put it gently, the world in which I live disapproves of boys who are emotionally attuned to the girls and boys around them, rubbing their backs when they get emotionally hurt or asking if they are okay. Boys who are emotionally super-smart are regarded as girls – and, ironically, possessing that kind of intelligence, as you might know, is not well regarded in a patriarchal society.

Love is valuing others and being valued, certainly. I have learned that it is many other things too. I speak to ten people – for instance, ten men who grew up without biological fathers – about what it is they mean when they say they love another person or love something, what love looks like and what it does, and think we have covered as much ground as we can. But I go on to ask another ten people – for example, ten female and male university students, with or without fathers – and have to agree I did not consider ten other things love looks like and can do.

In short, despite my convictions about the value of love in life, to state with absolute certainty what love is or what it is not, what it makes people do or not do, and what is allowed and disallowed in its universe of acts, thoughts and feelings, would be injudicious. Even so, what I can say with a degree of confidence is this: a world in which one half receives little love education is likely to generate unhappiness, if not outright threat, for the other half.

9 | Talking matters

Talking matters. Stated somewhat differently, talking matters over helps.

I do not wish to go into the considerable scholarly discussion in psychotherapy about why talking helps, except to point to what psychologists call a therapeutic relationship or alliance.[1] A *relationship* can be therapeutic. Due to the fact that an alliance can be healing and people can be trained to be good listeners, I submit that an experienced, expert therapist can be of great help in dealing with apparently common conditions like anxiety, and surely in managing serious ones like personality disorders and psychosis.

Just in case this is missed, it needs underlining. While a relationship can be a source of strain, it can also be healing. The relationship need not be with a professional. This is something I wish to stress and shall return to.

It may come as a surprise to some people that a certain reluctance about recommending psychotherapy has characterised my own life. I would even say, I have at times been dismissive of the psy-professions. Critical psychologists can be like that. My disinclination is attributable to a critical awareness of how psychotherapy has been appropriated by what is referred to as the 'psy-complex'.[2] As a profession, psychotherapy is too medicalised, elitist, and nurtures unwarranted power hierarchies. That is besides the fact that psychotherapy is unaffordable and adapts people to the world as it is, which is to say it is part of the neoliberal, capitalist machinery that excludes the majority of people and supports an unjust world. Poor and lower-middle-class individuals who could benefit most from it do not have the money to see a therapist. All that said, I believe that where a therapist can commit professional suicide by jettisoning the baggage of psychotherapy, and place their work in the service of the daily struggles of people and their life problems, therapy can be of tremendous use.

However, I am here not concerned with psychotherapy as such – not with whether or not it is possible to escape its Euroamerican ontological and epistemological framings, or tame its capitalist tendencies, not with the problems of its medicalisation, not with whether the talking cure actually cures, or under what conditions it works if it does, or if we should have more therapists in our country, or if training is appropriate, or with whether changing the language in which therapy is delivered would make it more African.

I am also not concerned with serious problems for which a person would need to see a clinical psychologist or psychiatrist, such as intellectual disability or severe bipolar disorder.

My concern is with what we might call everyday problems of living – for instance, anger, low self-esteem and relationship breakdown. There is no need to medicalise many of the problems individuals face in their day-to-day lives. Paying a professional to make you see that you need not fly into a rage if someone cuts you off in traffic is unwarranted. Consequently, it is not essential to call a psychologist. Help in such cases can come from speaking with someone who is willing to listen, in order to get some perspective on what has happened to you.

Although I have come to know the benefits of talk *in my head* intellectually, it took me, in my personal life, even with this information, longer to *emotionally* accept how much as a man I could benefit from others I trust if I was to talk with them, even when the talking was done in the company of a professional listener. So, even though I appreciate that verbally opening yourself up to being helped is beneficial, and having a person who listens can help you work through your troubles, it can still take a while to fully understand the immediate and more hidden and distant benefits of talking (including, in respect to the long-term benefits, the transformation of your masculinity). When I do open up, when I manage to overcome my resistance, I am always reminded that talking helps me to see more clearly. Even when it does not offer a solution, talking can make me see things differently. It can even help me to better understand what it is that I am feeling. (Of course, talking as a cure works just as well for a woman or child.)

The *relationship* itself, meaning the talking and being heard and being with attentive others, which implies empathy, is the 'magic' element. The illustrious American psychotherapist Carl Rogers said that a surprising discovery he made early on in his work as a therapist was that 'simply listening to my client, very attentively, was an important way of being helpful. So when I was in doubt as to what I should do, in some active way, I listened. It seemed surprising to me that such a passive kind of interaction could be so useful.'[3] From the perspective of a man experiencing psychosocial suffering, troubles in the spirit or relationship difficulties, he needs to seek an empathetic ear.

You need not be a therapist to realise the importance of listening in your own life. Alongside being receptive to the benefits of opening his mouth to discuss his difficulties, be they related to work, relationships, spirituality, sex or manhood, a man may also want to attend to the benefit of opening his heart (that is to say, learning to hear with his heart). Listening carefully to another person talking about their problems, or even their ordinary day, without being distracted or waiting to tell them about your day, hearing what they are saying but also what they are not telling you, takes practice. It took me what seems to be a lifetime to appreciate that being open to speaking, while not paying attention to what I am hearing, will not help me as much as if I were doing at least as much listening as talking. That, then, implies listening to other views in order to get another perspective on what concerns you, and make better sense of things. Sometimes, I have understood, I need to hear more and say less. That is what I have learned so far, but I know I am not as good a listener as I could be, for sometimes days or even weeks later, I get what the person I was sitting with was trying to tell me and that I did not hear at the time. There have been occasions when only years later did I get what a person was trying to say to me. It is a lifelong process, learning to listen.

Speaking of listening more and talking less also leads me to underline the fact that there are times when words are superfluous.[4] There are times when not talking at all, in the presence of another person, is what is asked for. Communication can be present in the quality of the silence. Just because you have many words (to speak about emotions, for instance) does not mean you have to use them all the time. You need not verbalise the trouble eating at you, but simply sit together with someone, allowing yourself to be held or to hold the other person.[5]

I may be misinterpreted, so let me stress that by talking I mean talking *with*, and not talking *at*. An exchange, not a sermon. The other person is also talking. You are listening. You want to solve the problem, whatever it is. Hence, whereas I am talking more about talking, listening matters as much as talking.

When I talk with you, I would like to find out what you think about my problem. I want to know what you feel. What advice you can share. I want you to help me. Help me see whether I am making sense. Help me make sense. I want to hear how you see the difficulty I am bringing to you.

When I say a man needs to talk with someone, it is as often as not taken to mean he should consult a psychologists or psychiatrist. Priests, rabbis and imams used to and continue to perform this role of helping people to make sense of events and issues in their lives. Sangomas (traditional diviners) and elders have done this work too. To be sure, when I say we need someone to talk things over with, I do not have *specialists* in mind. Specialists are fine. We need them. They are trained to listen. They are professional listeners. In my country we need many more such figures. Crucially, we need specialists who know indigenous languages, so that they can really hear what troubles men's hearts, in order that they can offer a vocabulary to men that can give meaning to life's messiness.

A man does not necessarily need to see a specialist to make sense of things, then. Most times what an individual simply needs are other persons to trust. That is the sum of it. If a man does not have a person he trusts, a person to be with when he needs an attentive ear and someone to whom he can turn in the permanent quest to make sense of life, that lack of trust in others is already a problem in itself. It contains the seeds of rage born from a sense of abandonment, a sense that nobody cares for him, and therefore the absence of social mutuality. According to one theory of psychosocial development, basic trust in others sits at the core of a well-adjusted ego, a secure identity.[6] (It is readily understandable that circles of trust can be expanded from close relationships to strangers and to social structures. The more we trust in, for example, the police, the more we are able to feel secure in our society. That said, in our society, given the levels of violence, we have to think critically about trust. Trusting blindly can get you robbed, raped or killed.)

In December 2020, I was once again reminded of the necessity for us, men, to have someone we trust with whom we can talk. It was nothing earth-shattering that made me recall this necessity to talk and be heard. A friend I had not spoken with for a long time was having difficulty in his marriage. I called him. His wife, whom I do not know as well as I know her husband, my friend I had not spoken with for months, was the one who asked me to call him. I had been at the couple's customary marriage ceremony and Western white wedding a few years before. That meant that all the rituals that form the foundation of marital life had been observed as they usually are. The wedding had been beautiful and enjoyable. The customary ceremony had been full of laughter, and a lot of clothes and household items had been exchanged between the different kin. (The exchange of gifts is what happens at the customary ceremony, known in Sesotho as *ho phahlela* [gift-giving]. During the event, *mokgoenyana* [the groom] and *makoti* [the bride] give gifts to each other's families. While *ho phahlela* is related to *mahadi*, it is not *mahadi* per se and instead follows that central custom.)

What all of the above implies is that I was among the people who had borne witness to the beginnings of a publicly affirmed cultural and legal bond between these two people. What I am learning is that witnessing our friends' relationships cannot begin or end with *mahadi*, *ho phahlela*, or the white wedding. It seems we have to continually ask of each other, 'how is your partner, how old are the children now, what is happening with the family?' if we do not wish to be caught by surprise, at the least. At best, it means we are tuned in to each other's emotional waves.

I do not know whether my long conversation with my friend over the phone helped him. However, I do know that we should have had that call much earlier. Many calls. How I understood the problem that my friend was having was that the problem itself was caused by a man and a woman *not* communicating with each other. It may sound like a self-help insight, yet without sharing thoughts and feelings, the idea of sharing a life together is severely challenged. Surely there is no relationship of equal intimacy without communication, where communication means being in verbal communion with each other. Sharing a life implies sharing our interior lives. All of it: the ugly feelings and joys, fears and positive states. Intimacy in modern culture means sharing our inner lives, I am afraid. If you do not want to be part of that kind of life – of love as sharing of ourselves – it may be best to make it known to others in your life.

At the same time, talking to others, friends in this case, means sharing the burden. It does not come easily to many of us, given the kinds of ideas about manhood to which we subscribe. However, friends are meant to be trusted. If your friends are not to be trusted with your emotional burdens, then you have to find others you can trust to help you make sense of things that trouble you.

As far as I could see, talking with each other almost certainly would have helped my friend and his spouse. (Of course, you could say, learning how to communicate is a whole education on its own. I agree.) In my assessment, there was an obvious misunderstanding between them of things I believe are straightforward. The misunderstanding was about how the mind works, at least according to psychology and, more so, psychoanalysis. In this tradition, the mind is known to be a trickster. It can hide things from 'us', the supposed owners of it. For example, the mind can repress memories. At times it changes painful memories into something different. Often individuals are not absolutely sure about why they act in certain ways, or like or dislike certain people or things. And sometimes we are confused about our own feelings. If memory is not always as reliable as we think it is, and we are never sure about our own likes and dislikes, and our own feelings can be confusing to us, the difficulty increases when we have to deal with other people's memories, actions and feelings. The point is that it is not unusual to misconstrue our own actions, thoughts and feelings. We are not masters of our minds and feelings, at least not always. And the trickster mind does hide things from itself and thus from us. What can help is to talk with people who may have knowledge about the things we do not know. And then we can make up our own minds.

In the end, though, whereas talking to another person we trust about life issues that trouble us can offer us insight, and even change how we think and feel about a particular concern, changing masculinity demands more than just talking with and listening to each other. Changes in gender ideologies, in norms, in family relations, and surely in economic policies and relations, as some examples, are necessary to effect the thoroughgoing transformation of the prevailing models of masculinity, which is to say paradigms of living and being that discourage men from talking.

10 | Listening carefully is an articulate act of love in action

Every man needs someone to talk with, as I have already said. Talking with someone else about your problems actually helps. I believe that.

More than talking, though, we all need to learn to listen more, because hearing what others have to say helps. The people we need to listen to are the women in our lives, family, friends, girlfriends, colleagues. Hearing them helps us build our relationships with them. Listening carefully is the most articulate act of love in action. I believe that even more. To listen is something I work on because, even at my best, I still catch my attention drifting even though I want to listen. That indicates that I am not fully present. It means I am likely to misunderstand. So, I know, learning to listen *fully* takes practice.

I know I have said something earlier about learning how to talk. Here I will say just one more thing. I find that it helps me see matters more clearly if I talk with someone. It helps me clarify what I think. Sometimes I find that I have a better grasp of my own feelings if I speak about them. I may have thought what an interaction generated in me were feelings of being upset, but during the back and forth of conversation I come to understand that what I was feeling was anxiety. I get perspective by hearing another perspective. I make sense of things in the world around me but also of what is going on inside me.

Actually, when I slow down my thinking, I find that it helps me see more clearly, even if all I am doing is listening to the other person talk. When I take time to turn things around in my mind, as you would do when you have *roosterbroodjies*[1] on the braai and turn them round and round, I appreciate the different sides of what's cooking.

A curious thing I have found about listening to another person is that my mind makes connections that go far beyond the topic being discussed. I have a feeling that this happens to all of us. You may have had the experience of listening to a conversation about sport and your mind drifts and you start to think of something that has nothing to do with sport, perhaps something that you forgot to do last week. Or you may be talking to your boss and your mind conjures a dream you could not remember that morning. The mind is always making connections between things at a subconscious level of which you are not necessarily fully aware. That may be one good reason for listening to others, because it may bring to the surface the latent connections the mind has been making.

Listening to others is helpful in more direct ways. Other people have different views from mine. They can – if my ears, and most crucially, my heart in concert with my ears, are open to what they bring – offer a different way to make sense of or fix my problem, or just to be. If that problem involves a relationship, it is almost 100 per cent certain that there is another viewpoint on the problem. I know it is not easy when you are not used to it. But what can you lose if you are already losing your way?

11 | Why does love hurt?

'Love hurts, love scars,' the hard-rock band Nazareth sang in their 1974 international hit version of Felice and Boudleaux Bryant's widely covered anthem.[1] The song expresses a particular kind of love: passionate or romantic love (instead of companionate love, sibling love, love between friends, parental love or godly love). A hurting, fiery love is, to be honest, a staple variety in the love-song genre.

There seems to be widespread cultural agreement that when it comes to this type of love, a risk exists for emotional turbulence when an individual is madly in love. It is crucial to underscore that it is psychological injury – meaning emotional pain, mental distress, verbal abuse, neglect and other forms of non-physical violence, instead of physical violence – with which we are concerned in this case. A culture that accepts that deep love can hurt, or will hurt, we must note, not only covertly reinforces emotional violence as part of love; it also suggests to us that psychological pain is not as bad as physical pain.

In their book *Masters and Johnson on Sexuality and Human Loving*, the acclaimed sex researchers William Masters and Virginia Johnson and their collaborator, Robert Kolodny, write: 'The great loves of fictions and verse have been romantic loves marked by a whirlwind of emotions from passion to jealousy to anguish.'[2] One undergraduate psychology textbook says that 'for many people, passionate love resembles a ride on a kind of emotional roller coaster – they experience intense joy if the feelings are reciprocated, and intense pain and despair if the feelings are unrequited'.[3] Therefore, it seems passionate love is perceived to come with the possibility of pain. (That is why the dominant narrative for this love uses the phrase *falling* in love; we risk falling and hurting ourselves.)

Do we not gain from assuming that love carries with it the risk of distress? Do not many of us suffer from unreciprocated love, the unwelcome absence of the beloved, the ending of love, losing a loved one? Pain is never far off in this kind of love.

With this assumption in mind – that being loved passionately by a man or a woman, and the risk of being hurt, can co-exist in the same relationship – we are in a position to ask, in what circumstances is the emotional pain that comes with love tolerable and when can it no longer be abided? What kinds of men and women *intentionally* hurt, yet passionately love at the same time? How are we to intervene if we find psychological violence and love in one and the same place? Psychological violence is taken to mean intentionally demeaning and abusive non-physical acts against another person.[4] The aggressor aims to hurt the mind or emotions. This type of violence is usually executed verbally, but it may also be expressed through gestures, silence and omissions. Threats, coercion, neglect and withholding affection are examples of psychological violence. Psychological violence may be the most pervasive form of violence in close relationships, if not in all interactions, because it is hard to define, and because quite often people do not consider it to be violence, and they do not seek professional attention when they are psychologically abused. And we must note that the consequences of psychological abuse do not stop at the psyche, for physical symptoms can result from it.

The co-occurrence of love and violence in the same relationship is not an unusual phenomenon. (Once again, we will do well to remember the co-occurrence of love and hatred within one person, starting with ambivalent love experienced in childhood.) In their study examining love among couples in which the male partner had been violent toward the female partner, Dalit Yassour Borochowitz and Zvi Eisikovits asked that very question: how can both partners speak of love in such violent relationships? They say they approached the couples with the assumption that the relationships were suffused with undesirable emotions. What they found instead was that most of the women and men in their study reported mainly positive emotions, and that that was the reason for the couple remaining together.[5] And in her study, Halimah DeShong states that love is a barrier that inhibits the ability of women in violent relationships to end them.[6]

It is not infrequent for many people who see their relationships as *not* violent to hurt the people they love. It is a rare intimate relationship in which people never *knowingly* use words or non-verbal acts to emotionally injure their loved ones. It may be that because it is not physical, this behaviour is bearable. It may not even be defined as violent. The reality is, our partners and we ourselves do not immediately up and leave when we hurt each other. We stay, even though we are wounded.

This is not to argue that staying in a violent relationship is sometimes a good choice, or that leaving is what everybody should always do. The reasons women and men stay in abusive relationships are complicated. Like many people who work against violence, I hold the view that women and men who get hurt have agency to make decisions about their lives. Anti-violence, pro-feminist work is work that puts people's agency at the centre, not the theory of academics or interests of advocates. I am, of course, also aware that agency is shaped by social structures, including patriarchy, capitalism and racism. Working toward a non-violent society and a mutually caring relational life between partners must move between what happens between two people and what happens in their society.

By paying careful attention to that dynamic of interpersonal and intrapersonal history, by listening closely to men and women who say they love each other even though they emotionally hurt one another, something of great significance can be learned. A problem I recognise in myself, and which I suspect exists in other critical scholars and anti-violence advocates too, is that we often bring out moral values, which we feel are superior, about what a good relationship is. While love is, among other things, a psychological state found within and between two people, it unfolds on a moral and ethical terrain. We bring to it what we see as right and wrong, good and bad. When our work is to challenge violence, any notion that we are morality instructors will trip us up, frustrate our work. We will make mistakes when we think we always understand, even before we take time to listen to others.

I must also state clearly that I am not saying some violence should be tolerated. Psychological violence is not 'better' than physical violence. It is an error, for individuals and society, to regard physical violence as more reprehensible than emotional violence. All the same, given the known levels of direct, sexual and physical violence, intimate and stranger-related, in our society – even without measuring the potentially high levels of psychological violence – we just want the violence to stop. We must reduce the high rates of violence, all violence, and particularly gratuitous violence.

However, it is true that we, the thinkers, the activists, the policymakers, always bring with us our moral evaluation of what love entails, what true love is and what it is not, but also what is and what is not violence. Sometimes, probably most times, the violence, like love, is complicated. What we need to do is understand the complication, and check our own moral high ground.

What, then, shall we do if we – those dedicated to eradicating violence from society, an impossible goal – find that love hurts, as the song goes? Shall we intervene, upon finally admitting that love and some form of aggression co-exist in many relationships? How shall we do this?

This reality, that some kind of violence is not exceptional in close relationships, may be troubling to many people. As I have indicated, though, the violence found in close adult relationships begins during the earliest relationship in life: between parent and child. Feelings of aggression in parents, and often overt aggression, are not uncommon. Children, too, experience feelings of aggression and exhibit violent behaviour against others. This is not a new hypothesis needing empirical support. It is common knowledge. The confusion I experience is about why I seem to expect most adults to have expunged all violence from their psyche or interpersonal life, when there was violence in their early lives.

To say violence is not exceptional in affectionate relationships is certainly not to argue that love always *has to* scar. Intimacy *does not have to* emotionally disfigure. I am also not arguing that we have to accept the fact of violence in our own intimate lives, although I have come to understand that anguish is familiar in love. This understanding makes me approach intimacy differently. On this basis, I wish we could be unafraid to talk with our children, with each other, precisely about the violence we inflict on each other, because we are intent on raising the young to be clear-eyed about relationships. As a parent, in raising a boy toward an egalitarian, loving form of masculinity, you would want him to know that such a masculinity does not mean he will not be hurt by others, or hurt others. 'Son, you can and may well get hurt by a loved one,' a parent might say. 'You will hurt others, too. What you need to think about clearly is when the hurt caused is intolerable. And you should equally know when the violence you have caused others cannot be tolerated. Be prepared to ask for genuine forgiveness. However, be prepared for the person you have harmed not to offer it to you.'

There is no life without suffering in one form or another. We do well to remember that simple fact. While I might not fully comprehend the emotional distress and financial pain of divorce, you might not totally understand the psychological pain of a couple who have experienced a miscarriage. Since there is no individual life that does not know suffering, there is no relationship that does not have the potential to collapse from the old pain of the individuals in it. It makes sense, does it not, that those with whom we are in relationships are the ones who make us suffer. It happens in a family. It happens in a group. It happens in a country. The 'enemy' is intimate, inside (the relationship, the family, the borders, the organisation or the 'kitchen'[7]). The question, if you are on the receiving end of love that hurts you, is this: is this the kind of suffering I can accept? Which is to say, what kind of suffering will I withstand and how much, when do I fight back and how, and how long do I have to fight before I have to leave?

12 | The world is not yet ready for loving boys

I may have had an inkling earlier, before he was born, maybe when I met his mother, but at some point I realised that bringing into the world a boy with my skin colour, but who would speak a mother tongue different from mine, would add one more trouble to his life's journey. I think to myself, how enviably beautiful is that skin that came out of the mother's womb; yet even that beauty does not come close to what I glimpse in his heart. Neither his beauty nor his heart will protect him, though. He will suffer.

Some of the suffering cannot be helped; it comes with being alive. All we can do is hope he can bear it well. Some of it will come from the choices we have made that led him to where he starts making his own choices. Some of the suffering, after that, will be of his own making. But there is also the suffering that will occur just because he was born a boy like him in this place, in this time.

He was three years old when the thought, steeped in a great fear about what was coming, pushed itself into my mind. I do not recall exactly what he was doing.

He is going to get hurt, this one, I thought to myself.

Perhaps it was one of the times when we went to the beach, which we did often, and as he was walking to the edge of the water I would hover close behind him. What to the other beachgoers was just another boy had become the reason for my joy, which intimates the reason for my greatest cares.

It could have been when I saw him spending time with his friends, and at a moment when I saw how free and full of life he was.

It might have been one of the times I dropped him off at the play-school.

What I know is that on one of the evenings, I put down some of my fears in my journal. I wrote that I watch as my three-year-old son walks to a place where he is going to get badly harmed. I feel almost helpless. *Almost* because, while I am still around, I will 'hold' him, speak to him of what I have seen, love him, and offer him what I know, even if he may still choose differently.

I have thought, this child is going to get injured. Surely, disenchanted. Possibly confused, a lot of times. The world is not yet ready for loving, free, kind, sensitive, smart boys like him. But what else to do than love him this way, unstintingly, always remind him how lovable he is, how beautiful his skin, what a kind boy he is?

There is a kind of suffering that is unavoidable for people like him, in the world in which he will live, unless something unanticipated happens between now and when he gets to adulthood. That is what I am learning from being a father to him: that there is no way to avoid that kind of grief. That pain may even be necessary to become the person he is pressed to be in his society. He can't but go there. Hurt awaits anyone like him who would grow up believing they deserve to be seen in their fullness. He must experience the frustration, even injury. It is not an injury that will be immediately visible to an outsider. However, as someone who knows how deeply and lastingly harmful being misrecognised can be, who knows men walking around with a raging sense of being unseen, I will see his confused pain without him needing to tell me about it. Even at his young age, it is clear that he is a thoughtful, kind, idealistic storyteller. He tells his play-school teacher and schoolmates that a volcano erupted in his backyard and dinosaurs chased him. We are told he likes rubbing his friends' backs when they cry, something culturally inherited from his mother. If he realises that he has unintentionally hurt you while playing with you, he will repeatedly ask if you are happy, and what he should do to make you accept his apology.

I said that my hope is that the suffering he will experience is of the kind that will open him even more to the world, push him to connect more to others even when they don't know that connection is what they lack, rather than the kind of suffering that will close his heart and make him fearful, angry or cynical.

From what I have witnessed thus far, with his family behind him, his storyteller's imagination, the girl- and boy-friends he is making, and the doses of good old luck he has had, maybe he already has much more than I ever had to withstand the inescapable arrows of life.

Of course the boy is going to get hurt. Racist patriarchy, you may know, does not care if boys like him cannot breathe. Women, I have been told, do not like men who are soft. The world does not always show kindness to loving boys with imaginative minds and compassionate hearts. While working to bring such a world into being, what we can do is bombard this one with as much love as he will need to love himself enough to withstand what's coming. We should do this for all boys.

13 | Producing and embodying the loving images we want of ourselves

A while back I saw a video of four Kenyan men, young-looking, addressing themselves to the Western world about the stereotypes of African men in Hollywood movies.[1] The video was posted in 2012. It has now been viewed more than 1.6 million times on YouTube. I am one of those viewers, watching it more than once because it provoked something in me.

The video begins with each of the men declaring, 'I am an African man'. One stereotype they seek to challenge is of African men as obsessed with violence.

The stereotypical representations of African men are something I know not only from YouTube videos, television, movies, print media, pornography and books, but as a lived experience with which I grew up. The very ways I breathe, walk, have sex, speak, get spoken to, dress, love and am loved have been marked by colonial prejudices about what I am and what I can be. The contents of my mind are still soaked in racist beliefs. It is only through struggle, at once psychological and social, creative and institutional, that we might be able to rid ourselves of such beliefs and free ourselves from prejudice.

The time when I, like all men similar to me, will feel completely secure, free from the blinding white gaze, is still in the future. But it is a future that won't materialise out of the blue. We have to want it and work for it. And this does not mean we have to stop practising a capacious kind of love – I could even say *botho* – and freedom in our lives today. While some things around us may not change as swiftly as we would like them to, the possibilities of a life where we feel we deserve unconditional positive regard and of shifts in the wider world are always present.

Years after the formal end of apartheid, I am still making my way toward 'I'. For, like all men of my shade, I continue to be part of 'them' – not yet entirely an individual. I remain unknown and unpredictable to some people when they encounter me. I can't be really known or fully trusted, even though I am the shadow tending the garden, the figure standing guard at the gate in a uniform, a speaker of parliament, a CEO of a major corporation, a father, lover, global football star. As is true for those men in the video and for millions of other men like me, being a stereotype remains a fact of my life that is hard to shake off – when I get followed in department stores, when white women hold more tightly onto their bags as I pass, when I hear car doors go click as I jog past, when I am thought incapable of looking after my child on my own.

Under these conditions, reimagining yourself as fully human, capable, hard-working, loving, caring, intelligent, knowledgeable, creative, joyful and all you can dream of, is nothing short of life-saving.

But as I said, I found that the Kenyan men's video provoked something in me, in the sense of being both generative and annoying. The positive aspect of the video was that it centred African voices and sought to undo stereotypes about men. That is undeniably important for anyone who believes in Africa and its men, women and children.

However, there are some negative aspects to this video. The main one is that it is not really addressed to African people. Its primary audience is the Western world, specifically a white audience in the United States, a fact evident in the description introducing the video. This audience is the one called on to stop the pity by the organisation that made the video, Mama Hope, as part of its 'Stop the Pity, Unlock the Potential' campaign.[2]

The simple message is that, even though there are organisations and individuals that help in working to change men in Africa and how these men are viewed in the United States and other parts of the West, it is really men in Africa who must themselves create many more and many different images, in videos, films, photography, fine art, books, news reports and through research. They must make the images of love, of sustaining relationships and of the kind of caring world they imagine. The more diverse and favourable the images, the better, for that is how stereotypes are undone and new subjectivities and relations can be made.

It is true that social media and the wide availability of smartphones have made it possible to stage, produce and circulate images of heterosexual men, trans men and other queer men like never before in history. Every image of a man that refuses typecasting does the work of contesting the image of African masculinity as not only coming in just one model but also naturally violent. Hence, African men need more representations that lay the groundwork for diverse patterns of masculinity to emerge, out of which a more caring version can materialise.

It is, however, not enough for Africans to just imagine themselves. Image must be made flesh. They must, that is, make and embody the images of love, of sustaining relationships and of the kind of world they need. That is always the harder project.

14 | If women stopped caring for men

Now and then I have imagined what would happen if women in this country were to stop caring for men. If for one month they said, 'We don't care'.

What would happen if they said, 'Take care of yourselves, your dogs, your houses, your sexual needs, your offices, your hospitals, your children, all your needs that you have burdened us with for so long'?

Can you imagine that? If they were to care only for each other; not for us, or for white men, and not for white women?

How would we react? I think at first there would be laughter. Bafflement would follow. If they still did not come back to their caring roles, anger would come next, and then bribery.

And we would be furious. How can they? Who do they think they are?

But then we would surely make promises of better pay. Maybe, for those who love us, promises of a more practical love.

And then, after trying to invent robots to have sex with, make tea and take care of our other needs, we would resort to the old forms of torture.

It is no secret that we treat those who take care of us badly precisely because we know, in our nightmares, that showing how much we depend on them would reveal how much we owe them. We must make them believe that their labour is worth very little. We must never let them fully grasp that their loving care is the only thing between here and hell.

Part 2 | Violence

Violence:

1. *(a) The exercise of physical force so as to cause injury or damage to a person, property, etc.; physically violent behaviour or treatment. (b) An instance of this; a violent or injurious act; a physical assault. (c) The unlawful exercise of physical force.*
2. *The state or quality of being violent in action or effect; great force or strength in operation; vehemence, severity, intensity. Also, an instance of this.*
3. *Strength of intensity of emotion; fervour, passion.*
4. *The action or an act of constraining or forcing unnatural change upon something; specifically, (a) misinterpretation or misapplication of a word, etc.*

—Lesley Brown, ed., *The New Shorter Oxford English Dictionary on Historical Principles*

The World Health Organization defines violence as: The intentional use of physical force or power, threatened or actual, against oneself, another person, or against a group or community, that either results in or has a high likelihood of resulting in injury, death, psychological harm, maldevelopment or deprivation.

—Etienne G. Krug, James A. Mercy, Linda L. Dahlberg and Anthony B. Zwi, eds.,
World Report on Violence and Health

As a point of departure, let us say that violence is present when human beings are being influenced so that their actual somatic and mental realizations are below their potential realizations. *This statement may lead to more problems than it solves. However, it will soon be clear why we are rejecting the narrow concept of violence – according to which violence is somatic incapacitation, or deprivation of health, alone (with killing as the extreme form), at the hands of an actor who intends this to be the consequence.*

—Johan Galtung, 'Violence, Peace, and Peace Research'

15 | 'I am more scared of them'

'**I** am more scared of them.'

This is what Adande Tyokolwana says in a video hashtagged #IAriseAndSpeakOut, made by the MultiChoice Group for the Uyinene Mrwetyana Foundation in 2020.[1]

In August 2019, Uyinene's life was cut short by a post office worker, Luyanda Botha, at the Clareinch post office in Cape Town. The 19-year-old University of Cape Town student had gone to fetch a parcel at the post office.

In a country that daily experiences gruesome attacks on women by men, Uyi's murder captured the headlines in a way only a few incidents of violence had done before.

A university student at a top university who goes to a post office to fetch a parcel and ends up dead in the post office will generate fear in many women at universities, in women anywhere. I can die a violent death at the post office, on an ordinary day; I can die going about my routine daily business. That's what a person may feel. While it remains a hypothesis why the killing of Uyi galvanised the righteous rage of thousands of women and tipped over into public protests against men's violence against women, Adande Tyokolwana's words touch on the daily emotion that not only she lives with, but many other women too. Fear.

I am more scared of them.

'Them' are men, of course.

Men have become phobogenic objects.

Women are scared of men. And women's fear of being violated by men means they cannot love freely. It is the well-composed man women think they know, behind the counter, at work, as much as the stranger at a deserted train station, in a parking lot, who poses a risk to them.

A society in which women are scared of men is not just a terrifying and maddening place for women. It also throws up questions about whether we can love when we are afraid of being close to those among whom love may be found. About the reduced likelihood of friendship between genders. The absence of playfulness. Love under threat.

How does an individual find or nurture love in a society where fear is pervasive? Can a scared person genuinely and willingly care for another? It does not sound possible, for fear does not care. Scared people do not care. What they want is to stop being scared. Only then can they start to care about matters other than being frightened.

It seems to me that love coming from a fearful person is love under duress, obligated intimacy, care that is coercively extracted. The 'best' care you expect from obligated care, which includes paid-for love, is care as duty. That is why they teach front-desk workers at airports to smile. Why they teach receptionists at hotels to appear welcoming. Why they teach assistants at clothing shops to ask in a 'happy' tone if they can help you with anything. They are paid to take care of customers. That is what is called emotional labour, a key task in neoliberal, capitalist service industries. Service industry care workers and other low-paid and precarious care workers live with the insecurity that they will lose their jobs, not receive their bonuses or be disciplined if they show what they really feel, which could be tiredness, anxiety, or anger about something that happened to them the day before. They have to lock that away. As customers we also do not care about their emotions, except to be served with a positive attitude.

Like the badly paid, precariously employed and job-insecure care workers, day labourers, hotel cleaners, restaurant waiters, academics on short-term contracts and domestic workers who live with job insecurity, women in a violent society live with physical and emotional insecurity. They are scared of being attacked, robbed, punched by their partners, harassed in the street, flashed, coerced, hijacked, raped or murdered. Their lives are marked by fear, sometimes vividly close up, sometimes under the surface and unconscious, but constantly in the news, and always in the air.

When women are scared of men in their workplaces, it affects their well-being, of course. And that has repercussions also for the productivity and well-being of the organisation as a whole.

When the women are scared of the men of the same race as them, the race is sundered by fear. We cannot take care of one another. We cannot be free with one another.

Blackness is supposed to indicate solidarity, I am told, which is to say a kind of affective and practical bond. I believed it. What I did not reckon with was that solidarity is love in practice, making affection visible. You have to do it again and again. Do it until the fear dissipates.

When the presence of men in a place, a taxi, train, club, street, generates fear in a woman, her breathing is constricted. But when women fear me as a man, my world is also impoverished and darkened in profound ways. I cannot play with them. They cannot be free with me.

This is important enough to underline: the realisation that women are scared of men has brought forth the insight that they cannot be playful around and with men. Play is disabled by fear. The one cannot exist when the other is in place. When children are unable to play or are prohibited from doing so, they are also denied a vital learning opportunity. At the same time, fewer opportunities to play imply reduced opportunities for the body to develop without undue hindrance and for the brain to grow. The same is true for adults: without opportunities to play, our chances to learn are encumbered, our bodily and mental health is impeded, we stop growing, biological deterioration speeds up, and love has a decreased chance of flourishing.

16 | Men who speak with fists

I met Pearlie Joubert in November 2012 at the Queen of Tarts café in Observatory. We had a conversation-slash-interview-slash-ideas-storm about a project on how to start a social revolution. I do not recall the details of all we spoke about, or what I said to her. It was something about fathers who have precarious employment or are unemployed, and the structural violence that underpins and feeds their own interpersonal violence. Something, then, about the violence arising from social structures that burrows into men's veins and infects their inner lives, and the violence they take out on others or themselves, some even taking their own lives sooner or later.

What made me want to meet her in the first place was an article she had written a few years earlier, in 2007.[1] The article, titled 'Men Who Speak with Fists', had stayed with me for two reasons. First, it told a story of an almost uncontrollable drive in some men to control women. Second, and equally sharply, it portrayed some men's need to learn, to reference Thich Nhat Hanh one more time, other ways of 'how to fight' with mindfulness.[2]

The annual '16 Days of Activism for No Violence against Women and Children Campaign' had started the week Joubert and I met. We did not talk about the campaign. The article she wrote was, however, relevant to the 16 Days Campaign. It is relevant to the campaign of last year. And this year's too. It will be relevant to next year's campaign. And so, in fact, it is relevant to all the other No Violence Campaigns until there is no need for a campaign against violence.

As we spoke about a social revolution, the 16 Days Campaign was, then, in the background of our conversation. In the times in which we live, all conversations about this campaign are at the same time conversations about men – which is to say, today, all conversations about men's love and men's masculinities have to face up to the fact of men's violence.

In Joubert's article, what was as memorable as the men's violence against the women they are close to was what the men she interviewed told her. As I said to her in in an email, what struck me most about the men was the apparent inarticulability of their emotional and motivational lives, the 'not-knowing' how to speak of their inner lives, rage, pain, frustration and the sense of emasculation that they could only restore by beating 'their women'. It was in using violence that they showed their ownership, dominance, manhood.

'Sipho says *he doesn't know why he beats "his Emily"*.' That is how Joubert wrote about one of the men.

Chris James said to her, 'Halfway to work, I realised that I'm not satisfied *because I didn't manage to have my say.* I went back inside the house and then I exploded and I punched her in the face and told her that I've had enough of her shit. I exploded. I did not have my say.'

Like me, you may want to say, what the hell! I wanted to cry, to plead, 'Lord, help the women and the men'. I wanted to be roused and enraged. But I knew. Do we all not know? We have been here. We have seen all of it. We have heard men like this. Men who want to control women and experience uncontrollable rage when they cannot do so. Although some researchers may feel men pretend not to know – how to speak of their anger, express feelings of being unworthy of love or control themselves – in order to not take responsibility for their actions, there are men who actually do not have tools to analyse their own emotions and behaviour. They do not know – and violence gives them a sense of mastery.

I know about not-knowing, not having a voice, being at the mercy of others. Though I have raged inside and wanted to explode – because I did not know how to articulate what was inside me and why I was so enraged – and I did not get a chance to speak my mind, I hope I will never use my fists to speak. That is really what I wish we men would and could say, before we turn violent.

You learn to speak. You learn a new language of emotions. It is not b-s. Without language, there is only a raging sea inside.

Who has never had that feeling of dissatisfaction and unfinishedness and smallness and ugliness when you want to feel big and beautiful? The sense that you could have said it differently. That you could have said it better – and won the argument. Could have dominated, appeared man-lier. Or sexier, smarter, cooler, more knowledgeable, more desirable. Who hasn't?

Are these men victims too, then? Is that what I am saying?

Well, no.

Well, yes.

As Joubert observes, in part these men's stories are about 'poverty and its devastating effects'.[3]

The trick in separating the abuser from the victim-who-is-also-an-abuser is to know when it is one and not the other. What is required is to prevent the boy from becoming a victim in the first place, so that the abuser does not get born. If a boy is raised in an abusive household, there is a likelihood of him becoming an abusive man. But because some of us will be raised in just such violent homes, if not violent neighbourhoods where we witness abuse, we need an education in how to fight mindfully, to speak with care and understanding.

17 | Violence wears many faces

I have held back from defining violence up to now. Given that many equate violence with aggressive physical contact, this is a good point at which to bring forth other interpretations of it. And there are many. In the epigraphs to this second part of the book, three characterisations of violence were presented: one from an English dictionary, another from the World Health Organization (WHO), and the third from the field of peace studies. I will limit myself to considering these.

In the Oxford English Dictionary, violence as injury, or as damage-causative physical force, is prioritised, perhaps because this is the most common understanding of the concept. Rape is an example of this form of violence. Other examples include causing injury to a person with a sharp object like a knife, or a blunt instrument like a brick, slapping them, running them over with a vehicle, strangling them, kneeling on them, pushing them forcefully, or holding their face under water. This notion of non-fatal or fatal injury or damage to the body appears in the majority of definitions of violence. When the media report the number of people who have been killed or injured in a shooting attack or bomb explosion, the underpinning definition of violence is this.

The Oxford English Dictionary also includes something that is often referred to in media reports: damage to property. This notion of violence is, of course, tied to economistic views of property relations. It is a curious idea – unless one takes for granted the idea of private property. Anyhow, when you damage a building you are, from this perspective, not merely doing violence to the building, but by implication doing harm to the owner of the building.

It is the three other definitions offered by the Oxford English Dictionary that add something which is absent from many of the definitions that come to us when we commonly think of violence. In the first two of these, violence is equated with force, strength, intensity, fervour and passion. Most of these terms can also be positive. Intense emotion, for example, is taken as violent emotion. The last definition of violence in this dictionary touches on constraining or forcing change to happen.[1] This is also unusual in everyday understandings of violence.

The definition of violence used by the WHO, which is commonly cited in public health interventions, underscores the explicit inclusion of power relations in addition to physical force.[2] In this view, intentionally injurious acts as a result of power relations between parties are deemed to be acts of violence. It is not obvious in the definition whether the power is unequal, and whether the violence is directed only from the powerful to the powerless. Nonetheless, the inclusion of power itself is significant. In feminist theory, rape is related to unequal power relations between men and women. This implies that the rapist does not have to physically attack or hold down the victim. Neither is a threat necessary for there to be rape. All that is required is for there to be absence of consent.

An insight to be derived from the WHO is its recognition that injury-causing acts can include physical and psychological acts of commission (hitting a person or telling them they are stupid), but crucially also acts of omission (starving a child or neglecting them). They can also include use of language to hurt, or emotional withdrawal.

Johan Galtung's conception of violence has opened up a different tradition of thinking about violence and peace. Galtung calls on us to consider much more than just body count and injuries to a person, the body or property in our approaches to and work against violence. An example he gives of a need for a wider conception of violence is this:

> If a person died from tuberculosis in the eighteenth century it would be hard to conceive of this as violence since it might have been quite unavoidable, but if he dies from it today, despite all the medical resources in the world, then violence is present according to our definition.[3]

The implied question in this instance is, why is this form of violence, otherwise known as social injustice, not always readily perceptible? The simplified answer is, because it is usually part of the 'normal' way the world appears to us. We might say, that is the way things are. Actually, a great many resources are used to keep our attention away from recognising the violence inherent in social structures.

Even then, when it becomes unavoidable to see what has happened as violence, such violence is often not regarded as direct violence deserving resources and attention (for example, the violence of a young man who fatally knifes another person). Nevertheless, we must underscore that when a woman is about to give birth, yet the nearest hospital will not help her deliver her baby because she does not have medical aid, violence may not be detectable to the eye but is present, keeping people like her out, sometimes to the point of killing them. The same general idea applies to issues related to unfair discrimination on the basis of race, sex, bodily ability, age and so forth. If a person dies or is harmed when the death or harm could have been prevented, violence is present although indirect. All of that means unfair economic discrimination is a form of injustice. Unfair discrimination on the basis of dis/ability is a form of structural violence. And the same holds for other forms of unjust discrimination. All are held in place by actual or threatened violence, inscribed into structures. This understanding of violence as part of systems has yet to permeate societal consciousness. In a country where capitalist economic rules are part of life, you would expect many people to immediately recognise capitalism as a system kept in place by state-legitimated and -sponsored violence, not merely impoverishing the majority but often causing death – and the killing of mineworkers at Marikana, which I discuss later in this book, is a clear example – or letting them suffer homelessness.

When we recognise that violence can be baked into rules, institutions or policies, we become aware that this is in fact a violent society where laws give rights to only some people. Which rights are granted to whom is characterised by an element of arbitrariness – the right to vote, work or have shelter. There is violence in an economic and political system where company executives, politicians and government directors are handsomely rewarded while teachers, domestic workers and nurses are paid much less. People might not even think to raise this, because many of us take it for granted that company executives deserve to be highly paid, whereas domestic workers do not. A substantial amount of the hidden, indirect violence emanates from how the world is organised and who runs that world. It is the dominant groups, including those in political and economic power, who enable this form of violence, because of what the powerful have decided either to do or not to do.

Galtung also draws attention to psychological violence in a way that is usually occluded in statistical reports on violence or government policies. In distinguishing between physical and psychological violence, he refers to 'the basic distinction between violence that works on the body, and violence that works on the soul; where the latter would include lies, brainwashing, indoctrination of various kinds, threats, etc. that serve to decrease mental potentialities'.[4] From Galtung's contribution, what we are enabled to see is not only psychological violence highlighted more visibly, but also institutional and cultural violence. It is, however, his elaboration of the idea of structural violence, which encompasses or is linked to the other insidious forms of violence, that is of import to some of us. Recognising that violence can be indirect and take the form of structural violence, we can now add symbolic, environmental, epistemological and other forms of violence to our definition of violence. Ultimately, given this understanding, we grasp that a person does not have to be raped, shot or punched for violence to have been done to them.

Having presented some definitions of violence, I must now restate the fact that violence has always been part of us. The distinctiveness of our own society is the level of violence present in it and, as media reports sometimes claim, its (apparent) senselessness. As the *World Report on Violence and Health* observes, 'violence has probably always been part of the human experience'.[5] The report does not seem to want to fully admit the logical conclusion of this opening statement, which is that humans can never completely eradicate violence. We kill other animals to eat. States imprison people who transgress their laws, and sometimes death is the penalty for unlawful behaviour. Nations war against other nations. Within a nation, a group may fight to take power. Civil war is a common occurrence in some countries. Gangs or other types of collective will fight for ascendancy. We dig the earth and pollute it for economic gain, even while we depend on the same earth to sustain us. Parents discipline their children, often using corporal punishment, even while loving them. Some violence, such as kill-ing lambs to feed ourselves or jailing terrorists, seems to makes sense. All of that seems to point to the inevitability of some forms of violence, direct or structural. The implication is that human existence has always taken place in a world in which violence is normative, lawful and sometimes nec-essary. And in turn this suggests that violence will always be part of our relationships with others, and those we love and who love us may be the same people who carry out violent acts. If they are not violent toward us, the ones who love them, they can be violent toward others.

As part of human society, an individual can never entirely escape vio-lence. The only question is, then, the sense, type and quantum of violence you can live with. Since you cannot immunise yourself against violence, you have to reflect on what is acceptable violence, what you can endure. It seems that what some of us want is that violence not be directed at us, that it not come from those we love or those who belong to our groups. That, however, as already indicated, is itself a limited condition that can only be temporary, since violence is always happening to others, if not to ourselves. We have to think, therefore, along the same lines that the Reverend Dr Martin Luther King Jr articulated in his long letter from the Birmingham jail: we have to want to reduce violence not just because it is violence against us, or against women, or against queers, but because men's violence against women is violence against all of us. 'Whatever affects one directly, affects all indirectly.'[6] Decreasing the likelihood of violence in society reduces the chances of violence against any one of us as individuals.

18 | 'Brothers, check yourselves!'

It was a Sunday night in March 2015 at Azania House, University of Cape Town.[1] A young woman told the house of how some nights previously, in the middle of the night outside the building, a male student had hollered at her and said, to use her words, maybe her vagina should be occupied. The woman was part of the group of #RhodesMustFall students – the Fallists – who had occupied the building, which normally houses the office of the university's vice-chancellor and top managers.[2] The occupation and renaming of Azania House was intended to pressurise the university into bringing down the statue of the arch-colonial figure Cecil John Rhodes, which at the time had pride of place on the university's upper campus.

The woman spoke of how she was threatened with rape. She said she wasn't the only one who had experienced threats of sexual violence and bullying.

'Black brothers,' the woman then said, 'check yourselves.'

That was the moment, fastened to four words.

Due to the intricacy of intimacy and confrontation they convey, these words are memorable.

The young woman said she could not sleep another night at Azania House. She felt unsafe in the very space meant for students who dared to stand up against and to bring down colonial symbolic power and make the university a home for all.

She left.

It is not my intention to offer an extended reflection on the 2015 #RhodesMustFall uprising, although the events of that night bring into sharp focus for me some men's ideas about and relations to women and their bodies, about struggle, about freedom, about power. I have several times visited it in my mind, in academic discussions, in private ones, and in writing this specific moment in which a woman speaks of fear of harassment and violence, and wishes to leave the joint struggle to decolonise universities. For me it is a moment that sparks thinking about how we might work with men and boys toward a pro-feminist consciousness and practice. By pro-feminist consciousness and practice, I mean a sociopolitical awareness in men and boys that supports women's feminist struggles, and the behaviours that go with such awareness.

A moment like this is significant for those of us engaged in the pursuit of social justice in interpersonal and intergroup life, efforts to decolonise minds and society, and the work of trying to build safe, peaceful, inclusive and thriving institutions and structures. Such a moment, in which we witness threats of violence in the very place where there is supposed to be camaraderie, appears to be very useful for closely examining and trying to understand not just the psychologies of some men, but relations between men and women. A moment to build decolonised institutions. And it is also a moment that I have employed in considering precisely what is needed to draw men into joining intersectional, decolonial feminist women in their fight against a modern/colonial, exploitative, patriarchal, heteronormative, racist world.[3]

As it turns out, it is not easy to turn men into pro-feminists. I have tried. (I am still trying.) This difficulty in making men pro-feminist, making them see the personal and social benefits of gender equality, is, ironically, real even for those men who may have experienced oppression in their own lives as part of a class, culture, sexual group, nation or race. But I should have known. An experience of, for instance, white racism is not a sufficient condition to change a person into a fighter against all forms of oppression, and too often not even against white racism itself. Having suffered from exploitation as a blue-collar worker (for example, working for a bad male boss for low wages, for long hours, in unsafe conditions) usually does not in itself turn a man into an anti-capitalist non-sexist, let alone turn him against all forms of exploitation. The experience of social or economic injustice is not, on its own, guaranteed to radicalise a subject against that particular injustice or against other forms of social injustice. Something else, then – a deliberate education about the effects of the interaction of, for example, racism and sexism and capitalist exploitation on men's lives – is required.

In patriarchal societies, which include most societies in the world, pro-feminist men can be regarded by other men and women as an anomaly. Men who support feminism in patriarchal societies can be threatening to the status quo. In such societies men are encouraged and permitted to ignore women's voices and rewarded for doing so. In these societies, then, by definition most men are not inclined to support feminist goals, even when some feminists are willing to work with those same men to the benefit and health of men and boys.

I was at the occupied and renamed Azania House because of an invitation from a radical female African social psychologist and a queer feminist, both based at the university. I mention some of their identifications because as a cisgender, heterosexual man I take it as a privilege, as evidence of the possibility of trust, to be invited by queer and heterosexual women to support gender and sexuality struggles.

Both women were closely involved with the movement and in supporting the students. Because of reports of sexual harassment experienced by female student activists, they asked me to facilitate a discussion on patriarchal masculinities among the student activists occupying Azania House.

After a long and bruising engagement with the students, I would leave the space with a feeling that the night had been instructive and intense for me, no doubt. It was, however, far from a success in fulfilling its intention to shift the dominant male voices, meaning the most vociferous in that space. Although some young men wanted to hear more about why patriarchal forms of masculinity might be deleterious for the well-being of males and not only females, the feeling that stayed with me was that it did not seem as if we are very successful at getting into the heads of male youth, let alone changing their practices. Why, I would later wonder – as I have done so many times – do forms of domination persist within spaces precisely aimed at challenging domination? Why is there sexism in the very struggle against colonial, patriarchal oppression? Why is there violence among those who have been violated?

I admit it was with some trepidation that I agreed to facilitate the discussions among the #RhodesMustFall students. I asked questions about whether the students would be receptive to a discussion on patriarchal masculinities. It may be true that, wherever there is sexual harassment and other forms of violence, we ought to always be ready to engage with those who are violent and harass others. However, if under ordinary circumstances most men are disinclined to support anti-patriarchal interventions, the likelihood of turning away from patriarchal masculine practices decreases when they feel obligated to do so. Yet I agreed to facilitate the discussion, because I am persuaded by the view that employing processes such as working through our pain, and conscientising those who have been dehumanised by economic, sexual or racist ideologies, can help people come to realise that they won't be humanised by hurting others.

My engagement with men is informed by practical experience and by a theoretical appreciation of the workings of socioeconomic power and psychosocial pain. I mean that I am acutely aware of the permeation of structural power into subjective lives. Our emotional lives, feelings of insecurity or well-being, are not simply due to our will, to what we do or what happens inside us. What we do, indeed what we are, is constrained or enabled by forces beyond us. Environmental factors, where one lives, the education one has, the money in one's family's or one's own pocket, and the politics and policies of the country structure our lives, but not in a deterministic fashion. That appreciation therefore includes the knowledge that individuals have agency. While some of us do overcome the suffering we may have experienced, others may deal with their own distress and insecurities by wounding those around them.

I have been inclined to believe, wrongly as it turns out, that it should be evident to most victims of white racism that sexism is not a remedy for racism but rather its kin. I have also wanted to believe that individual men who injure women and other men would realise that they are not contributing toward overcoming the capitalist, racist and gendered humiliation they have suffered at the hands of exploitative, supremacist and patriarchal structures.

The assumption that those who have been hurt are supposed to comprehend the effects of violence, and thus should almost instinctively recoil from violating others, is what creates disappointment when we cannot help men swiftly transform their gender practices. A great feat of economically, racially and sexually violent structures is precisely to predispose their victims to hurt each other. Ironically, the violent behaviour of the (formerly) oppressed toward each other may sometimes follow the same lines as the violence of the (former) oppressor: the formerly colonised become neo-colonialists, those who were abused become abusers. The same holds for other forms of oppression: individuals repair themselves when they arrive at a psychosocial and sociopolitical place where they are enabled to recognise that, however much they have suffered, the hurt they experienced will not be palliated by making others suffer. I am aware, then, that individuals deal with the hurt they experience from structures and others in a complicated way – people don't simply rise up and direct their rage at the unfair structures and those who oppress them. Therefore, although it is dispiriting to encounter sexist men, unfortunately there is a rationale for intraracial sexual harassment and violence. This is not an excuse for male violence. Instead, it is on this basis that, in the face of frustration, activists, researchers and teachers ought to work harder and more imaginatively to find pedagogic and conceptual registers through which we can turn young men toward pro-feminist masculine consciousness.

The register I propose in engaging young men (and women) is, in other words, what might be referred to as a *loving situated pro-feminist praxis* – that is, ideas and action in concert – that centres the real conditions of lovelessness among young men in the work for harmonious, healthy and just gender relations. There is one other matter that needs to be dealt with before I elaborate such a praxis: the absence of a clear and positive image of men and how to educate them toward caring, happy, healthy and socially just gender relations.

What underpins my engagement with men is an evolving critical consciousness that incorporates anti-racism, feminism, situatedness and an awareness of the interpenetration of psychical processes and social facts. My concern with masculinities is also shaped by the ideal that men *can* grasp the fact that harmonious, egalitarian, caring and just gender relations are good for society, positive for interpersonal relationships, and life-enhancing for individual men and women. Of course, not every man or woman or group values things like equality and just gender relations. In fact, sometimes the majority in a group can value inequality and discrimination, apartheid being a great example of just such a situation.

There are two closely related problems we encounter when the absence of young men in feminist projects is examined. First, as I have already suggested, mainstream feminism, at least that which prevails in our society, does not have an adequate vision, strategy or language to conscientise men to live with changing women (that is, with women as they become conscious of their agency, become empowered) and to value socially just sexual and gender relations. The dominant feminist form of pedagogy and activism has a shadowy image of young men. It appears to be uncertain about the kind of future it imagines for them.

It is, of course, unsurprising that mainstream, non-feminist research and pedagogy in the social sciences and humanities, as well as the policies emanating from social scientific and humanities research, continue to largely overlook the ways in which young men are fundamentally gendered and peculiarly vulnerable to gender-related harm. Even where governments might recognise that men are disproportionately represented as victims of war, homicide and other forms of grave physical assault, or that men are not impervious to other crimes such as human trafficking and rape, government policies usually do not tend to consider men, in comparison to women, as appropriate beneficiaries of interventions.[4]

In contrast to non-feminist scholarship and teaching and activism though, feminist work is supposed to be interested in gender. Stated differently, although it places women and girls at the centre, the analytical interest of feminist work encompasses all genders and gendering, including the ways in which men, boys and trans individuals are gendered. Gender is not another name for women, but refers to the position of women within culture and social relations; and men are gendered – positioned in gender relations – as much as women. Yet, where it exists, feminist work on men, especially young men, tends to be largely indifferent to men and rarely life-enhancing for them, offering no progressive vision of masculinity. Certain groups of young men, in particular, tend to be predominantly viewed as perpetrators of violence, rarely as survivors of parental, partner, stranger, community and structural violence. Historian and gender scholar Lindsay Clowes has lamented that 'there is such limited discursive space (either inside or outside the classroom) from which to consider the possibility that gender inequalities are harmful to men (or that conversely gender equity has anything to offer men)'.[5]

The dearth of situated pro-feminist discursive space designed with boys and men in mind is partly due to the lack of activism, teaching and research that illuminates the harm done by patriarchal masculinity to men themselves, and not only to women and children. Scarce is the research that analyses men as simultaneously dominant, insecure, loveless. Also scarce are pedagogies that build on this research while pointing to the further work needed on contradictory male experiences of socioeconomic conditions at the juncture of dominance and subjugation. The potential active participation of young men working toward non-sexist communities may thus be undermined by the lack of pedagogy and research that adequately *situates* and meshes their traumas, feelings of being unloved and unlovable, struggles to survive, and violence perpetrated by and against them at the centre. In other words, there is a need for a situated, caring, critically empathetic, psychosocial, pro-feminist approach to masculinity, one designed with the struggle for meaningfulness, worth and recognition of male youth lives at its centre.

Many men are unimpressed by feminism, and much of feminism has tended not to be impressed by the trauma experienced by men. In other words, on the one hand, some feminists have been largely blind to, sometimes even unmoved by, the painful lived realities of men; and, on the other hand, most men have not been very enthusiastic about joining the feminist movement. Samuel Adu-Poku notes that 'the presence of black men in feminism is a complex and conflicting issue, particularly in a Euro-Canadian/American context'.[6] In similar vein, David Ikard and Mark Anthony Neal observe that 'though the black feminist movement has always had a spattering of black male support, most black men – then and now – view black feminism as "whitewashed" and anti-black male. It is hardly surprising, then, that black male participation in black feminism has always been a sticky political issue.'[7]

The distance of many men from feminism and the incredulity that attaches to male feminism hold even more power for male youth. So, while there is a view that men see the feminist movement as whitewashed and not for them, a different reading of the terrain reveals that there is hardly anything written on anti-patriarchal work that addresses young and old men and their concerns and hopes. African American cultural analyst bell hooks has been influential in how I came to be free to think of love in the lives of boys and men. She offers several insights into how we might unlearn patriarchal beliefs:

There is not even a small body of anti-patriarchal literature speaking directly to black males about what they can do to educate themselves

114

for critical consciousness, guiding them on the path of liberation. The absence of this work stands as further testimony validating the contention that the plight of black men is not taken seriously.[8]

There is a scarcity of pro-feminist manuals and spaces in society concerned with what to do when men are raped, assaulted, or simply maltreated by their parents or are without jobs. There are not many pro-feminist texts and spaces aimed at repairing men who are violent *because* they grew up in abusive homes, violent neighbourhoods and an uncaring society. The simple reason for not paying attention to men's and boys' victimisation and vulnerability is that nearly all of our attention is usually focused on men who rape, who assault others, who support the domination of women and girls, or who are oppressive. To be sure, there is no question that most rapes are committed by men against women. And most women, like most men, are killed by men. All the same, we must do more with the knowledge that boys and men, too, get raped. Prison is one space where men get sexually assaulted, but it is not the only one. The overarching point is that we can use resources that render feminism understandable for boys and men. The basic idea of feminism, that all are created equal and must be treated as such, may be resisted by some men. In such cases, feminist men and women who are interested in changing men need to take the sources of such resistance into consideration in their work and find ways to overcome it.

The #BlackLivesMatter movement in the United States and elsewhere, which arose as a consequence of the unending killing of African American men by the police, highlighted the banal neglect of men as victims of institutionalised brutality, and the racialised and gendered hierarchisation of pain as inscribed within class, gender and race. What pro-feminist transnational readings of the #BlackLivesMatter movement show is that African American lives, and specifically African American male lives, do *not* matter in the United States. But I am afraid this lack of care for black males' lives appears to be true also in South Africa, other African countries, Australia and across Europe.

The neglect of male fears and traumas may be due to a genuine lack of awareness of the pain that males suffer. This is my optimistic interpretation. However, I also know from reading and thinking about imperialism, colonialism, racism, sexism and capitalism that some groups (white children from upper classes, for instance) have been considered more vulnerable to injury than others. Power structures work to convince us that some humans are more human than others, and thus some deserve more of our empathy and care, while others are less deserving of these. In light of this social structuring of warm fellow-feeling, violence against some groups can be viewed as outrageous and violence against others as not so bad. Perceiving violence toward certain social groups as more deserving of our attention than violence toward others means that too many gender scholars and activists fail to fully acknowledge some men's vulnerabilities. In other words, a wilful ignorance of the pain of some people as also meriting our empathy (and more of our resources to deal with it) disables some activists and scholars not only from achieving a thorough understanding of the true extent of violence, of who suffers from violence, of the determinants and pathways of violence, but also from comprehending men's vulnerability and hierarchies of masculinity. hooks is arguing for reclaiming feminism that imagines 'a world where women and men can belong together'. She reiterates the obvious fact that patriarchal domination and men's violence can never be attenuated, let alone eradicated, unless men are offered opportunities to change. Her work on men also suggests that even the people who are revolted by men's violence against women are not always repulsed by their violence against other men. She argues that male pain must be given equal consideration to female pain:

> While some women active in the feminist movement felt anguished about our collective inability to convert masses of men to feminist thinking, many women simply felt that feminism gave them permission to be indifferent to men, to turn away from male needs. When contemporary feminism was at its most intense, many women insisted that they were weary of giving energy to men, they wanted to place women at the centre of all feminist discussions. Feminist thinkers, like myself, who wanted to include men in the discussion were usually labelled male-identified and dismissed. We were sleeping with the enemy.[9]

The hurt that male violence does to women may be all too obvious. But we seriously err if we believe we can overcome men's violence – including that against other men and the aggressors themselves – without fully recognising and admitting into our policies and work men's own experiences of violence, victimisation *and* psychosocial pain.

It is often thought that it is because I am male that I am interested in masculinity. A person can never say with absolutely certainty why she, he or they become interested in a particular musician (say, Chicco), a knowledge field (like cosmology), an object (for example, a brand of jeans), an idea, another person, whatever. We can come up with an explanation when one is required. We can tell a story about how, being from this part of the world, we came to love the hairless Donskoy cat breed or the poetry of Su Tung-po, the classical Chinese poet. We can explain our love for a particular designer label or model of car. But that does not mean that individuals fully understand all the facts and circumstances that have influenced the development of their interests, trajectory and desires. Nor are they knowledgeable enough about their inner life to understand the dynamics of their fascinations. Without sounding a little too precious, then, although the male body I am in, that is me, may have something to do with my interest in masculinity, I suspect that interest came via my concern about *our life together as women and men*. I feel it came from wanting to know how we came to be in this shape.

Another explanation is that I have thought about and travelled to other countries that appear to care about their people, or where levels of direct violence are low, although the two are not to be conflated. But I have asked myself, how great would it be to live in a country like the latter, if not the former?

All of that points to the need to make more men (and more women) care a little more about our lives together as women and men. We must care about what makes men act with aggression toward women, especially those they say they love. If we are going to change men, even while conscious of the fact that we might not change all of them, we have to care and make men care about what they do to others, to each other and to themselves.

'I have never raped anyone' is not an achievement.

20 | Why is there violence where we expect to find love?

I can imagine a future where developments of the Fourth Industrial Revolution (4IR), like machine learning and big data computation, will have made it possible for people to find perfect love, not only with human-oid robots but with other people. I can envision that, in such a future, a human being could be enabled to ascertain whether the other human they select as a potential long-term partner, and who may declare love for them, might end up violating them. People would be able to rule out potentially abusive mates. This could be of incalculable help in drastically reducing violence in our society, perhaps even changing how we love.

However, I do not have the skills to develop an intelligent machine that would help to control or predict violence in relationships. Neither should you come to me looking for how to end violence by men against men, against unknown women, against children or against the planet.

I have learned, though, that if you bring up a child in a war zone you are more likely to create a warrior. But that is not the only reason why children grow up to love violence, for even in violent countries like this one, we do get a Desmond Tutu. In other words, we can still nurture non-violent masculinity, solidarity among the genders, support for one another, empathy and compassion, even in a country like ours.

It is common cause that, according to some people, the only antago-nistic force against violence is tougher policing – which is to say, a larger police force, increased militarisation of society, more prisons, more lethal arms, weapons that can inflict even greater destruction. In this worldview the one with the biggest muscles or weapons wins. Many individuals, groups and countries believe that. Not just gangsters, but army and police generals, presidents of countries and multinational corporations believe it. So do ordinary men and women you might walk past in a supermarket: violence has to be met with more violence.

Other people believe love will conquer all. That is the staple of films and literature, although these works tend to concentrate on passionate love to the exclusion of the many other kinds of love. I know of no government that believes that. I do not know whether feminist and critical psychologists believe in the idea that love can undo violence, even if it cannot conquer all, as the saying goes. All the same, it is my contention that it is worth critically analysing the potential of love as a force to alter boys and men, to transform masculinity, and thus to shift social relations between the genders.

It is infinitely discomposing, although the term does not cover all of the feelings I wish to express, to see love where one expects to find mostly violation, meanness and lack of empathy. It confuses some people when they see *botho* among the poor. This is due to the belief drilled into us by hegemonic capitalist thought that we, as individuals, have to want, or we are nothing, which is to say that material deprivation is the same thing as psychosocial or cultural ugliness. Journalists, scholars and politicians who may well frown at the misery caused by capitalist exploitation (and even support pro-poor social welfare policies) can be conduits of this belief: that is, that emotional misery is not as bad as economic misery. We come to expect to find rape among the poor; we anticipate that there will be more of the experience that nobody cares, which is to say lovelessness, among poor people in informal settlements; we may even hope that the people in townships will feel ugly. But it is when I see companionship in a 'poor couple' that I am reminded that it is not poverty that leads to sexual violence. Too often, it seems, it is because we have been taught that economic poverty leads to bodily and psychological violence that we imagine we can only find stories of abuse and despair where people live in squalor, or in a violence-wracked area. Consequently, we fail to see wells of affection in a place where we expect disaffection. We ignore lessons that care in action often entails something other than an expensive gift. Even where there is material want, belonging can be a spiritual bulwark. Even where there is destitution, we must find true intimacy, we must not give up on love.

There is a reverse story. We do not expect to find violence where there is wealth, in middle-class and rich homes which look wonderful from the outside but where there is viciousness within. Where there are expensive objects and yearly vacations to exotic destinations, but the torture is as sophisticated as it can be fatal. Stating this can provoke incredulity. But the disbelief stems from miseducation: because everything looks great from the outside does not mean that all is well inside. The way we present our lives to the outside world can be different from what really goes on in private. And the more successful we look, the harder it can be to tell others about our suffering.

Why, then, is there violence in some lovely-looking homes? Let us once and for all dispense with the view that violence is confined to poor households. It is not true that there is no violence among the affluent sections of society. A close look reveals that underneath the appearance of happiness the reality is complicated, but that reality can be as dire as in ugly-looking homes. The simple fact is that men's will to dominate women is found in all kinds of relationships and homes. That fact intimates that our instruments for understanding and preventing violence, in its different guises, have to be targeted at all homes and relationships. (Although we are concerned with homes and relationships at this point, violence is found in other institutions, spaces, events and interactions.) At the same time, we ought to expect to, and usually do, find the need for affection and loving relationships in men just as in women, regardless of where they live or what rung of the economic ladder they occupy. One reason why there may be more violence in less affluent homes and relationships is that lack of money is *one more stressor*, and a key one, in people's lives in our society, where money is a chief form of power. A lack of money not only increases the number of causes of conflict, but is at the root of other causes of conflict. Yet while lack of money can add to life-stress for those who are poor, it can be used by those who have it, while others around them do not have it, as another instrument of control. On the one end of the spectrum of this money-related control, the control can be imperceptible. The less economically well-off partner may even be happy because of what the money they receive can buy them. That is to say, because there is money a partner can be happy in an unequal relationship. On the other end of the spectrum sits economic abuse. In such cases, some men overtly use money to have women do what they want, control their behaviour or punish them if they stray out of line. What all this is intended to communicate is that the desire to have control over others leaps boundaries dividing the absolutely destitute, the economically poor, the middle stratum and the economically very rich. It is also to say that we ought to remind ourselves why being truly valued is so necessary for all, regardless of economic station in life, and why it is necessary from early in life till the end. It is because love, as what we can call emotional wealth, is a resource that can act as a protective barrier in times of stress for everyone.

I want to say one more thing about money before I move on. Money can also be an object behind which men can hide so as not to deal with their feelings. It can allow some of us to refuse to 'engage' emotionally. It as if some men's viciousness toward women who demonstrate love for them is a kind of refusal to believe they can be loved or emotionally gratified for just being alive. The violence appears to communicate that the love and objects that surround the couple or family are not enough, that the experience of lovelessness from an earlier period perhaps is so deep that you cannot see the love right in front of you – even though you need it. (It is important that none of this is read as an excuse for men's violence. It is to suggest that we cannot understand men's violence until we deal with these emotions.)

It is my view that violence is the antithesis of love. By understanding and valuing another person, love appears to me to be the most vital force against violence. I know I may sometimes sound like an optimist, full of hope, idealism and unwarranted belief in people. I know that we can and do hurt people we love. I am aware of the many reasons men aggress against women. It may well be because of the immensity, inconstancy and inexhaustible intricacy of our affective lives, the fact that others affect us in ways we do not always readily comprehend, that we cannot but hurt them. More often it is because we do not take enough care; but sometimes it is because we want to injure them in order to witness the depths of their affection for us. We hurt those we love because we want to be loved more – more intensely – even when we do not love ourselves, to make up for the hunger we carry inside ourselves from an earlier period.

I am, then, not naïve. The force of love can bring ill consequences. We can be maimed, brutalised, and our lives ended by those who claim to love us, for among the people who love us are those who can injure us. Sometimes the person who violates me is the same one who once swore to love me.

However, we have neglected love as a transformative social and psychical force in our work, and in academic and policy studies dedicated to men and violence. Such neglect is incomprehensible, for we already agree that colonialism and apartheid were systems aimed at dehumanising men and women. Colonialism did not have any love for the kind of humans we are, and did not want us to love ourselves either. Apartheid found many ways to show us that it did not love us, and did not want us to love even our own skins. All of us, women and men, need love in our lives. If this is so, it suggests that those who preach, teach, write, or make policy about men and boys cannot ignore love in their work with men and boys. The question to ask at this juncture, though, is, what kind of love?

It is a commonplace that violence is not a rare phenomenon in love or intimate relationships. At this point, it is worth repeating what I said previously. While the phrase 'intimate relationship' is a handy one, to assume that just because two people are 'together' they are in an *intimate* relationship can be misleading. To proceed on that basis to study why there is violence in an intimate relationship thus takes us further and further away from the primary fact that there may be no real intimacy in the relationship. Studies on intimate relationships do precisely that, often taking for granted that a more or less steady relationship between two people involving sex or living together as spouses is defined by intimacy. Sadly, there are intimate relationships *without* intimacy, if we understand intimacy in the way Lynn Jamieson described it a while back:

> What is meant by intimacy is often a very specific sort of knowing, loving and 'being close to' another person. The self-help books advocate talking and listening, sharing your thoughts, showing your feelings. This is the type of intimacy I call 'disclosing intimacy'. The emphasis is on mutual disclosure, constantly revealing your inner thoughts and feelings to each other . . . Mutually shared intimacy of this type typically requires a relationship in which people participate as equals.[1]

It is for this reason that, in my efforts to understand violence in relation-ships, my focus is on situations where the word 'love' is used explicitly, where a man says he loves a woman. I want to try to clarify the specific relationship of intimacy I have in mind, namely, an equal love relation-ship; I want to consider whether or not equality is presumed to exist in an intimate relationship. If, however, intimacy does not necessarily presume equality of partners, I want to know how the partners justify to themselves and live with tacit inequality. The complication we sit with is obvious, given the foregoing definition of intimacy: people can have a 'love relation-ship' without loving; or there can be happiness in a relationship without gender-based equality. And this may be an important clue as to why there is violence in intimate relationships. That is to say, in our time, when fem-inism – the theory and practice informed by discourses of equality – has decisively shaped gender relations even while it faces ongoing resistance, intimate violence is created precisely because there can never be real inti-macy where the partners are unequal.

I am aware that this repertoire of practices of intimacy, of mutual self-disclosure, sharing one's feelings and thoughts, was developed in a particular culture, although globalisation of images has made the reper-toire available to billions around the world. Since this ideal of romantic love comes from a culture that many people in our country may not share, it means that when people are in a relationship they may not have in mind, nor expect to experience, an intimacy of self, or to regard each other as equals.

Previously, I have asked: do men need (this sort of) love, this kind of intimacy? Critical scholars of violence, like critical scholars of mas-culinity and critical psychologists, rarely ask this question. I am not sure whether that neglect means that we, critical academics, think love is not worth studying, or whether the sentiment is that focusing on love in men takes our attention away from more important topics like social equality. It may also be due to our natural suspicion as critical scholars about what individuals say (and certainly what they say about love), a suspicion that is not altogether misplaced. However, I assume that the lack of attention to love *as* love is because of the fact that, among those of us who study intimate relations, there is already an expectation that there is always a possibility of aggression, even where there is love. That violence is all too common is a fact. But there is, as I have said, a need to be open to the unanticipated, and to recognise love as potentially transformative for men.

In the context of a society saturated by violence, there is an as yet unresolved difference between how love is analysed by, say, critical scholars of men and boys on the one hand, and how love is understood by the men and boys themselves on the other. There is a gap that still needs to be bridged between how love is theorised by, say, a feminist psychologist and by those for whom she is fighting. This is no mere academic concern. In the area of love, to try to understand violence one must face theoretical and political certainties lying side by side with everyday experiential contradictions. There are uncharted territories, numerous gaps and abundant slippages in our maps of understanding.

But let me underline this: objective social inequality between women and men is a huge contributing factor to men's violence against women. It is critical to recognise this.

The fact of objective gender inequality between men and women notwithstanding, we must not close our minds to other drivers of violence. Levels of economic inequality are implicated in violence. Alcohol, too. And the inefficiency of the criminal justice system when it comes to apprehending, disciplining and rehabilitating those who commit acts of violence. A society's generalised support for the use of violence to resolve conflict, or to demonstrate power, is also a factor. In a racist society, unfavourable attitudes toward black lives and the death of black people cannot be discounted. Lack of impulse control plays a part. Individual men's belief in rape myths is also likely to dispose men to rape.

I have said that I can imagine a future where 4IR helps humans find their perfect, non-violent, loving partners. I am sorry I do not have the skills to develop the technology to realise that future, but I am not ruling out someone else creating such a technology. It will still have to deal with the question of lies that people tell to achieve the goal of finding partners. I also do not have a formula for how to eradicate men's violence in relationships. None exists at this point in human life. What I have done is to ask questions, even if they may have looked nothing like questions. That is also to say that what continues to trouble me, in the end, is how perturbing it is to face the fact that violence can exist in what are called intimate relationships, that hurting others can live alongside declarations of love for them.

What I find, for myself if for no one else, in this troubling fact is that I still do not fully understand why men hurt women, yet if I am to move closer and closer to knowing anything real about men's love and men's violence and men's identities, I must remain open to finding unanticipated stories, surprising answers, the unexpected.

21 | Really nice guys

Alles ist gut (*All Is Well*) is a searing German film written and directed by Eva Trobisch, her first feature-length movie, first released in 2018. It is, among other interpretations, a film about the many sides of silence.[1]

The main protagonist is Janne, played by Aenne Schwarz. Janne is about to begin a job as a temp in a publishing company. After a class reunion party, she is raped by Martin, who, she will find out, is her future boss's brother-in-law. What follows is a slow-paced story in which Janne acts as if nothing happened.

The film is about what not speaking about sexual coercion does to a woman, when she cannot even name what was done to her as sexual violence. The violent sexual act is treated as though it is not really violence, yet the viewers are left in no doubt about what they have witnessed. When Janne and her mother have a sauna together, and her mother asks about the bruise on the side of her face and what happened, Janne lies. Despite her mother's repeated questions, she opts to say nothing happened. When her would-be boss, Robert, asks about the bruises, she says nothing. Her boyfriend also does not get told the truth. Although they were financially insolvent before the rape, the couple are shown to have had a well-functioning relationship. What Janne wants is to go on as if all is well.

But rape alters the future and the self.

The first time Janne meets Martin after the rape is at the theatre to which Robert has invited her, because his partner is feeling unwell. At the theatre, Janne spends an uncomfortable period of time sandwiched between her boss and her rapist. After the play, Martin approaches her and wants to talk. She elects to talk about everything but the violation. And she offers her cheeks to be kissed by him, although rather hesitantly. Only when she is walking back from the theatre alone, in a telling scene, does her body shake, and through her gestures and guttural sounds we are given a sense of what is happening inside her. This is the one scene where it is evident that everything happened, that all is not well. The second time we see her unable to keep things inside, convulsed with tears, is after she has been working late at the office and Martin comes in.

Janne has to see her rapist nearly every day. Martin and his victim work together at the publisher. It seems to me that the director wants us to see Martin not as a monster but as an everyday man. Actually, the very first time we see Janne and Martin in the same scene in the film, before the rape, a character called Sissi says Martin is a reasonable guy.

Janne's boyfriend also says he is really nice. Janne agrees. Really nice guys rape, the film wants us to admit.

On later occasions when they meet, after the rape, Martin is apologetic about how he acted. On several occasions he wants to talk about what happened. What he is after is absolution; in effect he wants Janne to recognise him as the nice guy she and others say he is. He may even want *her to say* he did not intend to assault her.

When your rapist asks pardon from you, that entreaty is added to the unarticulated sense of defilement, the shame with which you walk around. How can such a nice man do such a bad thing? Who can believe it? I must be in the wrong. I led him on.

Janne will find out she is pregnant. In addition to the violent act of rape, there is that to deal with. She has an abortion. And that, too, is one more thing to add to the consequence of the rape.

She tells Martin about the abortion. Her boyfriend only finds out when he has to pick her up from the abortion clinic because her mother, whom she had called, is away and cannot fetch her.

The sexual attack and its effects are made all the more terrible by the slow and terrific way in which the film develops. The 'non-violent' assault itself is preceded by scenes of sharing cigarettes, dancing, and Janne inviting Martin to sleep on the couch after the party. It is because the rapist is such an ordinary man, a nice person, one whom a woman can trust because he is white-skinned, tall, plays with a cat, wears nice, just-conservative-enough white shirts, that we are led to understand what the sexual assault does to Janne's sense of things around Martin and her work.

I had watched the movie months before. I decided to watch it again in December 2020, to remind myself what it was that had left an impression on me.

In watching the effects of Martin's rape on Janne, part of my mind is not only on her but on white women who are raped by white men known to them, white men who look nice, respectable. I am so engaged precisely because of what I want to learn of women who look like me who are raped by apparently respectable men like me. To see Janne being raped by Martin prods me to ask another question that has troubled me for a long while. How many white, middle-class women choose to pretend all is well when they have been raped by white men they know? The silence is not only in movies.

I take it seriously that *Alles ist gut* is a German film, set in a country where, even after taking in many refugees since 2015, whiteness, racialisation and racism appear to be not as prominently discussed as they are in the United States and in my own country.[2] To consider the German context of the film implies that I hesitate to analyse it from my own situatedness in South Africa, with its particular history. I am also aware that the sexual violence dramatised in the movie may have little to do with the Germanic whiteness of the protagonists. In Germany race may perhaps have nothing to do with how sexual violence occurs.[3] That said, history reveals that some core ideas about racial superiority, ideas which enfold whiteness as a desirable, non-violent status, were manufactured or 'refined' in German intellectual thought and perpetrated on blacks and Jews by Nazism, the twentieth-century apogee of racist thinking.

Ironically, in the former colonies of Germany and other European countries, racist ideas have long and overtly structured our identities, explicitly directing our choices regarding who deserves our love, who gets to share our bodies and who is suspect. Racism has everything to with trustworthiness, lovableness and their opposites, for 'race was made through rape in very direct and deliberate and indirect ways', as Pumla Dineo Gqola has incisively argued.[4] The truth is that it is not only in the former colonies but all over the world that racist patriarchy is evident; with a little scratching beneath the surface, one soon realises that white niceness is often part of the cultural myths and beliefs that silence abused women. It is not only the 'enslaved', dirty, unrapable women who have no recourse to speak of their rape by white men, but curiously, as we see in the movie, desirable white women, too, who are shamed into silence.[5] It is knowledge of how whiteness is shaped in a world structured by race that prompts me to want to know: what might be the effects on white victims of being raped by nice, familiar white men? I would like to see and read more of these stories, about the silences around rape of respectable white women by men they know, stories such as that told in broadcaster Tracy Going's memoir, *Brutal Legacy*.[6]

In bringing to mind places where racism was once law, I wonder whether it is because much more is to be gained than lost that the pain of sexual violence is dwarfed by the rewards of whiteness, where white women who are raped by white men they know do not tell of their rape. You may recall that in such places, at one point black men were imprisoned and murdered on the basis of trumped-up accusations of the rape of white women. The rape of white women by men who are regarded as not white, which is to say in that sense rape by a stranger, is the rape that can be spoken about without any hesitation. The black man is, to most white people, the unknowable stranger. He is also, by the way, not quite human, a lower animal, which already surfaces images of bestiality.

In these places the structuring force of racism convinces us that only poor black women deserve rape, since their bodies exist to serve others, even if against their will. Having been violated, they cannot be articulate about their pain. They are structurally voiceless anyway. Even now, after the formal demise of legalised racism, dog whistles abound about black men as the intruders and the embodiment of rapists, and black women as unfeeling animals who cannot be raped.

What I see in the film, beyond Janne's story, is that, in certain cases, women choose not to report being raped by white men, nice men, respectable ones. I have little direct knowledge of those cases that will not be readily found in the police reports or newspaper pages. I suspect it happens more often than the statistics tell us. It has to be hidden.

When other forms of abuse of women are added to the sexual violence – the emotionally belittling words, verbal putdowns, gaslighting and financial manipulation, the everyday micro-forms of control and ill-treatment, quite often followed by niceness and appeals for understanding – there are grounds to suspect that there are more women who suffer in silence. That is why I have now and again wondered why women who appear to have good families, are educated or have a good job do not seem willing to report abuse they have experienced. What prevents them from saying, me too, a nice man I know raped me? My boyfriend made me do things I am ashamed to speak about. My co-worker was sexually aggressive toward me. Why are there more reports of sexual offences against poor and less educated women than against these other women?

What the silence of a raped woman in *Alles ist gut* communicates to me is not only that much is unwell between nice white women and nice white men. I know this is not breaking news. But being aware of the misogyny, sexual exploitation and coercive sex visible on pornography sites (which it is best not to cite), where white men are subjecting white women to degradation, deception and humiliation, I am surprised at the relatively low numbers of reported rapes among white women in the country. While sexual assault may not be readily found in the statistics, it is to be found in books like *Brutal Legacy* and *Of Motherhood and Melancholia: Notebook of a Psycho-Ethnographer*.[7] What the silence also communicates is the need to look for it, to open it up, to incorporate it, old news though it is. What I suspect is that there are possibly many other women, surely not only one white woman in a film in Germany, but in particular women of a certain class, of all colours, who suffer in silence from the aggression of the nice men they know.

22 | 'There was nothing suspicious about him'

Just as in matters of loving and being loved, vulnerability is baked into trust. And as with love, trusting others and being trusted do not headline news make.

The closer the attention I pay to news reports of violence, the more I realise there is one other thing we could use but are not getting help with from African social scientists and humanists. We could use the help of these experts, who are employed to explain our society and our subjectivities, to *write for us*, not for each other – but that is not help I am asking for at this moment. Of immediate concern in this reflection is the help we could use in the form of *productive, creative thought* that seeds how, within a context of pervasive and gratuitous violence that characterises society, we might repair psychosocial mutuality – assuming that such thinking, or its effects, reaches those who desperately need it.

It is common cause that violence has become part of the ambience of our lives. Less common is the understanding that because of this ubiquity of violence, trust connections – which are interlinked with other affective attachments like love – have been extensively damaged. The impairment of trust as social capital can be traced back centuries. We could not trust the racist, colonial and apartheid governments, because they were not elected to care for us. Exploitation, theft, corruption on an industrial scale, oppression in various forms, and different refinements in methods of humiliation – these were at the core of what those governments were about. There was also segregation, the ideology of superiority of some over others, and the internalisation of inferiorisation in many. The use of violence to ensure that these aims were achieved was part and parcel of that centuries-old history. These governments simply could not be trusted, of course.

The reality of oppression and cruelty could not remain out there, only touching the surface of our skins. The historical lack of trust in the whites who governed – or rather misgoverned – us under duress would seep into our interiors. And so our psychosocial relationships with whites were sullied. Many feared their barely concealed violence, the constant threat they posed. We learned that their animus could be unleashed at any time. Encounter by encounter, our trust in whites was eroded.

What could we do, though, having been pauperised, dispossessed of the land, and forced into labouring for white capital, but rely on whites to employ us? We had to survive. We may not have fully trusted them, but we needed food, medicine, shelter.

As intergroup trust decreased, intragroup mutuality increased. Or at least, that was what was supposed to happen. We were supposed to rely even more on each other. And very often we did. Racist segregation created forced intimacy. But the daily humiliations of the white racist structures seeped into black lives. A man would turn against another with deadly violence if so much as his shoe was stepped on. Violent death and injury were mundane aspects of life. We had our own internal tribal hatred. Politically motivated violence morphed into interpersonal violence. We witnessed horrific acts of violence, like necklacing, perpetrated against our neighbours. There were *izimpipi* (traitors) and *askaris* (turncoats) who betrayed us. The effects of the savage laws had long been injected into our bloodstreams.

Yet the new government led by the African National Congress (ANC) that came to power in 1994 did not seem to realise the imperative of repairing the broken trust between the people and the state. There was also never any society-wide effort to rebuild trust within communities, a much harder task. It was preposterous to assume that, on its own, the demise of apartheid would automatically repair our brokenness, our mistrust of each other and lack of confidence in ourselves. And as people living in same country, we cannot do without nourishing trust in and for each other. As part of the process of turning us into a non-violent society, our social relations with each other still need repair, because there has been immense historical trauma in our society.

As is well known, not too long after Nelson Mandela became president the country would learn of the massive corruption that characterised the ruling party. And things would get much worse in this regard under the presidency of Jacob Zuma, who was implicated in state capture alongside other financial and political elites. The government was eventually compelled to institute a judicial commission of inquiry into corruption.[1] That is to say, on top of the historical mistrust of government we had inherited, the new government could not be trusted to manage our political economy, let alone help us restitch our frayed psychosocial ties.

All of that constitutes one line of explanation of the violence that is endemic in South African society. But we need to remember that to advance a historical explanation of this pervasive violence is not to excuse the violence.

Turning to history to find the roots of how we became what we are does not negate the reality that men pose the greatest risk to women, to children, to other men. Men are a risk even to their own lives, for they get fatally injured and commit suicide at higher rates than women. Men who subscribe to the notion that men have to dominate others by any means at their disposal, who believe that they must be in control over others or they are not men, embody the highest risk.

What baffles me is that despite the historical roots and omnipresent risk of violence and victimisation, many of us live as if we can trust men, both strange and familiar. We live as if violence only happens to others – until it hits us. Leaving aside those who have little choice but to stay in violent homes, to venture out across a veld soaked in risk, or to live with a forlorn kind of trust in those who pose a danger to them, it may be that those of us who behave as if the world is to be trusted make calculations about the risk we face. In most cases these calculations are correct. But sometimes, too often, they are disastrous.

At the same time, in the better-off suburbs, the common sight of private security companies being employed to protect residents from crime and violence is an indication of the fear and mistrust present in these suburbs. In the poorer areas, community policing and vigilantism are evident – signs of awareness of the apparent risk. In any event, the clearest indication of the reality of the risk we live with is found in the high rates of murder, assault, rape and aggravated robbery in the country.[2]

What I have learned from the time when the Covid-19 pandemic first made itself felt in South Africa in March 2020 is that, along with government leadership and institutional efficiency, trust is vital. Trust is critical not only in interpersonal life but in a democratic society, to enable it to quickly overcome a massive health challenge such as the pandemic. Trust is also a key ingredient when a society is faced with other big social and health problems such as violence. To overcome a danger like the coronavirus or widespread violence, there needs to be a high level of trust in government. Trust in science and in institutions is also important; that is, believing that scientists and other people working in these institutions are doing their jobs to the best of their abilities.

How might we understand trust at its most basic? Many definitions and ideas are available. One definition regards trust as 'an expectancy held by an individual that the behavior (verbal or non-verbal) of another individual or group of individuals would be altruistic and personally beneficial to himself'.[3] Another view is that trust is 'a constellation of beliefs regarding the extent to which others are or will be concerned about one's personal welfare and best interests'.[4] Yet another interpretation links trust to social capital and even economic prosperity, taking trust as 'the expectation that arises within a community of regular, honest, and cooperative behavior, based on commonly shared norms, on the part of other members of that community'.[5] And, finally, there is the psychosocial developmental idea advanced by Erik Erikson:

> The firm establishment of enduring patterns for the solution of the nuclear conflict of basic trust versus basic mistrust in mere existence is the first task of the ego, and thus first of all a task for maternal care. But let it be said here that the amount of trust derived from earliest infantile experience does not seem to depend on absolute quantities of food or demonstrations of love, but rather on the quality of the maternal relationships.[6]

In sum, trust begins at the earliest moments of a baby's life. Parents – usually mothers but sometimes fathers and other adults who help raise children – are the foundations of an individual's development of trust. And as Erikson also said, 'Mothers create a sense of trust in their children by that kind of administration which in its quality combines sensitive care of the baby's individual needs and a firm sense of personal trustworthiness within the trusted framework of their culture's lifestyle.'[7]

Trust is always relational, while including the confidence one has in the self. Indeed, what happens in early life 'forms the basis in the child for a sense of identity which will later combine a sense of being "all right", of being oneself'.[8]

Trust entails beliefs and expectations of civility. Trust is linked to social norms. And, once again, trust, like love, always involves vulnerability.

To return to violence, trust presupposes that another person or group will not harm us or treat us cruelly. Especially in the case of those others who are close to us, family and friends and neighbours, we are more likely to trust them because we feel we know them, and therefore expect them to have our well-being at heart. But what if evidence shows that those we are supposed to trust under normal circumstances are the ones who do harm to us? What if you live in a society where a significant percentage of those who are not to be trusted when it comes to hurting you are those you know – or think you know?

Studies indicate that 'outside the realm of relationships, trust acts as a social lubricant that promotes cooperation between group members, sustains social order, and permits beneficial long-term exchanges that otherwise might never occur'.[9] The relational nature of trust is not confined to one-to-one connections but extends to larger groups, society as a whole, perhaps even to the planet. We have to trust, as far as possible, those with whom we share group belonging and the world, such as work colleagues, or fellow members of our own race and ethnic or religious group. Conversely, we tend to find it difficult to develop trust in people we categorise as belonging to other groups, because we frequently assume they do not share the same worldview as ourselves and thus will not act altruistically toward us or look after our interests.[10] Nevertheless, if we belong to one society, even if it is one with a history of racist and sexist antagonism, we have to develop some level of trust for the society to function more or less smoothly. But our society appears not to function smoothly. Its dysfunctionality exists both on a large scale, as we have witnessed on many occasions even after the demise of apartheid, and in everyday interpersonal contexts, on a scale too overwhelming to survey here. Given the magnitude of this violence, one can easily become numbed by it, thus neglecting to pay close attention to individuals, to small events. But we must.

This meditation on trust was brought to mind by a news report about a serial killer in a place called Mthwalume, in KwaZulu-Natal.[11] Admittedly, the case is an exceptional one in which an individual man killed many women. Even so, in my country, sadly, the killing (and rape) of women by known and unknown men is not that rare.

Forty-one-year-old Mduduzi Khomo was the prime suspect for the murder of five women in the area: 16-year-old Nosipho Gumede, 23-year-old Neliswe Dube, Nosipho's sister Akhona Gumede who was aged 25, and Zama Sylvia Chiliza, aged 40. An unidentified woman believed to be in her late thirties was the fifth of his victims. The police found the burned body of another woman in the same vicinity, but believed she had not been killed by Khomo.

The sketchy details of the case are that the suspected killer had been employed at a newly constructed petrol station on the R102 road. He began working there in December 2019; he was first employed as a security guard at the petrol station and then promoted to petrol attendant. Four months later, in April 2020, the first victim was reported missing.

Most cases of violence against women are never satisfactorily resolved. The perpetrators are very rarely apprehended or convicted. In this instance, though, the perpetrator was found. Khomo confessed to the murders. He then hanged himself while in custody.

What interested me in this case was what the people who 'knew' Khomo and were interviewed for a newspaper report said about him. When asked to describe the killer, the manager of the petrol station where Khomo worked said, 'He was a very quiet guy. There was nothing suspicious about him.'[12] A female employee at the petrol station said something similar: 'nothing was off'.[13]

The question the journalist asked these people may have been misleading. Presumably the two were asked whether there was anything suspicious or 'off' about the killer. In my experience it is rare to have a killer wear a big sign indicating that he is a killer. Even if he wore a T-shirt with the words 'I am a serial killer' on it, we would not believe him.

What we must ask ourselves is not whether another person exudes serial killer 'vibes', or whether something about him appears to be 'off', or whether he looks suspicious. What we need to understand is how to go about *thinking about risk in this society*. A person who happens to have known a Khomo-type murderer (who evokes nothing suspicious) must ask themselves, why did I feel the person who turned out to be a serial killer was to be trusted, in light of the rates of violence in the country? Am I just trusting as a person? What kind of people do I trust?

The more complex a society becomes, the less certainty there is about others' trustworthiness, and the more time it takes to know what others are capable of. We cannot, in an impersonal society, know each other until death do us part, one might say. Even when we do know each other, we can never have all the information about each other. This is all the more so in a society where the empirical reality is of increased levels of violence, and where relations between men and women are, with difficulty, changing rapidly. Why do we think that men and women will be immediately knowable to us, unless we already know that they have not killed in the past and can be sure they will not kill in the future? Why do we *not* think there is always a risk, when it is clear that risk is present?

It seems that for the individual, what is needed is to be aware of the risk and do whatever is necessary to reduce it. We know that men are a risk and at risk. At the level of government, we need to reduce rates of violence and thus the level of vulnerability of individuals. For this to happen we need a government and other key state organs that pay attention to masculinity as a risk to health and to society. There cannot be rebuilding of social mutuality until this risk is attenuated. When the state fails to understand what is going on, and hence fails to protect us, when it is undependable or inconsistently reliable when it comes to meeting our basic needs, especially the need for safety, we have to do what we can to see to our own security needs, to depend on ourselves. We have to manage the risk.

Yet we must trust some people, just as we have to 'trust' some objects, like this chair on which I am sitting, which I must trust will not collapse under me. We cannot but trust (or act as if we trust) some institutions, because we depend on them. Take this example of how we cannot altogether avoid trusting. I once flew to a country on the other side of the world where the people speak a language I could not understand. I had a bilingual dictionary – that is how long ago it was – and hoped they spoke English (which I understood a little). I had paid many euros for a hotel via an internet-based service. It was the first time I had used the service, and

I was worried about whether it would work. When I arrived, I showed the receptionist my passport. They asked for my credit card, and told me my room was ready. That is the story. Nothing untoward happened.[14] I had taken several risks along the way, and things had worked out the way they were supposed to. But at several points I had been aware of the risks, and that I could perhaps lose money.

In that transaction, as in many ordinary ones, I was reminded how we (have to) depend on others not to swindle us. Trust in others and in services, many of these now provided via the internet, is vital to a predictable, safe life. We have to live as if others, whether they belong to an out-group or we see them as part of our in-group, are trustworthy. To trust is therefore always to take a risk. (The same applies to love: to love is to take a risk.) We put ourselves in a vulnerable position when we choose to trust. (The same holds for love: we invite vulnerability when we open ourselves for love to enter.)

The more we believe we know others, even though our knowledge of them will always be partial, the less risky we feel it is to trust them. But that does not mean there is zero risk; it simply means the risk appears low. Remember this conversation between my partner and me?

I ask, But you don't think I can hurt you, do you? That I can kill you?

I don't know. You *never* know. She stresses the words, dragging out 'never'. Maybe there are circumstances we haven't tested you under.

But the probabilities? I ask.

The probability is low, she responds. But there is always –

Ja, I know, I say.

There is always a chance, she says.

I can hurt you emotionally, yes, I say. Not kill you.

I don't know, she says.

I don't feel that I'm capable of killing you.

You never know with perpetrators, she says.

You never actually know, I say. But why is that? I mean is it the length of time –

I think I meant that even with the length of time you can never fully know what another person is capable of.

I am *not* arguing for a society of mutual suspicion. Suspecting all men of nefarious intentions would make life difficult. That would be essentialising men as naturally bad. It is also true that in any society it is a minority that kills. Also, while many men are complicit in control, violence or coercion attached to currently hegemonic patriarchal masculinity, a very small number of men actually are hegemonic.

I should also stress that the case of Khomo is exceptional, because there was a pattern to his behaviour. He was a serial killer. The risk, in this case, is different from the risk in cases where a man is relatively close to his victim, and may even be an intimate partner, not a potential serial killer hidden in plain sight.

I *am* suggesting that we have to engage with our notions of trust. We must talk about the fact that we never totally know men (or women). And a recognition that we always operate under conditions of uncertainty in our interactions and relations with others has implications for our social and intimate life.

Never being able to fully know others is understandable – except when lack of knowledge comes with increased risk. In that case the bar must be set higher. We have to think about the fact that there is always a probability that others – including our boyfriends, girlfriends, relatives, children, colleagues or spouses – can harm us, a fact that is evident in the police statistics on crime.[15] In our society, that probability is higher than in many other societies. I am suggesting that certain forms of masculinity pose a risk, and that to reduce the risk to ourselves we must fully understand that masculinities come in different forms, and make the masculinity that endangers people unattractive to boys and girls, and to men and women, too.

I am arguing that we have to think about our relations with each other. I am suggesting that we are in need of repair of social trust. It should be obvious that while reducing the likelihood of violence is important in itself, the reduction of violence also facilitates the restoration or increase of trust and social mutuality in society. I am always holding on to the hope that we shall find ways to repair ourselves so that we can redevelop relationships with each other. And I am always looking at how we might engender more caring masculinity as we raise loving boys, as a way out of, and even in the face of, the violence that endangers our lives.

23 | They don't teach about sexual consent at university or at home

Where did you learn about sexual consent? How do you understand it?

These were two of the questions I asked students at Graham House, a men's residence at Rhodes University, as we did an exercise on putting things in the #ConsentBox[1] and throwing out other things.

I had been invited to the university in 2016 by a woman and a man (which is important to note), Babalwa and Sbu, to give a series of presentations and to talk with students.

Sounds elementary.

At some point we get taught about sexual consent. And then we build on that for ourselves.

I had anticipated, from a combination of extant literature and experience, that most students at that university had never had any explicit dialogue on sexual consent. Had never been taught about what is and what isn't sexual consent. I am afraid I wasn't proven wrong.

I never got an education on sexual consent at university. But that was in the 1980s. I also never got it at home. Or at school.

I do not think many universities had courses on sexuality, let alone on sexual consent, when I was a student. You could say I went to university at a different time, that things have changed. You would be mistaken. As far as I know, few universities today, in the twenty-first century, have a systematic and consistent education programme for their students on the ins and outs of sexual consent. The lack of sexual consent education is not confined to Rhodes University.

The dialogue with students at Graham House left me convinced that intensive, ongoing, expert and, to be sure, sociopolitical education campaigns on sexual consent at universities are long overdue. One student at the residence said this was the first time they had had any such dialogue, and, he went on, it is too late to change what young men like him understand about sexual consent. He was earnest, and angry, and sad, almost in despair. This student was not from a township school. His point was that this is a dialogue he had needed much earlier in his life, in Grade 7 at the latest. I think so too. But I also think it is never too late. We need to give young men like him, and women like those with whom I was in conversation that night, an education that aspires to make more and more real the values in our Constitution about equality. If we do not, who do we hope will teach young people how consent is knitted in with femininity, masculinity, gender and sexual power?

I had been both excited and a little apprehensive about the dialogue I would have at the women's residence, Victoria Mxenge House. I had initially been invited to speak to the male students and that was what I had prepared for. That was also what I told the female students when I took my place in front of them at their res, since I could do nothing else after I was told they were waiting for me. And were they!

Why was I apprehensive about the dialogue with female students? Part of my anxiety came from the fact that the public lecture I had given at the university on masculinity and sexual violence had ended on a somewhat sour note. I had been unable to come to a satisfactory point of disagreement – agreement was not going to happen – with a combative student who insisted that masculinity is, by nature, violent. I disagree, of course.

I opened the dialogue by speaking frankly to the students about my trepidation. I told them I had been under the impression that I was invited to their university to have a set of dialogues with male students on masculinity and sexual violence. I said that, in my estimate, the subject of sexual consent with female students would best be discussed with someone like Danai Mupotsa or Pumla Dineo Gqola, who would be at the university the following week. I still think so: that these thinkers, whose work I do not just know but can never get enough of, are best placed to talk to women about sexual consent, perhaps even to anybody who wants to learn. This is not modesty on my part. I say it not only because each of these feminist thinkers is among the best in their field, but also because they *know*.

But two female students had a short answer for me: to paraphrase, we want to hear what a male person like you has to say on the subject. That is how they put it.

Well, what could I say? I am one of those – a human male.

It is true that I can never know if I did a good job representing the male of the human species. But after a night and a day of letting what went down percolate through my body and mind, what I told anybody within earshot or on my Facebook page was that, following what I had thought was an informative discussion with male students, the dialogue with the women was one of the most incredible dialogues with students I have had in my career as an activist scholar. Possibly ever.

It wasn't because I am a really good teacher. It was because of the students. It was an intense 90 minutes. It was emotional. It was eye-opening. I don't think you would be able to get that dynamic in a traditional lecture room set-up. Maybe I should do this again, I thought. I am not sure that universities, even better-off ones like Rhodes University, are providing some of the life education these women are looking for. Knowledge about how to survive what are meant to be the peacetimes.

I am incapable of communicating what an impression our dialogue has left on me. Besides getting a clear appreciation of the need to keep talking to young women and men about masculinity, femininity and sexual consent, it seems to me that in the area of sexuality, violence and gender, there are significant differences between the concerns of female students and male students. There are worrying differences between how some young men and young women at university think about a 'no' and a 'yes', about relating, about emotions and about freedom. What was supposed to be simply a dialogue about sexual consent opened up into a discussion that drew in the students' views on their relationships with their parents, unequal treatment of siblings by mothers, absent fathers, being single parents at university.

To start a discussion about sexual consent can never be a simple matter of talking about how a no is a no. That is why the female students spoke candidly and critically about the disjuncture between the lessons they received from their parents and where they were now. To speak about consent is ultimately to speak about how we are raised, the ways we play, what we are looking for when we go out to a club or party, the balance of power between men and women, how we live with each other, what we believe about women and men, and, of course, our fantasies, fetishes and fears.

What would I do with this knowledge if I was a university manager? I would pay close attention to what students say about their lack of well-founded, affirmative education on sexual consent. I would initiate regular sexual consent teach-ins. I would call on the amazing feminist teachers we have around us to help me put together programmes and to show me how to do this well. I think Rhodes University can use more of these dialogues. I suspect many other universities can, too. Heck, the entire basic and higher education system can use well-designed training on sexual consent.

•

I did not know about the House of Yes or the idea of 'consenticorns' until late 2020. I got to read about both following an email from a journalist, Catherine Del Monte. Consenticorns are consent guardians associated with the House of Yes, which was created in 2007 by two friends, Kae Burke and Anya Sapozhnikova. Their website says they 'just wanted to make art and have a good time'.[2] The space they created is described in this way:

> We are a collective of creatives, performers and innovators who live to support artistic expression, performance, nightlife and community. Our home is the House of Yes in Bushwick, Brooklyn – our venue and incubation space fuelled by passion and designed to inspire. Together we build intimate experiences, spectacular entertainment, killer parties and outrageous events anywhere and everywhere.[3]

Del Monte was working on an article on consent, specifically the idea of consenticorns, for *Maverick Life*, a supplement of the newspaper *Daily Maverick 168*. She had been looking for an academic to respond to some questions she had about consent. She had contacted several of the well-known feminist scholars in the country, but none had the inclination or time to do what she needed. She was eventually directed to me by Floretta Boonzaier, a professor of psychology at the University of Cape Town.

I was happy to be interviewed on the topic, because I have strong views about academics and the necessity of engaging with different publics via the media. More importantly, I had been thinking and engaging with students about consent for a while. I had also recently been working on online materials on sexual consent for young people with my intern, Pascal Richardson. Among the thoughts I have on this subject is that it is an error to categorise sexual consent as a verbal act, limited to what happens in private between two people, where one person wants to have sex and the other has to give or withhold consent. That had become exceedingly clear to me since that conversation with female students at Rhodes in 2016. The idea behind sexual consent runs through what university students feel and do about, say, going out to a club; it informs the tacit understanding about our dress choices. Consent is about a natural right to one's body, what a person is entitled to do and not do with it. It is not just about sex.

When I received Del Monte's invitation, I sought information about the House of Yes. It is a New York club where supposedly anything goes. I read about the idea of consenticorns. I read what the philosopher Slavoj Žižek had written about the notion after Del Monte had pointed me to his newspaper article.[4] I went back to what I had said publicly about consent and to some of my private notes in my journals and diaries.

The journalist had several questions for me. I have decided it would be a good idea to present these questions as she sent them to me, and my responses to them, so that after reading them you can read her article, 'Beware the Violence of Intimacy: On Consent and Safe Spaces', to see the story she told about the club House of Yes and consenticorns, and how she wove my responses into what she wrote.[5]

What is consent?

There is what consent ought to be. And getting it right is utterly important in countries wracked by rape and violent, coerced or non-consensual sex. South Africa is one such country.

Then there is the messy fact of what is consent in practice. And that messiness is found everywhere in the world. Without the mess, play is inhibited. Not all of us enjoy sex with robots.

In relation to sex, consent refers to voluntary, verbal, explicit, and freely given agreement to have sex. That should be normative. What should go into laws, policies, and codes. What teachers and parents ought to teach and impart.

In practice, though, things can get very complicated, actually. I once read a study where one of the participants said consent is a butt lift. That's when you lift the butt and allow your sex partner to remove your underwear so that penetration can be effected. That is sort of explicit and voluntary, but no words are spoken. In real life there are many such situations where an explicit yes is not uttered.

Why is consent important?

Show me a country in the world where there is perfect equality among the genders, and I will show you a place where consent is not important. The basis of consent is negotiation, and negotiation assumes equal negotiators. Only if we are sexual equals can we give consent freely. So consent is important because ours is an unjust, unequal world. And the larger the inequality in a place, the more social injustice there is in a country, the more vital the need for consent is.

But the opposite is often the case. The more powerful the men, the more they feel entitled, the less they think they need freely given consent. Harvey Weinstein. Bill Cosby. Jacob Zuma. Jeffrey Epstein. R. Kelly. There are many whose names we know, who felt they can take what they want. And many others whose names are not in the media.

There is another version of the same theme. The more a man believes, implicitly or overtly, in a hierarchy of natural rights between men and women, the less likely he is to prefer 'unruly' women, women who do not want to be ruled by men, and as such the more he will use violence when he doesn't get consent.

How nuanced is consent, i.e. where is the line?

Utterly vital though it is, in many situations consent can be quite tricky. We should exclude situations where non-consent has been expressed, whether in the form of 'no' or non-verbally. That out of the way, consider other situations. You can give consent but yet not want to have sex. Why? Because the motive is to please your partner. Or you can want to have sex, but not certain acts, like anal sex or someone asking to come on you. But, for whatever reason, you give consent because it is easier to say yes than to say stop. Perhaps one of the most troubling moments for many of us is when we give consent even when we don't want to, because we want to be liked. That, I am afraid, is the complexity of humans and their psychological life that makes consent a difficult rule to fit all times and all situations. Humans can and do often enough give their consent even though they may not want sex.

Given the context of South Africa's GBV [gender-based violence] pandemic, what do you think of this 'consenticorn' concept? What are your thoughts on the Independent's *author calling it 'commodification of intimacy'?*

First, the person who said this is the philosopher Slavoj Žižek. He is a contrarian and performer, among other things. He is interesting to read and listen to, but we should not give all he says too much attention. Of course, he has a point when he says neoliberal capitalism commodifies our intimate life. At the same time, it is also the case that the rapist can be somebody with whom you are intimate. This predicament is all too common in South Africa, one that even first-year philosophy students understand. So when a writer says beware the commodification of intimacy, I say beware the violence of intimacy. I do not want a sexual bouncer when I am having fun, of course not. But until violence is exceptional, we might not need consenticorns per se, but consent compacts may be necessary.

Do you think that this concept of 'consenticorns' could extend beyond the nightclub scene somehow and be beneficial in everyday society?

I have been thinking not about consenticorns as such, but something along those lines. In a study we are undertaking on masculinities at universities, we would like to train what we call sexual violence preventionists. We are still in the thinking stage, so there is nothing to report. But the work we see these preventionists doing is to prevent sexual violence, along with other forms of university male students' violence, before it happens. Training people and doing campaigns around consent is part of that work.[6]

24 | Jeanne and Emmanuel

'I am the one who killed the parents of this girl.' That is Emmanuel, a character in the film *Kinyarwanda*, in a scene toward the end of the movie. The girl in question is Jeanne, the daughter of Emmanuel's former employer. Shot on location a decade and a half after the 1994 Rwandan genocide, *Kinyarwanda* was the directorial debut of African American film-maker Alrick Brown.[1] Released in 2011, the film won a clutch of awards, including the World Cinema Audience Award at the 2011 Sundance Film Festival and the World Cinema Audience Award at the 25th American Film Institute Fest. Weaving together several stories, reportedly based on true accounts of survivors, the filmmaker seeks to tell the story of this horrific and historically momentous event.

One of the stories the film portrays is that of the characters Emmanuel (played by Edouard Bamporiki) and Jeanne (Hadidja Zaninka). The film fleetingly suggests to the audience that Emmanuel has feelings for Jeanne, who is in a relationship with another young Hutu man. In one scene the film shows Emmanuel watching Jeanne arriving at her home with her parents, his face changing from a lustful, toothy expression to seriousness on realising that Jeanne's boyfriend is with them. In another scene, in the chapter of the film called 'Guns and Cockroaches', Emmanuel is shown hanging out with two other young men with machetes. One of the young men asks Emmanuel if he has a girlfriend. Emmanuel lies. He says he had one, but got rid of her because she was half-cockroach (meaning part-Tutsi and part-Hutu). He is referring to Jeanne. With Jeanne having been brought into his mind, Emmanuel says perhaps they should go and pay her a visit one last time, so that he can give her one last kiss. One of his companions asks if Emmanuel would really kiss a cockroach, and adds that one does not kiss a cockroach but rapes it/her, a sentiment with which Emmanuel agrees. Can we interpret these scenes to indicate that a feeling that appears to be opposed to another feeling is already kneaded together with it; that an act of hatred is sewn to a hunger for love, if not lustful desire?

I am not offering a detailed reading of *Kinyarwanda*. The film came into my mind as one of the readily available texts that try to draw our attention to and assist us in thinking about hate and trauma on such a huge scale in society. At the same time, the film is a story of individual lives. The stories of Jeanne and Emmanuel are among the main ones in the film.

The first time I saw the movie I was left with a great deal of dissatisfaction and a question which I find hard to resolve: whether some things, like genocide, are unforgivable. The same question can be asked about murder, I suppose. When is murder forgivable? What makes it possible to forgive a rapist?

After seeing the movie I was left grappling with the (im)possibility of forgiveness. I spent days puzzling over the question of what makes some people, and not others, able to forgive. I asked myself about the conditions of asking for forgiveness and agreeing to forgive (or not). I was not so much interested in whether forgiveness is necessary in order for a person or group to move forward in the case of colossal atrocities like genocide, ostensibly the main subject of the movie. Instead, I mulled over why a victim, a woman, would forgo what we can call a natural right to want to hurt those responsible for her injuries, physical or emotional, or for the death of loved ones. What I was interested in were the personal stories. If a man has killed my daughter or raped me, why would I forgive him? If I do manage to forgive him, what stories do I have to tell myself to be able to do so? In other words, what enables a person to overcome their need for vengeance, what makes it possible to forgive those who have caused you pain and suffering, and what are the specific conditions that make it easier or more difficult to forgo the desire for retribution?

In my view, it seems reasonable that a person who has been violated or seen his child disfigured would want vengeance. Given the rationality of the desire for revenge, forgiveness appears to be an irrational response to gross intentional injury. In light of this assumption, we must always want to understand why those who have been deliberately maimed, oppressed or maltreated do not in turn want to see those who made them suffer also suffer.

Stories of those who have been made to suffer help us to understand their pain and its resolution or non-resolution. A novel or film is particularly good at doing this, because it has a neat beginning and end and offers opportunity for analysis. Armed with tools for critical analysis, we can weigh the rationality or irrationality of forgiveness versus revenge.

Consider the very scene where Emmanuel says to Jeanne, 'I am the one who killed the parents of this girl'. In the same scene he also says the following: 'From my heart I ask for forgiveness.' It is worth quoting the words Emmanuel is given to speak in this scene, within which his plea for forgiveness is embedded. He says:

> I stand before you, accepting accusations of all the wrong I did. Because I actually did them. I don't remember the number of people I killed. This is the right time to condemn myself, because during that period I made a bad decision and betrayed Rwanda. I ask for forgiveness. [*At this point the film cuts back to the moment when Emmanuel and his companions burst into his former employer's house and, among other things, he says to Jeanne's father, 'I want your cockroach daughter'.*] I am the one who killed the parents of this girl, looted all of their property. From my heart I ask for forgiveness . . . Please.[2]

I watched *Kinyarwanda* as part of my preparation for a trip to Rwanda in 2018 for an academic symposium organised by Pumla Gobodo-Madikizela, of the University of Stellenbosch, on historical trauma and memory and living with the haunting power of the past.[3] I still had to settle on what I wanted to say about historical trauma, memory, and the past itself. I had known about and read some articles and reports on the Rwandan genocide, watched several television reports, heard academic presentations on the genocide, and familiarised myself with the economic and political developments in the country under Paul Kagame's long presidency. This is the context in which I came upon the film.

I replayed this scene several times in my mind. I watched it again while rewriting this reflection. The character of Emmanuel – as a man, in what drives him, in what he is asking for when he asks for forgiveness from Jeanne – is of particular interest to me. But I was also, of course, interested in the response of Jeanne, who is in this scene in the film, standing in front of him. I was interested in her as representing a young Rwandan woman who had been hurt by a Rwandan man, in her as a woman standing in for women who have been hurt by men; in her case, a hurt most cruel and rather complicated because of its politically symbolic quality, but of course also personal.

This is what Jeanne says to in answer to Emmanuel's plea: 'From the bottom of my heart I am giving him pardon. And you will be a friend to me as you once were to my mother and father. And I will respect you.'

I confess that I was unable to relate to this. Why would she forgive him just like that? Where is the tension? What is the backstory that brings her to this moment?

Although I have read about Rwanda's *gacaca* courts,[4] and I want to believe this forgiveness is possible – I have to – I found both Emmanuel and Jeanne at this point in the film hard to believe, their words too contrived. His plea for forgiveness, with its reference to Rwanda, sounds as false as her words that she will respect him. Why is there a need to befriend and respect the killer of her parents, besides pardoning him?

I have therefore not found a way to make sense of her answer, as I cannot believe her. Is this merely a case of bad writing on the part of the filmmaker? This is the most probable answer. The film is unconvincing.

And yet, I came to learn something during my visit to Rwanda. We were taken to one of the villages where perpetrators live side by side with survivors whose families have been massacred and women who have survived the horrors of the genocide. We had a meeting where former killers and survivors spoke with us. I am afraid I did not learn about forgiveness, if that is what you are waiting to hear me say. I realised that there is something deep I cannot understand about the country, about the men and women who spoke to us. Maybe the film is unconvincing. But so were the Rwandan women and men with whom we spent time. What makes it possible for some women and men, who have a right to hurt their violators, to end up giving up on wanting to hurt those who have hurt their people, their parents and themselves? How are these women and men able to integrate trauma into their present lives, and to live well with and beyond the memory of a hurtful past?

Let me say this again. It may be a failure of the film that it evokes my suspicion of the plea for and granting of forgiveness. However, I concede that it may be the result of a certain incredulity on my part, due to how forgiveness is represented and flattened out in this movie. There is also what I experience as a lack of empathy in the film, and an absence of rage expressed by those who have been hurt. Why is this woman not mad with anger? Why is there no space in the story for creative tension that enables the woman to be mad? In denying her what I feel is her right to rage, the filmmaker is also denying us, the audience, a chance to experience anger against the killer and to have an opportunity to work through it in our own time.

In thinking of and intervening against men's violence, what we need to create and to allow is a space for victims of the violence to be incensed. To be very angry is human. So is the desire for vengeance.

At the same time, it is true that this very human quality of wanting to rage and *not* to forgive can sometimes be destructive. Rage can wreck not only those at whom it is directed; it also burns the one in whose chest it blazes. And the fire can take a long time to douse. It is well known that it can take much longer to understand the emotional and mental injuries underlying our fury than it does to recover from physical injuries we have suffered. In my work to comprehend the sources of men's violence, I am aware of their difficulty in dealing with ongoing humiliations and shame, degradation that sometimes turns into anger, and anger that can turn into violence. We have a right, when we are wronged, abused or injured, to be angry. But we must identify the source of our anger, so that we are more deliberate about what to do next.

As a man, a young man, I found these wounds always wanting to erupt into rage that was uncontrollable, burning everything in its path, burning me. Sometimes this did happen. For some reason I always managed to get on top of the rage, I am not entirely sure how. All I can say is that I am here, largely intact: that is the evidence I present. My survival may have had less to do with my own wits than with chance – chance is not to be discounted in determining where we end up, the many little probabilities that shape the course of our lives. It may have been thanks to others around me. I know that, since April 1994 and the arrival of political freedom, the ease with which we as a society have talked about non-violence, peace and forgiveness has not brought inner peace and self-forgiveness to many of these men. I have participated in many discussions on these and related topics where the intention is to transform men and masculinities. But even when Nelson Mandela (who championed peace and reconciliation) was president, I had a nagging thought-feeling that perhaps the aggression experienced by young men was not strong enough (given the structural conditions to which society subjects them), that it could be much more powerful, and that it could be better redirected away from the young women and other young men who are now its recipients. It could, I feel, be better directed toward those who deserve it, to the women and men who produce and perpetuate their abjection.

What I am doing here may be somewhat unusual. I am not offering any answers to the main question I have posed: how does one live with the memory of being hurt? The answers to the question of what to do when we have been hurt, some of which I have offered so many times, seem too easy and overly reasonable. I will offer them again in contexts and on platforms other than this, but it is not the answers, not the glib explanations, nor the theoretical formulations that I want to present here. What I want to do, rather, is to stay with the troubling questions and the troubling emotions. What does it take for some men and women not to avenge their injury? Why is this good, for whom, and under what circumstances? I am interested in a certain set of feelings connected to being hurt and wanting to hurt back; I want to understand what enables me to quickly integrate some memories of hurt, but to take longer to deal with others. Because such feelings are hard to measure, difficult to fix in place, to know once and for all times when and by whom and why they will be caused to bubble up.

Even though I keep saying 'I', I am not always talking about myself. I am also trying to put myself in the place of the young man on a street in Addis Ababa who jumps on another and starts punching him. Or the young men in an H&M store who apparently go mad and pull down the clothing racks in protest against the racist fashion adverts made by the store. Or the policeman who kills his lover and children. Or the man who rapes the student. Or the husband who pushes and kicks his wife. But even if I am trying to be this man and to place myself inside his feelings of hurt or shame or humiliation, which turn to anger and rage and aggression, in order better to understand his trouble when he is feeling hurt, it is an emergent pre-social truth that I am trying to track. I am trying to perform a kind of inward-looking psychological ethnography. But as embodied truth, when the self speaks to the self, this subjective knowledge never stays in one place forever.

It is true that there are times, which do not seem to have a very clear pattern that I can put into a single shape, when I have wanted to hurt someone who has hurt me, when I have barely contained my aggression against those whom I feel have wanted to humiliate and shame me, or have wounded those with whom I identify. Sometimes it is a stranger who is the object of this barely held-back rage. But at other times, I am ashamed to say, it is someone close to me whom I want to hurt, because they have hurt me. Are these not similar to the feelings that have impelled Emmanuel? Are these not similar to the feelings many men have? Are these not what cause some men in South Africa to inflict harm on their partners and on strangers? Do similar feelings lie below the violence of men in the United States, in Pakistan, in France, in the Democratic Republic of the Congo, in Rwanda? How, precisely, do we give up what we might refer to as 'the natural right to righteous vengeance' – or, expressed more palatably, the right to justice? How does one learn to integrate these feelings of being hurt, perhaps even learn to live with those who have hurt oneself or those for whom one cares?

The notion of giving up one's right to payback was best articulated by the former archbishop of Cape Town, Mpilo Desmond Tutu. For those who may not be familiar with him, Tutu was the chairperson of the South African Truth and Reconciliation Commission (TRC). He is closely connected to the concept of forgiveness and reconciliation in democratic South Africa. In an interview in 2012 on PBS in the United States he was asked, 'What do you actually do when you forgive someone'? This was part of his answer:

Well, basically you're saying, 'I am abandoning my right to revenge, to pay back. I mean, I have, I, by the fact that you have abused me, you have hurt me or whatever it is that you have done, you've wronged me, by that you have given me a certain right, as it were, over you that I could refuse to forgive you, I could say I have the right to retribution. When

I forgive I say I jettison that right and I open the door of opportunity to you to make a new beginning. That is what I do when I forgive you.[5]

Why would one give up the right to retribution? Tutu's words are powerful, and even make considerable sense at some level of consciousness. And perhaps they allow us to imagine the kind of human being that Tutu is seeking to hail. But I would like to contrast this powerful sentiment and the heights which Tutu wants us to reach with what Winnie Madikizela-Mandela said about the TRC. Madikizela-Mandela had been angry, I suspect, about being subjected to the TRC for her apparent role in the torture and murder of a 14-year-old activist named James 'Stompie' Seipei in 1989 by members of the Mandela United Football Club, which was associated with her name. Speaking later to a television news channel about the apartheid security agents who testified at the TRC about having murdered her driver and blown up his body, she said:

We were expected to listen to this, listen to this TRC confession and then forgive. We were expected to forgive, forgive this type of thing, forgive this type of situation where you don't even have a grave, where a man proudly says in the hearing, 'there was a toe left, and that toe was blown with a hand-grenade'. You can imagine the glee with which they [were] doing that. And what type of human being is expected to forgive that?[6]

To understand forgiveness is a very difficult thing. Equally or more so, you can imagine, when you bring to mind a moment when you were badly hurt, such as when a close one was blown up by a hand grenade. It requires intense psychical and moral energy to forgive. At one moment, then, forgiveness is an ordinary human response; but at another, in response to certain wounds, especially when no reparation has been forthcoming, it feels that it is too high a mountain to climb. We are told that we have to let go of our anger and hurt in order to be free. Yet payback against those who have injured someone is celebrated in films and in television series. We know it is a virtuous thing to forgive, but vengeance can assuage some of the pain. Against all this, there is a fundamental question with which I have endlessly troubled myself in my thinking about boys and men. It is a question grounded in the persisting context of historical, transgenerational, multiple and ongoing traumas that have shaped and continue to shape the lives of children and adults, women and men in this society. How do I better understand, critically and generatively, the circumstances that cause some men to desire to hurt others and to act on that desire, while other men manage not to do so?

25 | Is the lesbian an alibi for an untenable model of masculinity?

I had just received the book about Zanele Muholi's exhibition at the Tate Modern Gallery in London.[1] I was reminded that while violence against lesbians is commonplace, it seemed that as a country we could not fully process the horror of it. It may be that we did not want to confront the fullness of the terror to which lesbians have been subjected.

Has the horror gone away? I do not know. Actually, I do not think it has.

Why have there been so many sexually and physically violent acts against lesbians over the years? I do not know. However, I have sought to understand the terroristic violence perpetrated by men against lesbians.

I have written about the killing of Zoliswa Nkonyana in 2006 and the conviction of four men for her murder.[2] In 2008, former Banyana Banyana star Eudy Simelane was murdered and two men, Themba Mvubu and Thato Mphithi, were sentenced to life imprisonment and 32 years, respectively, for the murder. In 2011, 24-year-old Noxolo Nogwaza, a member of the Ekurhuleni Pride Organising Committee, was raped, then stoned and stabbed to death. Reports are that on the evening of her rape and murder she had been with a friend at a bar, and a group of men had an argument with her and friends of hers. In 2019, 25-year-old Portia Simphiwe Mtshweni was murdered and mutilated in Tweefontein, Mpumalanga. In 2020 Liyabona Mabishi, aged 16, from Nkanini, Stellenbosch, was stabbed to death. On and on, so much death and other forms of violence against lesbians. As far as I am aware, many of these cases in which lesbians are raped or murdered are never resolved, with no arrests made or prosecutions pursued.

Once again, I think social inequality between women and men contributed to this violence. Men's violence against lesbians is misogynistic violence and sexualised violence. There are links between the two – and one might say, sexualised violence is misogyny.

There are other drivers of the rape and murder of lesbians, though, including support for the use of violence as a means to resolve issues, attitudes toward black lives, attitudes toward women as a whole, attitudes toward different sexualities, economic inequality and poverty as an intertwined pair of factors, alcohol and other drugs, mental health issues, the weakness of the criminal justice system, and the dominant psychology of men. Regarding this last factor, it would seem that visible lesbian sexualities are seen by some men as challenging the prevailing heteropatriarchal norms of masculinity (and femininity) and the perpetrators' perceived loss of their power as individual men, whether that perception is correct or not. The figure of the lesbian is thus of central significance when we seek to understand the violence of individual men against women generally, and in particular against women who do not sexually love men. In that way, the figure of the lesbian may help us to comprehend the undoing of ascendant heteropatriarchal masculinity. That is, it helps us understand the unmaking of the dominant straightness of some men. The lesbian is, in other words, an alibi for a masculinity under perceived threat. She is a subject who arouses, or rather multiplies, feelings of psychosocial insecurity in the dominant form of masculinity to which some men subscribe.

I did not always understand what the fact that a woman loves another woman has to do with my masculinity. I do now. It is knowledge that can be of use to every man. We, all men, particularly those who are heterosexual, need to be among lesbians, to listen to them, to understand the terror which men like us have caused them. To be among lesbians, to listen to the life stories of lesbian women, to do more than just not kill them, is to begin to open ourselves to learning how to unmake masculinity, a masculinity that is obviously untenable, and therefore to begin the work of remaking men. For the rest of us (such as mothers of boys, heterosexual women and persons of other genders) who are desirous of remaking their masculinities, the least we can do is leave lesbians to enjoy the freedoms all of us are promised in the Constitution.

26 | Will we reduce rates of rape of women and children when we cannot face prison rape?

From my pre-teen years till my early 20s, I grew up in a poor, rough, violent neighbourhood. I grew up with many unmet basic needs but also so many fears. One fear that haunted my mind was being knifed and dying violently. I will never forget Herman, an older boy who used to bully me and whom I wished dead, actually dying in front of me and the other boys in the neighbourhood. That evening, Herman had been bullying me. He would taunt and push me and run around the block laughing. The next time he appeared around the corner he was staggering toward us, holding his chest. He flopped down next to us. Walking nonchalantly behind him were a couple of guys, *ditsotsi*,[1] as we called guys like that. I may be wrong, memory is a devil, but I recall one of these *'sgebengus*[2] not even hiding the knife he had in his hand. They just walked past us, daring us to do anything. Herman was on the ground struggling to breathe. Blood was spurting from his stab wound. The ambulance arrived too late. I don't know if the murderers were ever arrested. Violence and death had always been part of our lives. For some people, our lives did not matter as much as the lives of white people in nearby Germiston or Alberton.

Another fear I had was of being arrested and ending up in jail. It was not as if I was a fearsome *tsotsi* or the hardened member of a gang. I did carry a knife at some point in Grade 7 (what was referred to at the time as Standard 5), when I was newly arrived in the township and another boy, Budou, was bullying me. To be sure, we did not call someone like Budou a bully, for there were too many people like me who were 'bullied', children and parents. To be harassed, pushed around, tormented and have your life restricted was simply a fact of life.

My mother took the knife from me, and whipped out of me the habit of walking around armed with a knife. The lashing came after I had stabbed another child, who, fortunately, was only slightly hurt. For the whipping I thank my mother, although I do think hitting children can lead to them being violent. I am afraid her form of discipline may displease a lot of anti-violence activists, critical childhood scholars and feminist thinkers. But when your son carries a weapon in the township or in the streets of an American city, it is likely to end badly, and all means necessary should be used to protect him.

Long after the bullying had ended and right into my twenties, I walked around with this internal terror of imprisonment. I don't think I was at high risk. In fact, when I think of my young self I recall being what was called *ibari* (a dolt), the opposite of street-smart. I was new in the neighbourhood. I came from what was then a small rural area, Maboloka, in what is now the North West Province. But I was a quick learner – hence the knife. Soon I was a regular like the Katlehong-born boys you can see on most days on the front *stoep* of a local general store. I liked soccer. I hung out on the street corners. I hunted wild rats. I fantasised about girls. I watched Chinese kung fu movies at the local bioscope. I got into fist fights with friends from the neighbourhood and group fights with the boys from other neighbourhoods. I had good grades at school, sometimes. I went some days without food. I participated in protests against the municipal council, our school principal and the unfair education system.

You did not have to be a hardened criminal to be criminalised in my country back then. For some young men, it is as if the new country continues to treat them as potential criminals. And when you live in hard and unforgiving places, your one mistake can end up being your costliest. And when there is overcrowding, with you and your sisters, cousins, aunts, grandmother living in a four-room government house or a leaking shack, you can confuse the wrong crowd for the much-needed support you seek. Under these circumstances it is not that hard to end up dead or in prison, and I am not always sure which is worse.

The life conditions that increase our likelihood of ending up in prison are a theme in the documentary *Taking Off the Mask*, about which I was invited to share my reflections when it was launched in 2020.[3] Co-produced by Azania Rising Productions and Just Detention International–South Africa, the film casts light on sexual violence in male prisons. The story revolves around Isak Sass, a rape survivor.

As in the township in which I grew up, people live hard lives in Chicago, a township outside Paarl in the Western Cape, where Isak grew up. The probability of ending up dead or imprisoned is, in my assessment, a little elevated in these places, higher than when one grows up in a middle-class neighbourhood such as the one where I live now, where most people are well-off.

There is a point that needs highlighting in relation to the probabilities attached to different neighbourhoods and classes: the reality of differential chances. Not just of imprisonment but also of injury and premature mortality; of receiving good education and quality health; of work-life success and psychosocial well-being. In contrast to Chicago where Isak grew up and Katlehong where I spent my teenage years, in Pinelands, an old suburb of Cape Town which I now call home and where my son is growing up, the world is more forgiving. There are many good schools within a few kilometres. The University of Cape Town is a 30-minute walk away. In this place we do not have to struggle for survival. We do not have to fight off others to satisfy the basic needs of life. The streets are clean. There are times when I step out into the street – for example, when I have to take out the garbage for collection or walk to the local supermarket – and there is not another soul in sight. Squirrels dash here and there, crossing the road and running up and down the pine trees. No one eats squirrels, I think. There are many trees, more than squirrels, people and cars combined, I think. The place is so quiet that several driving schools bring learner drivers to practise driving around here.

The fear of imprisonment with which I grew up was a fear of loss of liberty, that I could be arbitrarily imprisoned. It was also fear of the fact that I would be raped if I ever made one bad move and ended up in jail. Isak says as much in the film: that, as a young person, you hear that if you go to prison, 'you will be a prison wife; you will be raped'.[4]

How is it that we know that rape is rife in prison and yet it persists? Why is it that boys and young men who grow up in unforgiving conditions are more likely to end up in jail with conditions so wretched?

I have previously noted the high rates of rape in South Africa – and it is not surprising that I had in mind the rape of women and children by men when I wrote that.[5] There are no readily available, reliable data on rates of rape in prison; however, anecdotal evidence suggests that rape is rife there. I have wondered whether it is possible to reduce levels of sexual violence in the broader society when we live with the bitter knowledge that sexual violence, which appears to go largely unreported, is the fate of many men who end up in correctional centres. And is it not ironic that this is the name – correctional centres – by which prisons are called, yet instead of rehabilitating inmates these prisons will crush some of them? Correctional centres are supposed to correct behaviour, to rehabilitate individuals. But they do not give me the sense of being very good at what they are meant to do, given the trauma and violence that men like Isak, and reputedly thousands of others, are subjected to in jails.

While I believe that we have to hold on to hope, the truth is I see no basis for being convinced that we can reduce rates of rape against women and children, let alone stop rape altogether, when we cannot deal with rape against men in prison (and outside). Similarly, I see no reason to believe we can reduce violence against farmers, against farmworkers, against immigrants and refugees, against queer people or against any other group, when we cannot reduce violence against young men in jails (or poor neighbourhoods). This is to say, the different manifestations of violence are connected to each other by an invisible line. People who hurt, hurt other people. Hence, while there is hope that in the distant future we will see a reduction in levels of violence, it is a *critical* hope that I hold on to.

I have been reflecting about fear, the fear of death and the fear of ending up in prison that I carried in me when I was growing up. Let me now talk about another emotion that is not immediately obvious in the documentary. In fact you will not see it, but it underpins the fact that the film revolves around one man, Isak. Shame, like fear, is associated with masculinity, but I feel we discuss it far less than it deserves in unpacking masculinity.[6]

In order to make the documentary, the producers needed to find men who could talk about being raped without feeling debilitating shame. That is to say, men who were able to say: I was raped. A man who is able to speak on a film about being raped is, in my view, one who has managed to some extent to realise that the shame of being raped does not belong to him. Even though I know the shame belongs to the rapists, I suspect many men find it hard not to blame themselves. (Shame is also a key theme in the experience of women who have been raped.) Even though the shame belongs to the Department of Justice and Correctional Services for repeatedly failing to prevent rape in prison, it is hard to find men who will speak of being raped. But it is absolutely true that the shame belongs to the government of South Africa. The shame belongs to society as a whole for pretending that this does not have to trouble us, even when the majority knows it goes on daily.

As such, a man who can stand up and say, 'I was sexually violated' is courageous. We may concede that our government and our society may not be able to prevent all sexual violence, but they cannot even squarely face up to the fact that men are victims of rape. Even while we declare ourselves to be against rape, most of us know that we like things in black and white, where men are rapists and women are raped. That prevents us from looking the scale and complexity and outrage of violence in our society in the eye and saying we are truly in trouble.

I know that there are thousands of boys and men who are raped, in prison and around us, who live with the shame but will not admit it. They would rather remain silent than let it be known that they are also victims of sexual violence. In any case, who will they open up to when there are so few spaces and opportunities to speak of their ordeal? And thus there are many who carry around this wounding that may lead to them wounding others.

I think of Isak as courageous if only because I know I am not so brave. I squirm when I have to speak about male rape. Speaking out about one's own rape as a man takes incredible bravery, because the shame is so unspeakable. It feels as if it is located in the nucleus of hegemonic beliefs about manhood. Being penetrated without his consent, one might say, totally humiliates a man's masculinity. And for a man to say, I have had another man's penis violently shoved inside of me, I have had my manhood crushed, is almost unthinkable. Honest speech about male rape is, at the moment, apparently unwelcome to most of society. The courage of Isak is multiplied by the fact that in our society, while we rightly focus on the rape of women, we are not very comfortable when it comes to speaking about the rape of men.

Why is it uncomfortable to face the fact that men can be hurt as much as women? Why is there this binary way of looking at violence? It could be that some sections of society believe that men *deserve* to be hurt, injured, jailed, even raped and killed. This belief may be below the level of daily consciousness, which means covered in denial, but could be a result of the prevailing discourse of 'bad men'. The view of men as naturally bad or as deserving to be injured may not be expressed in progressive political circles. But the current scarcity of voices speaking about men as equally deserving of protection from harm suggests that violence against men is refused admission into wide social consciousness, regarded as not of major concern, or simply dumbfounding. It is not all men, not outwardly successful men, as far as I can see, who are believed to be unworthy of being protected by the human rights enjoyed by the rest of society. It is mainly poor men, in fact. Men in poor, violent neighbourhoods like Chicago. We do not have to worry too much when these men are hurt.

There is a deep paradox about this, in relation to the concern with changing masculinity. Poor men, those on the peripheries of good society, 'losers', homeless men – that is to say, broadly, those men who are seen as having failed the test of successful masculinity – are the ones regarded as deserving to be harmed or not supported. It is true that there are 'successfully masculine' men who are 'called out', but such men almost always have supporters, and if they are portrayed in the media it is in more rounded terms. But the underclass among men as a social category, those who are marginalised, are expected to suffer, stay silent, and their pain to remain out of our consciousness. We may want them to change (without making too much noise about the hurt they have suffered), but certainly not to revolt.

It is for these reasons that I applaud a man like Isak for his refusal to suffer in silence; for his willingness to say, I was raped and treated as though I deserved to be raped, as if I do not deserve basic human sympathy. If a man (like a woman in the same position) who has been raped does not deserve human empathy, then who does? If I am raped even though I am in this wrong body, will anyone help me and share the shame I am supposed to feel, but which I must refuse? Does anyone among us deserve sympathy if we do not regard all of us as deserving of care?

With these questions I am throwing light on several things. First, I am convinced that we will never stop, or at least drastically reduce, rape in our society unless we aim to stop or reduce all rape, including rape in correctional centres. It sounds so elementary: is it not obvious that if we cannot protect prisoners then we cannot protect any of us, for prisoners are in the care of the state? The care we fail to offer inside is connected to the lack of care for each other as members of society.

Second, I have done work, intellectual and practical work, writing and teaching and training workshops and media advocacy and group work, on how we in families, as community activists, influencers, researchers, policymakers, media users or teachers can encourage boys and men to talk about the fears, vulnerabilities, shame and humiliation that they experience. Working on the emotional lives of boys and men, educating them into a language of feeling, is important in itself. At the same time, emotional education is required, because individuals use violence as a language instead of words. That is, some men use violence to avert negative feelings, insecurities or a sense of their own nothingness.

The reality is that boys and men get raped. Many of us know this. Many grow up with this knowledge. We have to face up to it as a society. It is especially boys and men who grew up and are still growing up in places such as Isak and myself and millions of men have experienced, who need the encouragement and courage to open up. They also need to be given the language to speak of their inner lives. Only then, when we have the language and space to speak, can we reduce sexual violence done to all humans, men and women alike.

Part 3 | Masculinity

It is essential to understand clearly that the concepts of 'masculine' and 'feminine', whose meaning seems so unambiguous to ordinary people, are among the most confused that occur in science. It is possible to distinguish at least three uses. 'Masculine' and 'feminine' are used sometimes in the sense of activity and passivity, sometimes in a biological, and sometimes, again, in a sociological sense. Such observation shows that in human beings pure masculinity or femininity is not to be found either in a psychological or biological sense.

—Sigmund Freud, 'Three Essays on the Theory of Sexuality'

'Masculinity', to the extent that the term can be briefly defined at all, is simultaneously a place in gender relations, the practices through which men and women engage that place in gender, and the effects of these practices in bodily experience, personality and culture.

—Raewyn Connell, *Masculinities*

The person responsible for ensuring my smooth transition into manhood was incapable. So Oom Dan took it upon himself to oversee things.

—Thando Mgqolozana, *A Man Who Is Not a Man*

27 | Trying to transform men is not a futile exercise, but it is slow and difficult work

I live in a country in which violence is highly visible, and all too often gruesome, as were the murders in 2013 of 26-year-old Duduzile Zozo from Thokoza, Gauteng, who was killed and had a toilet brush stuck up her vagina, and Anene Booysen, a teenager from Bredasdorp in the Western Cape who was gang-raped and disembowelled.[1]

And yet violence is also so banal.

It never stops.

I have tried to offer my small contribution – how interminable and even despairing and infinitesimal it often feels in the face of such horror – by discussing, teaching, conducting research and writing, with the aim of understanding the sources of men's violence. I do this in the hope that we men, at least some of us, the ones who have used violence in the past, do so now, or will do so in the future, but who appear not to fathom its effects, might pause to reflect on this apparent attraction some of us have toward violence – if not for society, then for those we say we love and for ourselves.

The violence in our society, which means within us, within the self, is usually linked to the hegemonic understanding of what it means to be a man. Violence is a tool men use to reproduce their dominant manhood. But what they deploy far more often than violent behaviour is its unarticulated threat, which is present in the tacit right some men believe they have to dominate other people. Being a man of power, they believe, means being entitled to control others. The threat and the actuality of violence are ingrained in the currently culturally ascendant form of masculinity.

The link between manhood and violence is made in the *National Strategic Plan on Gender-Based Violence and Femicide*, to which I have referred in earlier chapters. In the *Plan* the terms 'masculinity' and 'masculinities' are mentioned more than 20 times.[2] The ties between the two phenomena – masculinity/masculinities and violence – could not be clearer. The authors of the *Plan* see 'ideas of masculinity that are centred on male control of women, male sexual entitlement, inequitable gender attitudes, risk-taking and antisocial behaviour' as an interlinked set of factors in gender-based violence and femicide. Its goal is therefore to shift society from patriarchal or violent forms of masculinity toward alternative, positive masculinities.[3] The inference I make is that the reference to positive forms of masculinity in the *Plan* opens up a space for us to consider the nurturance of loving masculinities, and the education of men to embrace vulnerability in their emotional and relational lives.[4] What I have been suggesting throughout this book is that men's violence can be linked to their feelings of love-lessness and disconnection, and to their understanding of 'traditional' masculinity as avoidance of vulnerability. The quotation marks around 'traditional' are meant to draw attention to misperceptions I have studied about the concepts of tradition in general, but particularly 'traditional' masculinity.[5] Simply put, one of my conclusions is that one rarely, if ever, finds masculinity (or men and women who identify as masculine) and femininity (or men and women who identify as feminine) without tradition, for the simple reason that gender is culturally constructed, and gender has its own traditions. The question to ask always is, within which tradition or culture is the masculinity or femininity, man or woman, in question situated, and how? Men's violence can be considered as an instrument to defend themselves against emotional vulnerability – I wanted to say emotional disability. These feelings may not be readily recognisable for what they are. A man might suffer psychically but not really know why he feels the way he does. He might feel a momentary or enduring disaffection, but remain unaware that this state arises from his psychological history. But even if he does recall how much he hungered for love in the past, it can still be difficult for him to fully admit to this kind of emotional suffering, for he probably does not have the tools to 'fix' the vulnerability – except by turning away from it or fighting it. As bell hooks says, 'being "vulnerable" is an emotional state many men seek to avoid'.[6]

A man who does not want to be vulnerable desires to be perceived as an immovable rock. That could mean he wants to be a tower of strength; but it can also indicate a person who does not want his 'stuff' – his pain, joys, plans and inner self – to be known, which suggests that he subscribes to a 'traditional' version of hard masculinity. In relation to love, avoidance of vulnerability implies conditional intimacy, if any real intimacy at all. Hence, according to hooks, 'the more patriarchal a man is, the more disconnected he must be from feeling. If he cannot feel, he cannot connect. If he cannot connect, he cannot be intimate.'[7] Here we can imagine a man who has lived believing that tender feelings matter less than being in control, because he grew up with little evidence of warmth. It strikes me that such a person may even be closed to all vulnerability, for having lived without love was already to experience painful vulnerability. Why would he open himself up to that again, when he knows there was no one to soothe him when he needed comforting in the past? And thus, since he is now in control of or can fight what threatens him, he will go to war against this vulnerability, too.

A man can never actually win a fight against his own emotional vulnerability, though. He can only avoid it or bury it deeper inside him. The only way of winning, if we stay with the language of war, is through changing our understanding of both vulnerability and how we fight. It begins by grasping why one is feeling vulnerable and why there is a fight in the first place. This fight within the self is between an unhealthy and a healthy attitude toward feelings about oneself, and toward anything that smells of vulnerability. Understanding vulnerability to be a crucial aspect of living fully with oneself and others is, in my reading, a better way of overcoming the worst of the suffering. Understanding the nature of our vulnerability as men implies accepting that as children we could not but be at the mercy of our parents, but also that as long as we desire to live openly we are vulnerable.

I have spent a large part of my working life reflecting on the apparent link between violence and masculinity; about the males who inflict most of the visible, horrifying violence on others; about the everydayness of horror, an awfulness that appears sometimes to lose its capacity to shock except in the most gruesome cases. But years since I first began to think of men's violence, I am still trying to figure out why so many of us, men and women, consider the word 'man' as if it is another name for dominance, for aggression, for control. Why does 'man' not mean kindness, sharing, understanding? It is not a crash course, this education in how men are made. It demands time.

Again, I do not mean to say it is only men who commit acts of violence. And I do not only think and research and teach and write about men's violence when I contemplate masculinity. I also reflect on their victimisation and vulnerability, of course; their relations with others; their relations with their bodies; their non-violent and even creative performances of manhood. I consider ideas about boyhood: boys' relations with girls and other boys; mothers and their sons. I investigate work, sex, fatherhood, inequality, culture, race and, of course, love.

There are some things regarding violence that I have come to see clearly. I have come to see that even though a person might be strangled to death or disfigured by acid thrown at their face, and their death or injury can clearly be tied to an immediate direct act of violence, inadequate consideration of the historical and contemporary structures and dynamics of society as upstream sources of violence may be the Achilles heel of violence prevention strategies. I have come to see that in a country like South Africa, one cannot fully comprehend the gender histories that form men and women without understanding the intersecting history of race and racism that has made us, the country and the world what we are. I have come to better appreciate that it is no easy thing to honestly question the cultural beliefs into which we are born and that suffuse our feelings, thoughts and behaviours.

When I do think about violence, I try not to forget to consider its place in and interactions with other aspects of men's lives. I remember the antecedents and reverberations of violence for men, for how they became what they are, and I think of what men could be if there were no aggression in their lives. I wonder what kinds of men are those in whose lives violence has no place, and what kinds of love are entwined with violence. With regard to love, I might ask: what is the source of and hidden meaning of this violence that is directed at the people we say we love – and maybe we really do? Why doesn't the blackness of men and the women with whom they share this blackness – the women who birth them, raise them, grow up in the same family with them, care for them, fuck them, and nurse them when their bodies are wrecked by disease – give them enough reason to reduce the violence? How is this blackness these men and women share, this beautiful idea of being which some people taught us can be our gift of a more human aspect to the world, not useful in preventing violence?[8]

(In passing, I must observe that I have witnessed, in real life and much more on user-generated pornographic sites, white men who commit the most horrendous sexual acts against white women, acts that I suspect are never reported as violence, or misogyny. Observing this unremarked violence, I have wondered why white women love white men who violate them, denigrate them, sexually abuse and exploit them. Who basically disrespect them, minimise their achievements and are ungrateful for the care they receive from them. Yet all the while these violated women perpetuate the lie that whiteness protects them. The same wonderment, of course, applies to women of other colours, nationalities and religions, classes and creeds.)

Violence is so all-consuming, routine and absorbing, colouring everything, inside and out, that in some way, eventually, we cannot think about anything other than violence.

How can we fully think of love in this country without thinking of violence, when each week we read of a boyfriend murdering his girlfriend, a husband murdering his family, a policeman killing men and women and himself being killed?

One should ask, how do I become a more caring, more compassionate human being in such a world?

We may not always fully escape these forms of violence. When we do so it is only conditionally, temporarily, in the in-between moments, the exceptional moments. If that is the case, what we must do first is seek and build temporary spaces of love, small zones in which we can nurture loving masculinities, more caring gender relations, where men and women are free to breathe. It is possible to strive to find such free, non-violent, breathing zones. Zones of understanding. Zones of sharing. Of friendship. Of reciprocity. Where we care for one another and for the earth. This is not a dream. It is what the love I have been pointing to is made of. The more such free, breathing zones we can nurture, the more nurturing zones we can protect from different kinds of violence. The more we can paint the world with solidary care, the more commonplace loving masculinities can become.

As I have said several times already, I have asked myself why some women love men who hurt them.[9] We must also ask a related question: why do some women love men who hurt other women? In no way is this line of questioning to be interpreted as blaming women who have been wounded for loving violent men. I also must not be interpreted as asking, why do women love men who do not deserve to be loved? What this question does point to is the complex reality of finding love in the same place as violence, while not ignoring or minimising agency.

Is trying to change masculinity without changing femininities and other genders – which is to say, without changing all of society's ways of relating to itself – therefore a futile exercise? How much can we transform the dominant way of regarding men and boys without transforming the way society regards families, relationships and its overall emotional life? In an editorial in a Sunday newspaper, documentary filmmaker Jacqueline Rainers asked a question linked to the central one we have been considering in these reflections: namely, what do you do when people tell you that your boyfriend is a rapist? Responding to her own question, she wrote: 'My rapist was a family member, so I know a little about what it is to love someone who hurt you.'[10] She was saying that we can be hurt by people we love. Family members, who are supposed to care for us, can wound us.

The dilemma of having to work out what to do about a rapist in the family, as a close colleague, or as a friend, whether that rapist has raped oneself or someone else, cannot be exaggerated. We, women or men, cannot always just go ahead and cut out 'loved ones'. We are not always in a position to leave family and others close to us who harm us while claiming to care for us. Even more haunting, because we cannot immediately leave such a situation, is the reality that 'forgetting' and working through the hurt can be complicated. The presence of the rapist is a constant reminder. It is a confounding situation. There will be no easy solutions, not only because of the proximity of the reprobate, but also because there are other family members, friends of the family and wider circles of people who make up our social networks that we have to think about and deal with, as victims of the rapist in the family.

As scholars and policymakers, we have the freedom to reflect on this entwinement of love and violence. It is always worthwhile in such cases to examine the structural conditions under which people are motivated or subtly compelled toward caring for those who hurt them. At the same time, subjectivities and psychological dynamics of relationships must not be dismissed. Explanations that reduce everything to the effects of social, political, cultural or economic institutions are as unhelpful as those that attribute everything to individuals and psychological factors.

The question of why some women love men who hurt them, or hurt others, can be reframed as, why are there men who, it appears, do not care for women (or children) who care for them? This lack of care is an intentional injury caused to them. Why, that is, do some men hurt those to whom they are close?

Men hurt women they don't know, too, of course. While some studies report that they do so at more or less similar rates to the violence they commit against women known to them, other studies show that stranger rape accounts for a higher proportion of violence than violence against women by men who are non-strangers. And other studies still present a different picture, with intimate violence reported to be higher than non-partner violence.[11] However, it is the hurting of women by familiar men that is perturbing, because it appears to challenge our beliefs, policies, rhetoric and actions as a state, society and individuals. For instance, in policies, in advertisements and in advocacy campaigns, it is far more common to suggest and represent the perpetrator as an unknown man, because it is troubling to portray him as a husband or grandfather, or a teacher, coach or boyfriend. To face the fact that we are likely to be hurt by those close to us – a fellow employee, brother, neighbour or member of the same congregation – is to confront how close we live to violence.

But do men actually dislike women (or children), or has violence so infected some men's psyches and social existence that the real struggle is to extirpate it from inside their minds and from our cultural midst? Could it be that men's violence is in fact present because men do not care?

Even though I take steps to clarify that my aim is to understand the conditions under which aggression and affection co-exist, I am sometimes surprised by the outrage I provoke when I ask women the question, why do some women love men who hurt them? I have become extra attentive to how I ask this question. When confronted with the fact that care co-resides in the same subject as wretchedness, that it is not only happiness we experience with those close to us, we have to find a way to either live with the predicament or escape it. To realise that affection co-exists with grief in the same relationship, we have to reckon with how to think of our relationships. I am not expecting any one woman or man to have an answer for all of us about how to make all men more loving and less violent. If it is emancipating, tolerable or sensible *answers* that I am after, because there is not one final answer, I am also trying to learn how we are managing to live a life where violence is so close by, so much part of the fabric of the world in which we live.

But still I wonder, what kind of love harms you? One answer I arrive at is actually a question, leading to further questions, for there can never be a final answer – except the extirpation of violence from our bones, synapses and relational life. That question is, can peace, love or joy even be found in a society in which there are so many able-bodied men without decent work, without being cared for, without the slightest prospect of living a dignified life, without education in how to care for others, without representation, without words?

This is not at all to say that men's violence against women is inevitable *because* they do not have decent work, or that men will become more affectionate when society becomes more socioeconomically equal. It is to say that these are the conditions under which men become men. To be sure, these conditions shaping how we act from moment to moment are forms of violence, too. The structural violence of policies, of institutions, of economic arrangements. The violence, that is, of systems.

While recognising the slow violence of structures, of the social conditions that form our lives, we must be clear that they do not determine every inch of men's lives. If they did, then among women who grow up in the same society as men, everything else being equal, we would witness corresponding rates of women's violence against men. But we do not – not in police data, at least. Women and men, it seems, experience and react differently to their social and economic conditions. That is to say, society – our parents, priests, teachers, media, peers, workplaces – constructs us to be different 'kinds', to think differently about what it means to be women or men.

I am aware that research indicates that men's violence is associated with their support of gender inequality, with patriarchal views and practices that hold and show men to be superior to women. I have repeatedly cited this research in my work. There is something I still believe about that association. However, it seems that things are more complicated than I have led myself to believe, especially in practical life. They always are. But they are also complicated when you look closely into what people report in the research.

A few years ago, in a survey of over 1 700 men and women that my students and I conducted, I found that the overwhelming majority of South African men and women report that they believe in the equal treatment of women and men.[12] Yet the country continues to suffer from high levels of men's violence against women. If a man can report egalitarian views and still commit violence against a woman, how is gender inequality precisely related to gender violence?

I believe I do not understand the association as well as I thought I did. The relationship seems more complicated. Equality is more complicated. The drivers and pathways of men's violent behaviour toward women are more complicated. Love cannot be completely disentwined from violence, it has been averred. Conflict and suffering come with being human and relating to others. There is no love where one of the parties never hurts the other party at all, for where else does our earliest suffering go? We already know that parents do experience violent feelings toward their own children, and that young children harbour rage against the parents who take care of them. I know it is an uncomfortable hypothesis to advance, that violence can never be completely divorced from love, from our being in the world. We should not be afraid to delve into the complications of human relations, though. We always need more understanding about our own mental and affective behaviour, our own and others' pain.

Here is another hypothesis. It seems that we will not be able to stop violence in my country, in the world, because those who govern the world are really not invested in equality, although it might be enshrined in their national constitutions. There is not enough money to be made (by the powerful) in equality, in equal pay for men and women, in smaller differences between the highest-paid and the lowest-paid. Unequal power is baked into our world. Men's violence against women is entangled with other forms of violence and power, such as structural economic violence. It seems that we shall not stop men's violence against women until we stop economic (and racial and linguistic and other forms of) inequality.

I cannot imagine our capitalist world turning away from inequality. South Africa is a poster child for economic inequality, 'with a consumption expenditure Gini coefficient of 0.63 in 2015', according to the World Bank.[13] The World Bank also says that 'inequality in wealth is even higher: the richest 10% of the population held around 71% of net wealth in 2015, while the bottom 60% held 7% of the net wealth. Furthermore, intergenerational mobility is low meaning inequalities are passed down from generation to generation with little change in inequality over time.'[14]

If imagining South Africa becoming more like Slovenia in terms of economic equality and more like Indonesia in terms of gross domestic product (GDP) remains a pipe dream, and men's violence against women is indeed predicted by a combination of economic inequality and poverty, does that mean trying to change masculinities is a hopeless venture?

Maybe.

I do not know.

Sometimes I feel we will not be able to change many men.

But how does losing hope help?

Yet even when we hope, we cannot but be critical. That also means, even while I might think love is an important social force, I ought not to yield to an uncritical attitude toward love.

We have to keep thinking, we have to keep trying to change ourselves.

I have to keep writing.

We have to ask ourselves the difficult questions about ourselves, questions such as how love is tied to violence.

We have to find new ways to understand love, ourselves, each other. And we have to keep trying to find ways to understand violence, to understand why some of us are so attracted to it, even when we claim to love those we beat up and all too often murder, if we are going to reduce it, to stop it.

28 | A few key ideas to consider when thinking about men and changing masculinity

I should go back so that I am able to move forward with surefootedness. I have pointed to some concerns I have with the term 'toxic masculinity'. Am I making too much of nothing? Perhaps it is useful to speak of the things men do as expressions of toxic masculinity. Perhaps the inner debate I am having is academic, and if people have found a vocabulary to make sense of men and what they do, that is good enough. Perhaps, toxic masculinity 'serves the useful purpose of promoting socially desirable behavior among males — men shouldn't be bullies, men shouldn't rape. What healthy mind would disagree with that?'[1] As some have noted, 'the term's current popularity is easy to understand'.[2] It is interesting that while it has some of its roots in the men's movement, which has tended to be anti-feminist, and regards hyper-masculinity (such as that depicted in images of gun-related mass murders in the United States and gangster hip-hop videos) as toxic, the popularity of the term shot up in the wake of the #MeToo movement, which is feminist-influenced.[3]

I am very aware that my concern that toxic masculinity is too much *pop masculinity* language – as in *pop psychology* – and has too little analytical rigour, that at best it offers us another rigid typology, is of a nerdy sort. The trouble is indeed that the term 'toxic masculinity', in its definition and use, does not show enough scrupulousness. It is also too static a term. Usually, it is used against *individuals*, which is to say it individualises the problem of men's *social* oppression and violence against women and children. On those occasions when it is used to describe problematic masculinity in regard to men as a dominant category (rather than a problem of gender structures, norms and ideologies), its target tends to be men who receive poor dividends from systems that uphold patriarchal masculinity – that is, men who may already be disadvantaged by racist, neoliberal, capitalist patriarchy. Increasingly, however, it is used to target men of power (even though that still means the hegemonic institutions remain untouched). In fact, a disconcerting view that can be found in the discourse of toxic masculinity is that masculinity itself, not a particular expression of it, is toxic. In this case there seems to be confusion between toxic masculinity and sexism or patriarchy. If toxic masculinity means not so much hegemonic masculinity (given that, hypothetically, good masculinity can be hegemonic) as sexist masculinity, patriarchal masculinity, racist masculinity, hyper-masculinity, colonial masculinity or even violent masculinity, it is preferable to retain these terms. Perhaps toxic masculinity encompasses all of these masculinities; but if it means every bad kind of masculinity, it means nothing at all.

The most important course to strike in such cases, where masculinity itself is seen as toxic, is to examine what we understand by masculinity (which I will do shortly). Is masculinity the same thing as men? Is it an attribute that an individual inherits with his body, just like a nose or toes? Does masculinity come with different genitalia? The answer, as I have said earlier in this book, is no, no, no.

What about trans masculinity?[4] Does the term 'toxic masculinity' then not point to something else – for example, a set of beliefs, norms, constructions or performances? Since (toxic) masculinity signals constructions and practices that females can and do embody or enact, does it not mean we have to change how we organise against behaviour and policies we see as objectionable, harmful?[5] Is it an ideology? Can anyone subscribe to the ideology of masculinity? Does it refer to psychical structures? Or is it social structures?

These are more than merely pedantic questions, for they have material consequences. Being painstaking about the language employed in thinking about changing boys and men and transforming gender relations is not only something that should be of interest to researchers. In the case of toxic masculinity, the term conveys, although perhaps unwittingly, an essentialism that can be risky, particularly given that many people collapse masculinity into maleness. When discussing a structuring idea (or, we might say, a positioning discourse in gender relations) like masculinity, we ought to exercise care not to fuse it with male bodies or men as such. The structures, the institutions that support oppressive masculinity, are what need to be demolished: collapse the gender structures that support the power of men as a group, transform masculinities. The language of toxic masculinity may be increasingly popular, but it fails to permit a good grasp of men's *social* or *structural* domination of women, just as talking about toxic whiteness fails to understand the *systemic* domination of people categorised as white over those categorised as black.

What precisely is masculinity? It is usually defined in a society by a set of attributes, roles, beliefs and expectations associated with males.[6] In other words, what being a boy or man means from the perspective of a group. Individuals internalise such ascriptions and views and what they have to do in order to demonstrate that they are masculine. All of this is not entirely wrong. However, the definition fails to account for some critical issues.

Masculinity is a pattern or configuration of behaviour. By behaviour, which is a term preferred by psychologists, I mean more or less the same thing sociologists refer to as practice. I mean not only *observable* reactions to the environment, because emotions can also be thought of as behaviour. That is, when you feel, think, or internally talk with yourself, you are behaving even if no one else observes your emotions, cognition and internal talk. Masculinity as a pattern of behaviour derives from an understanding of the concept of behaviour 'not to designate something concrete and thing-like that one could point to, but instead, like the concept of "algebra", a *system* that people use'.[7] You could then say that masculinity is an element within a social system.

While the configuration of masculinity is cultural in origin, it is processed by individuals who in turn contribute to and collaborate in its social reproduction in their everyday lives. 'Configuration' is an appropriate word, one used by many scholars of masculinity. A dictionary definition of it: '*gen*. The (result of) arrangement of the parts or elements of something; internal structure, conformation, outline'.[8]

The idea of configuration, or more fully a configuration of practice, is one that is associated with the Australian thinker Raewyn Connell. This is what she says, in a frequently cited paper co-authored with the American scholar James Messerschmidt, in which they are responding to the massive scholarship generated by an earlier paper written by Connell and her students, about the new sociology of masculinity: 'Masculinity is not a fixed entity embedded in the body or personality traits of individuals. Masculinities are configurations of practice that are accomplished in social action and, therefore, can differ according to the gender relations in a particular social setting.'[9]

Whereas it is common to speak of this or that type of man, the notion of types limits us because the term suggests that a man and his expression of masculinity are fixed. Patterns or configurations contain an inbuilt idea that we can have *another* design or can develop an *updated* or radically different model. We know that good men do bad things and bad men do perform good deeds. Men are characterised by contradictions, just as clothing patterns can be intricate and colourful. When we seek to understand men, the idea of masculinities as patterns of practice facilitates the hope that men can be turned from violence toward loving connectedness. We mean by this a patterning that can be affected by social institutions – for instance, the education system and the family – or by peers and individuals, and that is open to change. Culture and its institutions and interactions fashion masculinity. Individual women and men, households, schools, religions, social clubs and workplaces are continually engaged in designing and influencing the social structures of masculinity. We cannot therefore change masculinity without changing the cultural moulding of boys toward adulthood in institutions like families, churches, schools, universities, public spaces and workplaces.

To say that masculinity is a pattern of behaviour implies that it is not something with which you come into the world. It is not something you are born with. What you come with are your genes, body shape, eye colour and penis. It is necessary to underline, however, that masculinity, because it is a configuration of practice, can be expressed by individuals without penises. As for what we understand as masculinity, that you get from the culture in which you develop. Masculinity is something we assemble with the materials we find in the world, constructions that are processed by individual minds. The fact that masculinity can be expressed in female bodies appears to discombobulate some men, resulting in horrific acts of sexual and homicidal violence to 'correct' the unfeminine or homosexual behaviour of women. I have referred earlier in this book to the 'corrective' murder of

19-year-old soccerite and self-identified lesbian Zoliswa Nkonyana, outside a shebeen in Khayelitsha, a township outside Cape Town, in February 2006.[10] From an initial group of about 20 young men between the ages of 17 and 20 who were charged with the crime, 4 men (Lubabalo Ntlabathi, Sicelo Mase, Luyanda Londzi and Mbulelo Damba) were eventually convicted and sentenced to 18 years in prison in early 2012.

Instead of one configuration of masculinity for all men, there are many models of masculinity. The same applies whether one is considering Zulu, Luo or Afrikaner; Togolese, French or Nigerian; or white or black masculinities: these are ethnicised, 'nationalised' and racialised configurations of gender relations. This is not to refute the argument that ethnicity, nationality and race do influence the development and structuring of masculinity. However, because of, for example, the history of global and local racisms and racist categorisation, too often when thinking about men we fall into the trap of thinking of Nigerian masculinity as one model, or Afrikaner masculinity as a 'type'. On the contrary, there is no one single 'type' of masculinity in any linguistic or ethnic group, nation or race. What helps us is precisely understanding masculinities as sets of changing configurations rather than fixed types. Such an understanding enables us to see ideas about masculinity as contestable, rather than written in stone.

Masculinity is about power arrangements among men, and between men and women. Men are positioned in relations of power vis-à-vis other men, and in relation to women. Masculinities, to which men subscribe, are also arranged in some kind of order, a hierarchy, as Connell has also argued.[11] Some masculinities are seen as more desirable, imbued with 'higher value', than others. To contend that masculinity is about power also means that in any society, power determines what is the socially valued masculinity. The form of masculinity that the greater part of a society generally agrees to be desirable – meaning those things the majority sees as defining a socially successful man – is the masculinity that is in power. It is especially the part of society that sets the agenda and direction of that society that has the most influence over what is taken by the majority to be highly valued masculinity. In our society, or parts of it, men are or have been regarded as embodying successful manhood when they have gone through initiation and been circumcised in a traditionally accepted way, have money, occupy some position of authority, have cows, have good jobs, can beat other men, drive expensive cars, have sex with the women other men supposedly desire, have sex with more than one woman, own properties, are respected by other men, show a readiness to use violence, and fulfil other measures of manhood for people with adult male bodies. What this implies is that, in order to prove we are men, we will seek to possess or demonstrate those attributes that our society believes define manhood. This, in turn, implies that to understand why some men are violent, we have to recognise how they understand power, which is tied to their understanding of masculinity.

One route through which power works is force. The use of violence to enforce the law or to rule over others is an example of this. Another route consists of ideas, which are employed to persuade us of the rightness of power, or to challenge the powerful. What this means is that the hierarchical order of masculinities in a society, what is dominant and what subordinate, can serve ideological ends, either to support the existing order or to challenge it. When politicians in some countries condemn transgender individuals, what they are doing is using ideas of masculinity for their own politico-ideological ends. They are trying to shore up their power base by denigrating trans men and women. This is true also for religious figures who preach against women who love other women, or men who prefer to have sex with other men. They are using the dominant ideas about what it is to be a woman or a man to reproduce their religio-ideological positions on gender.

Since masculinity is made up of patterns of the practice of power, it stands to reason that society, small groups and individuals can change the patterns, and can shift the power. This does not imply that it is necessarily easy to do so. But we can. There are always forces at work and individuals who will fight to conserve what has existed before or up to this point, which we refer to as the way things have always been done, or convention, or law, or tradition, even if what has existed harms others. Yet there are always opportunities to change the way things have been done in the past. The beginnings of such change lie in appreciating that the things we believe define masculinity are always changing, even if this is happening on the margins of society, or is pushed by small groups of people, or if the reality is that it is not all men who will change. Not too long ago, for example, the idea of same-sex marriage was so unthinkable as to be punishable by law. But gay masculinity is now out in the open for some (not all) men, and gay marriage is legally acceptable in many parts of the world.

29 | The politician told students you can't ask for money from somebody who raped you

More than a decade ago, a well-known political figure in South Africa, Julius Malema, said to a crowd of students at the then Cape Peninsula University of Technology:

> When a woman didn't enjoy it, she leaves early in the morning. Those who had a nice time will wait until the sun comes out, request breakfast and ask for taxi money. In the morning, that lady requested breakfast and taxi money. You can't ask for money from somebody who raped you.[1]

At the time, Malema was the president of the ANC Youth League. His words were in defence of Jacob Zuma, the then president of the mother body, the ANC, who had been accused of raping a woman named in the media only as Khwezi. I do not know what the students learned from that. Was it that there are rules for rape?

What Malema was expressing to the university students was an example of a rape myth.[2] A rape myth is a 'prejudicial, stereotyped, or false [belief] about rape, rape victims, and rapists'.[3] Another way to define rape myths is as 'attitudes and beliefs that are generally false but are widely and persistently held, and that serve to deny and justify male sexual aggression against women'.[4] These prejudicial beliefs and attitudes function to shame victims of rape, shutting them up.

Like many people, I grew up in an environment replete with these harmful stereotypes. Because of current levels of sexual violence, I have little reason to believe that there has been a dramatic change in the prevalence and content of rape myths.

One of the early works discussing the attitudes and beliefs supportive of rape was *Against Our Will: Men, Women and Rape* by Susan Brownmiller, published in 1975.[5] The book would go on to influence a large body of research and the thinking of many women (and men) about how sexist cultural beliefs support rape and thus perpetuate sexual offences in a society. These beliefs also justify other forms of violence against women. Brownmiller wrote:

'ALL WOMEN WANT TO BE RAPED'

'NO WOMAN CAN BE RAPED AGAINST HER WILL'

'SHE WAS ASKING FOR IT'

'IF YOU'RE GOING TO BE RAPED, YOU MIGHT AS WELL RELAX AND ENJOY IT'

These are the deadly male myths of rape, the distorted proverbs that govern female sexuality. They are at the heart of our discussion, for they are the beliefs that most men hold, and the nature of male power is such that they have managed to convince many women of their validity ... They deliberately obscure the true nature of rape.[6]

There are many cultural myths and beliefs about rape. They are very hard to dismantle without deliberate, consistent effort to undo the attitudes and beliefs that shape the masculinity many men have introjected, often unconsciously, into their identity. Even when a man has gone some way in extirpating these myths from the self, there is the broader society in which he lives that reinforces them. There are many places where we see society's tolerance of such attitudes and beliefs.

Although some myths need work to uncover, others are easy to notice. Enumerating some of the myths of which I am aware in my society, which I do now, is not, I believe, gratuitous, if these harmful stereotypes are to be smashed.

- Women who visit men at their homes or hotel rooms are signalling that they want it because, unlike men, women are afraid to explicitly express their sexual desires.
- It is not rape if she does not say no or fight.
- A person who is about to be raped will scream.

- Women lie about rape to get back at men.
- It is not rape if there are no bruises or the perpetrator did not have a weapon.
- There is a typical behaviour of women who have really been raped.
- Men cannot control themselves.
- Good men, rich men, handsome men, do not need to rape.
- There is a typical rapist.
- When a woman accepts favours, money or gifts from a man, she owes him.
- No does not really mean no, because women want to be persuaded.
- She should not have gotten drunk, she only has herself to blame.
- Prostitutes cannot be raped.
- She should have known better than to walk in a dangerous place. She should not have walked alone at that hour.
- A healthy heterosexual man who says no to sex with a beautiful woman who wants to have sex with him probably cannot fuck, cannot keep it up, is secretly gay or has something wrong with him.
- Real men cannot be raped.
- It is men who cannot have women who rape.
- A woman wearing revealing clothes is asking for it.
- How can you say no if you are my wife?!
- A man wants sex, a woman wants love, and that causes misunderstanding and leads to her accusing him of rape because he only wanted sex when she was looking for love.

I could keep adding to this list. There are so many more of these prejudicial views around. You can add the ones you know. In fact, making a list in your head or writing them down for yourself may not be a terrible idea. One would do such an exercise as part of a critical education programme on sexualities and sexual violence, for oneself alone, or as part of a formal or informal group one belongs to, such as a church group, a class, a friendship circle or in a workplace.

The attitudes and beliefs described in *Against Our Will* and those I have listed in this chapter may be different in degree from those that Malema expressed – that a woman who is raped leaves early in the morning; a woman who is raped does not ask for breakfast; a woman who is raped does not ask for taxi fare – but they obviously are of the same fabric. All of them to a greater or lesser degree support sexual violence against women; all of them are used to protect most of us from acknowledging the true reach and impact of men's desire to control women's bodies and sexualities. Of course, these negative beliefs do not merely 'protect us', psychologically and socially speaking. Their key social function is to reinforce the core of men's relations to women: that is, one group's subordination to the other. Hence, the resistance to these beliefs that is necessary through social activism, teaching, writing and subjective transformation must direct its energies toward democratic gender and sexual relations that can challenge and dismantle the edifice of rape myths.

It must be clear at this point that there are many common, insidious cultural myths that calcify misogyny and add to the difficulty of preventing and reducing grave sexual violence and femicide. Setting out to expunge rape myths from one's masculinity, I contend, is not an easy task for most people, and certainly not a once-off task. A person who grows up in a culture suffused with these cultural beliefs – which implies most people – absorbs them into their consciousness. They may even sink into the person's unconscious. We might even say, with caution, that Malema may actually not have been conscious that these myths were part of his beliefs, of his psyche. Yet even when a man's critical consciousness with respect to gender and sexual relations has expanded, and he can immediately recognise a rape-supportive attitude in himself, he is influenced by other family members, friends, broadcast media, religious communities, films, advertising, social media, laws and education systems that constantly reinforce, or fail to discourage, these myths. Consequently, if we take as our duty the making of a better society, it is society's support of rape myths that we must challenge.

Two years after his statement to the students in 2009, after being taken to court by the human rights organisation Sonke Gender Justice and losing the case, Malema apologised:

I am sorry, sorry and very sorry about that. And commit not to repeat the similar mistake again. Issues of women are sensitive, and once a person says, 'I'm offended', it doesn't matter whether you are right or not, you must have the capacity to say sorry. I want to say sorry to the lady and to the Sonke Gender [sic], and I commit to pay them that R50,000 and pay legal fees for that case.[7]

I don't know whether the students saw that apology and, if so, what they learned from it. Perhaps those who saw or read about the 'mistake' may have said something like, men can learn; they can say sorry when they are wrong. Maybe they said, that was then, and all is fair in the heat of politics.

Gender and sexuality are never outside of politics, of course. Rape is never not about power. By that I signal the fact that our identity as subjects of gender power, our words, our beliefs, our acts, including words, our acts of sexual violence, are never *outside* power. We are positioned by power. Power is part of our being in a society with others. And I want to state again: power is not always negative. It is not only used to injure, subjugate or control. It can be and often enough is used to free others, to enable them, and to build space for more people to be happy.

I hope that, if not those particular students who listened to Malema, then, with the help of this reflection, other students, you the reader, will appreciate that rape is enabled by stereotypes about women and men. Rape myths have implications for all forms of violence against women and for broader social relations. Rape is connected to our thoughts, attitudes, feelings, beliefs and actions, which are products of our culture, and culture is infused with power relations. Whatever else we may feel rape is about, it is simultaneously about who has power and to what end they use that power.

I also hope that more of us will appreciate that the victim of rape is never to blame.

'She was asking for it' is the classic way a rapist shifts the burden of blame from himself to his victim. The popularity of the belief that a woman seduces or 'cock-teases' a man into rape, or precipitates a rape by incautious behavior, is part of the smokescreen that men throw up to obscure their actions. The insecurity of women runs so deep that many, possibly most, rape victims agonize afterward in an effort to uncover what it was in their behavior, their manner, their dress that triggered this awful act against them.[8]

What Brownmiller is alluding to here is shame. As Rebecca Helman has said, the shame belongs elsewhere: 'In my interviews with survivors of sexual violence I have heard of a multitude of ways in which womxn are resisting being shamed.'[9] The shame that is attached to sexual violence belongs with the person who holds rape myths, the rapist, and the culture that supports rape.

It may not be enough, but all I have is hope and a willingness to work against these myths and their effects, for I do not know if the students who heard Malema say he is sorry quite understand how our attitudes, feelings, beliefs and behaviour support rape and what they do to our society.

30 | 'Dad, look at me'

'Dad, look at me,' he says. Or, simply, 'Dad, look'. An injunction. But also a petition. He is about to jump. Or to do something else with his body.

Human beings, I now apprehend better than ever before, because of this *being* who hails me as 'Dad', *need* to be looked at in a certain way. Being looked at offers a way of looking at ourselves. Without the other to look at us, we travel blind. We need to be looked at, as we do not actually know how we look to others. Looking is a form of building the other's self. Love is to be found in a look.

It is also true, though, that looking can be used to crush the self. Hatred, anger, disappointment, disgust can be communicated with a look. It is not only joy, camaraderie, recognition, happiness, pleasure, contentment and care that are found in the way we look and are looked at.

I know that in order to experience positive affect in interactions with others, a person needs to be spoken to in a particular way and not in other ways, held in a specific way and not other ways, or, of course, looked at in a certain way. I know it not as a thought somewhere in my head, but as something that every human being needs – not as immediately as one would need water after a day without drinking, but as much more than 'mere' pleasure. Other people have an influence on our emotions and, cumulatively, on what we become.

Even though feminism teaches us we have to resist the male gaze, it is common knowledge that we dress up for others, whatever gender we are. We instinctually crave the father's gaze as much as the mother's gaze. We apply make-up and put on earrings and our beautiful shoes and check ourselves in the mirror so as to look a certain way for an imagined audience. Those of us who grew up under colonialism and legalised white racism wear certain clothes, and on Sundays put on our best clothes, because, somewhere deep inside us – the white oppressor's stereotyping gaze notwithstanding – what we wear makes us feel good, since others look at us with envy or a sense of wanting what we are wearing.

It was Freud, once again, who alerted me to the idea that being looked at is libidinally exciting.[1] I found this to be so. Yes, we get excited at seeing others look at us. It is, however, a very strange pleasure indeed, being looked at. At the same time, we derive from others' eyes more than pleasure. It is not just the psychical enjoyment that we get from being looked at by our fathers. We also seek something of this very 'excitement' in the eyes of the security guard outside the store, or of our co-workers. It is, then, not merely thrills that we get from being looked at. Rather, what we are looking for is something much more ontologically reinforcing. We want to be noticed. Humans are always looking for a kind of recognition that they exist.

We do not eat 'being looked at'. We do not smell it. It does not keep us dry when it rains, or safe from those who would hurt us – even though there is a way of hurting from not being looked at, or from being looked at in a way that misrecognises us, takes something from us. And yet, we put a lot of psychosocial energy into receiving looks of recognition, sometimes even of approval. Many of us will buy new clothes to appear pleasing to others' eyes. Some of us purchase beauty products to make ourselves look attractive. And others will even undergo plastic surgery to render themselves young and good-looking.

'Are you looking, Dad?' It's now an interrogative. But it conveys the same demand, the same plea. We express an imperative appeal. I propose that this exigent craving is part of the development of all children, of all of us.

LOOK. AT. ME. DAD. He stresses each word. Why should I look at him? Why does he want me to look at him? What does it matter if he manages to jump down the stairs and I don't see him? What does he lose? What kind of enjoyment does he derive from me seeing him drawing, writing his name, doing a somersault?

Because it is not just pleasurable to be present in the eyes of the parent. Being looked at by the other is libidinally exciting, certainly. We enjoy being looked at in that certain way: that is true, too. We want to be seen in a certain light, as it were. But then –

First, I remembered, I knew, that Frantz Fanon had been here before me. I reread that famous passage. But where Fanon writes: ' "Mama, see the Negro! I'm frightened" ', from Ratele, the boy, I hear, 'Dad, see this "Negro" '.[2] How amazing is he! And this is what I arrived at this time: if I don't *see* him, if I don't look at him in the way he is asking me to look at him, he will never see himself. He learns to see, which is to say learns to see himself, through my eyes. He learns to be truly himself, to have a *self*, apart from me, if I look at him. If the father doesn't look at the son in the way he is asking to be looked at, which is asking for help to put himself, to put *a self*, together, he will 'burst apart'. My eyes bring his self to life. I can help, in a small way, to make that self more loving toward itself and to others. Is it possible that I can build a loving man? Maybe. I think so. In looking at him in a certain way, I provide him with the ontological weight he needs to be – to *be* (fully himself) without paralysing doubt.

31 | 'I have never hit a woman' gets you no loving man award

I thought it was self-evident why declaring that one has never raped a woman is not an achievement. Apparently, I am mistaken. I should therefore explain.

Let us consider not raping or hitting a woman. You may have heard this before: in response to reports of a woman who was abused or murdered, a man says to others or himself, 'I have never hit a woman'. Yet it may not always be clear to all what this declaration of virtue fully implies.

A man who publicly announces that he has never hit a woman seeks to set himself at a distance from the other man, the violent one. His intention is to underscore his blamelessness for other men's violence. How can he be held responsible for another man's bad deeds? And yet he must have an inkling, which he disavows, that he is part of the same group as that man: men.

Declaring that one has never raped, or telling oneself that one is not a rapist, misses the point that all men and women are agents within a gender order. They are members of social groups. Men who terrorise women do so in order that the majority of men do not have to hit women and, paradoxically, so that other men can perform their roles as protectors of women. Of course, they may be naïve about their role in reinforcing the fear of women and the protector role of men. They do not wake up and say they intend to restore men's domination over women. However, there would be no need for a protector role if men did not socially dominate women in the first place, and hence feel entitled to women's bodies.

Rape has effects beyond one man raping one woman. When I learn of yet another rape, the appropriate response is not that *I do not rape*. I have to see broadly, to remember that rape is about men's power over women, which tacitly or overtly permits different forms of violence against women as a category. I have to remember that it is when non-violent means of controlling women fail that men's power resorts to direct violence. In that light, *not* aggressing against women is not an achievement.

I have heard a version of this statement several times in the course of my life: 'I have never touched a woman', or 'I would never raise a hand to a woman'. (And I have heard more than one woman say, 'He never hits me'. As in the case of men, this is not a great relationship goal for women. It is not a sign of a loving relationship. More crucially, it is not an attestation of equality in inter-personal relationships. Not being hit is far too low a bar to which to aspire.)

Every time you hear a man say he has never committed a violent act against a woman, the question you should ask him (and yourself) is, what is that statement intended to do? In other words, what does a man who says he has never abused a woman *want*, exactly? Surely it is not an award from you? Perhaps it is approval, which is close enough to a good man award; we therefore need to show why this desire for approval misapprehends what is at stake in men's violence against women.

There is a multitude of examples of this misreading. In her book, *Of Motherhood and Melancholia*, clinical psychologist and university professor Lou-Maré Kruger reveals an example of a woman who is being hurt in different ways, unsubtle and quietly horrifying, without, as it were, a finger being lifted. After presenting and analysing the story of Delize and Piet, in which the violence is physical, clear and easy to recognise, Kruger writes about Cara, a stay-at-home mom married to Johan, a very successful businessman, who on many days gives her a to-do list that is impossible to complete:

> Johan has not *beaten* Cara (yet); but burnt toast drives him to shouting and swearing; her car left in the driveway between errands will make him pound on his car horn; an open door or drawer is grounds for a kid getting ''*n goeie pak slae*' (a good hiding) and serving dinner in a tracksuit may produce a week-long sulk ... Johan checks the wetness of Cara's vagina after they have male visitors, so as to make sure that other men do not excite her.[1]

To state it simply, then, *not beating* a woman does not deserve a manhood award. It is what should be expected. The fact that a man does not slap or punch a woman is not on its own an indication of non-violence. It is not a sign of a loving form of manhood. You cannot write a film whose synopsis is 'he never hit a woman'; there is no story in not hitting a woman. Surely a man can write a more compelling story, not just about love but about his own life course, than wanting to be known for *not* hitting women. So, to begin with, a man has to do a little better than being satisfied with the fact that he has never raped, coerced, abused or harassed a woman. It is not something to be proud of. It is the barest minimum expected of everyone.

The fact is, there are millions of men who have never hit a woman and still manage to make women miserable, render them less than men, or continue to be complicit in their subordination. More crucially, millions of men have never raped women, yet women's fear of men and men's power over women are social facts of the world. There are many ways through which men hurt and oppress women, and overt violence may not always be necessary. Some of these are located in personal life, others in the organisation of society. Forcing a woman into marriage is one example of how women are oppressed without a hand being lifted against them. So is denying a girl an education. Then there is paying a woman less than a man doing the same work, so that she must be dependent on a man. Pressurising her to have children. Withholding sex as punishment. Lying. Controlling what she wears because religious or cultural norms say it is inappropriate for women to dress in certain ways. Not paying maintenance. Laws that favour men. Withdrawing emotionally. Ignoring women. Supporting stereotypes about girls' and women's abilities. Using money to control them. Not taking them seriously. Representing women in limiting ways in the media. Shouting at a woman. Not doing enough as a government to prevent women from dying during childbirth. Sulking. Making women live with fear so that they need men's protection against other men. Forcing a woman to have an abortion.

Speaking of forcing women to have abortions in order to hurt them, I am reminded of yet another story that made headline news in South Africa, that of the murder of Tshegofatso Pule.[2] She was murdered by Muzikayise Malephane. Malephane alleges that he was hired by Pule's boyfriend, Ntuthuko Shoba, who was already married to another woman. Of particular interest in this case is that Shoba ordered Pule to be killed because he did not want to become a father. Pule had previously been forced by Shoba to have an abortion, and her refusal to have another abortion may have led to the femicide.[3]

There are, then, many ways to hurt women. Not hitting them is only one. And not hitting is not, therefore, a sign of anything other than the fact that there is no physical violence.

Non-violence is supposed to be the default practice in a relationship. And, as I have already said, there are many ways to make each other miserable.

Raise the intimacy bar.

Not hitting a woman does not get you an award.

32 | Before death, before conception, in the many in-between moments, then repeat

When is the optimal time to intervene if you want to change men? This is a question I have asked myself more than once. I also get asked it by others.

My answer: *the birth room*. There is no better time to make men aware that many of the behaviours the majority of them tend to associate with real manhood are more likely to lead them to an early death, than when they are in *the birth room*. If we use the teachable moment when a man's wife, girlfriend or friend is giving birth, then we might start to see some changes in how men think about life and death. That is pretty much the answer I gave in response to the question when I was asked by some students after a talk I gave at Stellenbosch University. It was September, the month after Women's Month. It was also the month in which the national police ministry used to release their annual crime statistics.[1] The statistics are now released quarterly.

I was wrong, of course. But my mistake has nothing to do with being idealistic, or with whipped manhood, or even with notions that men ought to enter the labour room.

I am no idealist. I am a critical psychologist of masculinity. I do not know about being whipped.

That question – of when is the best time to intervene to make men less violent – is one to be kept in mind every time we read crime statistics issued by the South African Police Service (SAPS). Around the time of the talk at Stellenbosch University, the SAPS had released the 2011/12 crime figures. The report indicated 15 609 reported cases of murder for 2011/12, down from the 15 940 cases reported for 2010/11.[2] You don't need to be a statistician to know that this was an insignificant drop. That said, the number of murders had decreased by 27.6 per cent in the eight years from 2004/05 to 2011/12. That is a significant reduction.

But I was aware that things could change in the wrong direction. More crucially, what was needed was an even more dramatic reduction in violence. And that was, as far as I could see, not on the horizon. The simple reason was that there was fundamentally nothing the government and the police were doing to reduce violence. (There still isn't.) The drop in violent crime was attributed to better policing, but there were no rigorous studies to confirm the claim. It was therefore baffling to me why murders were down, because there was no intervention or coherent, substantiated explanation for the drop in violent crimes observed between 2007 and 2012.

So it was no great surprise when the figures began to go upward again from 2012/13. In 2012/13 there were 16 213 murders. This number rose to 18 673 in 2015/16. In 2019/20 the figure was 21 325.[3]

The high body count due to violence cannot, in my assessment, please any state concerned with the impact of violence on the social well-being of its people. Coupled with the equally high numbers of rape, robbery, assault, theft, housebreaking and carjacking, news about violent and non-violent crime can be depressing.

What continues to worry me is what the police statistics usually do not show; you have to unpack them to see something disturbing if you are interested in patterns of violence. The statistics do not readily show, for example, who perpetrates murder and who gets murdered. You can infer some things from reading the maps of murder in South Africa, which have to be studied alongside other research. Thus, in the Western Cape, for instance, your chances of dying a violent death are greater in Delft, Harare, Nyanga, Mfuleni, Mitchells Plain, Philippi East, and other places near these areas, than in Camps Bay, Simon's Town or Fish Hoek. Tembisa, Katlehong and Kagiso are among the areas in Gauteng that have high rates of murder. What the maps suggest is that you are most endangered if you live in predominantly black (including coloured) areas, especially if you are in the Western Cape. Violence stalks black neighbourhoods.

What you still won't know, though, is that dying young from murder is largely the lot of black males. That understanding comes from the surveillance and research work that has shown a consistent distribution and pattern of violence mortality over the years.[4]

During any given year, the likelihood is that the majority of the people killed will be young black men in poor black areas. That signals five factors: youth, race, gender, economic status and neighbourhood. Young black men in low-income neighbourhoods constitute a group whose death rates have been highest for a long time in South Africa. Black men start dying from violence in their teenage years. The most dangerous period to be a young man is, however, in your twenties. And, although most men may be unaware of the quality of their breathing, they won't breathe easily until they get past their forties, if they ever do. The ease with which black men's breath can be cut short was magnified for the world in 2020 when a 46-year-old African American man, George Floyd, pleaded, 'I can't breathe' on the tarmac outside a shop in Minneapolis, Minnesota, while white American police officer Derek Chauvin knelt on Floyd's neck till he died.[5]

The lack of awareness and care about how close to death young black men walk each day has absorbed my attention for a long while. That lack of awareness and care contributes to the probability that South Africa will not and cannot bring down the body count to the hundreds, rather than thousands, within the next few years. But if men were shown how death stalks their days, it might just help to save a few more lives.

Of course, the problem is much bigger than one of awareness or simple policing. But that is not the reason I think my answer to the question posed after my talk at Stellenbosch University was wrong. The reason is also *not* because the levels of murder in South Africa will be drastically reduced by recruiting more police, shooting criminals and giving them harsher sentences, as opposed to encouraging men to witness the pain and miracle of birth on its own. To be sure, perhaps what we need is *smarter* policing – not more guns but *preventative* interventions. But somebody suggested to me after I had answered the question that the best time to intervene to save men from an early violent death is *before* conception. To save men from an early grave we need to intervene before children are conceived, before sex, before the ideas of boyhood and manhood congeal, before they die. Figure 32.1 presents some of the life moments at which this intervention

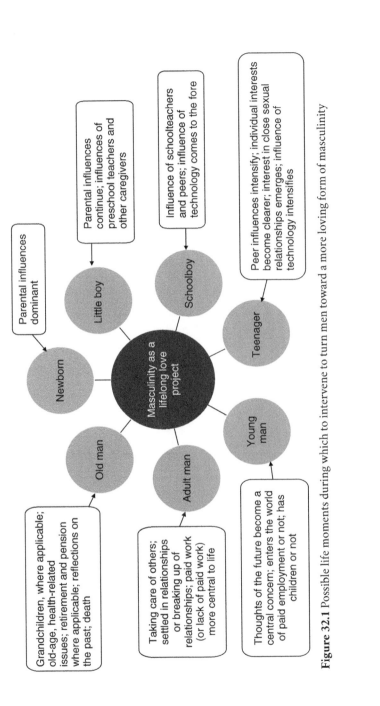

Figure 32.1 Possible life moments during which to intervene to turn men toward a more loving form of masculinity

can occur. What ties all of these moments together is love. I do not think that is too much to ask. Love boys so that they can become loving men, live well and perhaps even thrive.

And on and on, over and over again: before death, before conception, before injury, in the many in-between moments, then repeat. For the sake of loving relations between us.

33 | Baldwin was a full man

It is common for societies to erect boundaries, one can even say invisible prison-like walls, around the identities they create. That is, there are invisible but real borders around identities such as adulthood, whiteness, South Africanness, manhood. By this I mean that if you are an adult, it is expected, even demanded, that you not behave like a child, even if childlike behaviour may be good for your mental health. Or, if you are a white person, you are not supposed to behave like black people, whatever that means. It is therefore inevitable that a certain restrictiveness is built into masculinity as an identity. To be successfully masculine, meaning hegemonically so, you have to stay inside the prison walls, not act queer or feminine. In his essay on James Baldwin, Teju Cole writes about another kind of restrictiveness: the limitations imposed on black bodies by racism. To be more precise, the essay is about the time the gay black stranger, Baldwin, who was already famous, first went to a white town, Leukerbad in Switzerland, in 1951, where for two weeks he stayed at his lover Lucien Happersberger's family chalet in a village up in the mountains and wrote the essay 'Stranger in the Village'. While Cole, who obviously admires Baldwin, will not surrender the beauty of any great art, he seems puzzled by the writer's self-abnegation in the face of the art of a Rembrandt, Dante, Bach, Shakespeare, or the cathedral at Chartres, because Baldwin understood that the blues are not below Bach. 'But,' writes Cole, 'there was a certain narrowness in received ideas of black culture in the nineteen-fifties.'[1]

This idea of a received restrictiveness applies so well to what we become as men, and not just to how we become black; that's what I thought as I was reading Cole's essay. True, I do not know when we are ever men and not part of a given culture. And from the other end, of course, there is never a moment when we are just part of a cultural group and not part of a gender group. We are always more than any one thing at any moment, although the situation can make one kind of identity more salient than another. All the same, there is a certain conventional constriction in affects, attitudes and acts when we consider what we are allowed – and allow ourselves – to feel as men and women. Included here are the positions we hold (for example, regarding marriage) and what we do in our lives as members of the gender category with which we identify. It is this narrowness that a man needs to loosen in himself, if he is to be a different person – we might say, a 'non-traditional' man.

While Cole was concerned with the black body, I was thinking of the constricting ideas of masculinity that we inherit from our fathers (and grandmothers, mothers, neighbours, priests, uncles, teachers, coaches, grandfathers and aunts) that then shape our bodies and behaviours, keeping us within an imprisoning masculinity. While Cole was writing about the writer who knows himself to be so much more than the ideology of white supremacy would allow a black person to be, I was thinking of why he is saying nothing about Baldwin as a man who loves men. He could have said more about Baldwin as a man, I felt, but no matter. I guess I could say something here about the love letter Baldwin wrote to his nephew James – that is how I refer to it – because that shows another kind of love and the man Baldwin was. But another declaration will have to suffice for now.[2] It is enough to simply state that, even in times like those in which he lived, Baldwin was, as C.L.R. James might have said, a full man.[3] That, to me, means a beautiful man, a free being. We can use a few more Baldwin-like men here.

34 | The masculinity of a man who is a boy

In my country, for centuries adult men were regarded as *boys*. I have been talking a lot about men and boys. The difference is clear to me. Yet, while for some people the difference between men and boys is obvious – and, to be sure, *botho* means respecting people who are older than oneself – for others it may not be so.[1] In fact, it was not unusual for many white men and white women to refer to adult men who worked for them as boys. This was intended to infantilise and demean them. We could say, then, some people do not have *botho*.

Is calling a grown man a boy not a provocation, a form of psychological violence? How can a person to whom this is done not be enraged? How do we turn around, then, and claim the men who have been violated like this are violent, as if we do not know the shame they and their forefathers had to endure in order to survive?

I have wondered, that is, whether some of us still believe, deep inside our unconscious minds, that some men are boys. I have also wondered, given how parents can transmit their experience of humiliation and shame to the next generation, whether some men continue to carry intergenerational shame. Could it be that this history of inferiorisation, of dehumanisation, is still to be excavated from inside some of us? Could it be that some of us still believe that we are not full men?

For a grown man to be seen or to talk about himself as a boy is more than seeing him as a subordinate. It goes beyond the relationship between a boss and an employee. Its main objective is to degrade, to wound his manhood, to cast the individual out of the category of grown-up men, out of adult masculinity. If you refer to an adult male as a boy, not in a playful manner but in a serious tone, repeatedly, while giving him instructions or rebuking him, he cannot be your equal. He needs your tutelage. You are the parent, he is a child, even if he may be older than you in age. In fact, we learned that even white children can call old men boys.

I am not talking of men such as Chris/Lumkile, the main character in Thando Mgqolozana's novel *A Man Who Is Not a Man*, although the character tells us about the ways a particular culture, that of amaXhosa, ritually produces men, and how that ritual can sometimes fail and hurt its subjects.[2] I am talking about how racist ideology, entwined with ideologies of capitalism and patriarchy, has constricted the ways in which we regard ourselves. Have the long-tailed effects of these ideologies chained us, shaped us into believers that we were, and maybe that we still are, not men, not quite? Is that one of the reasons some of us cannot but be violent?

Could some of us hold this view of ourselves, perhaps below the level of consciousness, that nothing matters *because we do not matter*? That because the world does not care for us, we cannot care for others? Is that why some of us are violent toward others, even toward those who want to reclaim our inherent dignity as men, those who love us, which is to say women close to us and our own children?

That is essentially what I said to the audience at the Apartheid Museum in Johannesburg a few years ago, when we celebrated another Human Rights Day and I was asked to speak on the question of the black body.[3] A dark way to celebrate.

Maybe, I think, some of us turn violent against black women because of this abject struggle to rise to the level of a man, to prove we are not boys, to prove that we are men. The systematic dehumanisation of men and women of our skin colour began hundreds of years ago, here and in other parts of the world. These men and women were regarded as nothing but beasts of burden and breeding animals. That ideology of dehumanisation brought together economic exploitation, racism and patriarchy in one cruel, anti-human system. It is an ideology that has not completely died. Men and women all over the world are still exploited for their labour and their bodies because of how they look.

Could it be, then, that some of us continue to doubt our humanity, even while the countries we live in have long since stopped enslaving people like us and colonising our lands? This is not to suggest that racism is dead. And, of course, capitalist exploitation and patriarchal domination are facts of the world in which we live.

Even if the ideology that sees people of my skin colour as inferior is objectively garbage, there may be some of us who believe in the superiority of those regarded as white. Even when we know that some of our ancestors and some of our parents and some of us fought against white racism, it may be that some of us still doubt ourselves, haunted by the fear that we are not fully men.

I see two struggles that we are still waging at present. And that present has a history, of course.

One struggle is outside, against the material conditions in which some of us continue to live. These conditions themselves can be dehumanising. The other struggle is inside ourselves. It may even be harder than the struggle to obtain what we need to live.

But what precisely does it mean for a man to feel that he is not quite a man? It means we have already dehumanised him, explicitly or in our thoughts. With dehumanisation comes the idea that this *thing*, this not-quite-a-man, cannot feel pain. *It* is not like us. *It* is only partly a man, and so morally uninjurable.[4] *It* is underserving of all that comes with human morality, consciousness, freedom. Studies have shown that some people believe people of colour feel less pain than white people.[5] This has been shown to be particularly true in the case of men of my skin colour, who are seen as not characterised by what makes other humans human. Pain is what humans feel. And human freedom is, by definition, for humans only.

The dehumanised thing is therefore beyond human society, below it, outside it, not a part of it. And dehumanising a human being has far-reaching implications, some of which still characterise the world.

To be not a part of human society means being beyond the social facts of powerlessness, of unfreedom, of captivity, of helplessness. For the man who is not quite a social being, the understanding that he is not one of us is beaten into him so that he learns not to expect worldly delivery from the world of beasts, or empathy for his subjection. He will imperil himself if he even thinks of himself as a man. How can he think, let alone think that he is a full man? To show that he can think for himself, and thinks of himself as a man, would go against how others see him and want him to see himself.

That is what puts him in danger, because it disturbs their view of the world in which they and he live.

The man who is not a man is dead. Even while he works and makes money for others, he is not really alive. This shadow is also a potential danger, to himself and others. The danger arises from the fact that psychological (and often enough bodily) violence has been implanted in him by a world that continually debased him, until he stopped believing in other ways of being in the world. That is why getting him to expunge the violence from his interior will demand remaking him.

The question of what it means to think that a person is not quite human can be posed about the status of women. At the same time, women must also contend with the violence of men like us, who are in a similar position to themselves. In addition to the violence of a white racist society, they carry the burden of the violence of their men. The loathsome violence of men who look like me against women who look like me feels more despicable, yet more explicable.

Yet our aggression toward women is not entirely out of the ordinary. After all, we are men in a sexist and not only racist world. In this world, women's sexuality, like their non-reproductive labour, is one of the things that must also come under men's control.

As not-quite-women and not-quite-men, we are supposedly uninjurable, even though these men who are not fully men and women who are not fully women are integral to the economy of a country. Injurability is a notion that deserves thinking about in relation to masculinity and femininity. The perceived uninjurability of bodies like mine is one of the afterlives of slavery and colonialism. The dehumanisation of some men is associated with the callousness and brutality with which they are treated.[6] Dehumanisation flows from moral exclusion, the process which enables the slave, the oppressed, the other or the black to be 'perceived as outside the boundary in which moral values, rules, and considerations of fairness apply'.[7] Once you are morally excluded, you do not matter; your whole life does not matter. You can be raped, maimed, murdered – anything that is done to you is permissible.

All that may be a fact of history: that we were once dehumanised, that too many of us continue to be dehumanised.

But we should stop believing the lie, if we ever did, if we still do.

We are full men and women.

The standards we use to measure ourselves cannot be defined by others. For if you have not thought about what is the most valuable thing for you as a person, the thing you cannot live without, chances are that you will sooner or later become very distressed, if not a straight-out failure in your own eyes and, surely, in the eyes of others.

35 | Mr President, end patriarchy?

History may come to regard the fifth president of our democratic society, Cyril Ramaphosa, as one most distinguished by the constant attention he has paid to the issue of gender-based violence and femicide in South Africa. Politicians have contributed to the miserable conditions in their societies – and such unhappy conditions were evident in this country under Ramaphosa's predecessor, Jacob Zuma – and I do not have great trust in the words they utter. It takes a whole machinery to implement the promises they make. Nonetheless, while other presidents have mentioned it now and then, President Ramaphosa appears to take every opportunity to bring attention to the scourge of violence in South Africa. In contrast to the second president, Thabo Mbeki, who was preoccupied with women's empowerment, Mr Ramaphosa is particularly concerned with violence against women and girls. There are many instances we can point to that indicate this concern. For instance, at the beginning of 2021, while addressing the nation about the second wave of the Covid-19 pandemic, he referred to gender-based violence and femicide as the second pandemic. The *National Strategic Plan on Gender-Based Violence and Femicide* contains a foreword by him in which, among other things, he states:

> The unacceptably high levels of gender-based violence and femicide in South Africa are a blight on our national conscience, and a betrayal of our constitutional order for which so many fought, and for which so many gave their lives. South Africa holds the shameful distinction of being one of the most unsafe places in the world to be a woman.

We have amongst the highest rates of intimate partner violence, and recently released data from Statistics SA show that rape and sexual violence have become hyperendemic.[1]

Every sentiment in that statement is one I share. It is pleasing that the president uses words and phrases like 'the shameful distinction of being the most unsafe place in the world to be a woman', 'hyperendemic', and, elsewhere, 'queer or cis' and 'deep crisis'. I also believe that if we cannot now, under this presidency, move the needle toward a more non-violent society, we will be set back for decades. It is gratifying, therefore, to hear a man in such a powerful position speaking out against men's violence with such words. It is some kind of progress.

But turn and look at this: in his political overview, given on 7 December 2020 to the meeting of the National Executive Committee of his party, the ANC, President Ramaphosa referred to the government's adoption of the *National Strategic Plan*.[2] Among other things he said:

While there is much more that government can do and needs to do, social mobilization remains the most important and effective measure against GBVF. In effect, we need to change our society, *end* patriarchal attitudes and practices, and adopt a zero-tolerance towards GBV in communities and social institutions.[3]

I totally support some of the things the president of the country said. But then he also said we need to '*end* patriarchal attitudes and practices'. Taken together, the words 'patriarchal' and 'patriarchy' are mentioned more than a hundred times in this book; that suggests that the domination of men over women is a problematic that exercises me. But can we really end patriarchy in attitudes and in practice? I doubt it, and I do not think I am the only one who does so. Maybe even the president himself, and some in the ANC, do not believe it. However, it is his job to project confidence and hope that we will end the violence. I do not have to. And so I can say, the president is being unhelpfully overconfident. We should not believe Mr Ramaphosa when he suggests that we can 'end patriarchal attitudes and practices', not because he is a liar, but because ending patriarchy is unlike demolishing a building. There will be no big explosion. Patriarchy is built into our society, into ourselves. To end patriarchal attitudes and practices, we must end society, end the way we are.

I want to say something about these doubts. I have found that, though it will lose you votes, it is necessary to be careful not to speak in such overblown terms in the course of anti-patriarchal and anti-violence work. I, too, have been guilty of making over-optimistic claims, even while a part of me is aware that, given the nature of our society, our goals may not be achievable in the next 10 years, 50 years, even a century. When we come to patriarchy, meaning men's power, we should try to be more focused in order to make gains. Instead of speaking of *ending* patriarchal attitudes and practices, we should understand what it means to bring about such an end to men's power.

Forget that the party in government, the ANC, at the top of which sits the president, is a masculinist, heteropatriarchal organisation. ANC officials are repeatedly accused of, for example, sexual violence or harassment toward women.[4] The women in the ANC have been shown to hold patriarchal views.[5] The ANC has not always been resolute in dealing with such leaders. It looks like a need exists to tackle patriarchal attitudes and practices within the ANC before even thinking about addressing the problem in the wider society. Although the male-heavy leadership of the party has changed over the decades, ending patriarchy implies the ending of masculinist heteropatriarchy within the ANC as it exists. (Needless to say, patriarchy is evident not only within the ruling the party.)

It is my contention that the state, and government, are to a large degree heteropatriarchal institutions. It is not just that men have dominated and dominate most of the highest leadership positions in government and in the different arms of the state. Changing society will entail redesigning the state itself. Patriarchy is built into the foundations of whom we automatically regard as suited to lead us and run our affairs, whom we view as naturally competent, or whose voices carry more weight in meetings.

I would hypothesise that were we to ask a representative sample of people in our country whether the country will be able to end men's power, a minority will agree that this is possible. At best, progress toward ending patriarchal attitudes and practices, if they will eventually be ended, will be much slower than the current pace at which gratuitous, horrific violence plays out on a daily basis. It may be decades before patriarchy is decisively weakened, which means, in this equation, decades before our daily newspapers include far fewer reports of gender-based violence.

I attempt to visualise in my mind's eye a future society in which patriarchy is dead. But try as I might, I cannot see such a society. A phrase like 'ending patriarchy' is at best, therefore, just a careless use of words.

The same holds true for violence. Aiming to completely end violence is setting up an impossible dream. War, conflict and fighting have always been part of the human world. It is unlikely that we will completely eradicate them. These are phenomena whose pervasiveness and magnitude we can, at the best of times, *reduce*. We can work toward having far lower rates of murder and rape. We can build more institutions that engender trust. We can nudge more boys and men in our society toward embracing kindness.

The same applies to patriarchy. Ending it means imagining a new, non-patriarchal social order. And this means fundamentally overhauling the power relations and the cultures of gender inequality. Given what came out of the *National Development Plan 2030* – which is very little, in practice – we should not hold our breath as we wait for a new, non-patriarchal society to arrive.[6] For that reason, I am afraid we are setting ourselves up for a long period of outrage and despair if we use words so carelessly. What it is possible to achieve, though, is fewer unequal families, more feminist-empowered schools, more reflective boys, more egalitarian workplaces and a media that projects different gender relations. And, while these are not easy goals to attain, making progress toward any of them will be a step toward a new gender order.

It may seem that when I argue that utterances like smashing patriarchy in practice are overblown, I am speaking against myself. Let it be very clear: I live with hope and work for a society where men's violence is less common. But I do not think violence is going to end. The world believes in violence. The powerful countries are those with the biggest military forces. In such a world, violence sets the rules. So does it set the rules in our society. But as far as our society is concerned, there are additional reasons why we are not going to end violence or patriarchy. That knowledge gives me little confidence in us becoming a non-patriarchal society during Ramaphosa's presidency, or even in his lifetime. He has to set less grandiose and more attainable goals. So should we.

There are many reasons that lie behind this apparently bleak outlook of mine, my lack of confidence that we will *end* violence and *eradicate* patriarchy in our society – or the world for that matter. This is so even while I nurture a little light of hope that we can, in time, have an ethical, peaceful and loving form of masculinity as the hegemonic masculinity. I am very aware that such a pessimistic attitude appears to contradict the faith that keeps me working with boys and men to transform gender relations.

The first reason, as I have said many times, is that violence and the threat of violence are central in power hierarchies. They are the first and final instruments of control in, for instance, ideologies and structures of anthropocentrism, capitalism, racism and patriarchy. An instrument that these ideologies and structures regularly utilise to assert or perpetuate the power of one group over others – an instrument that in fact constitutes their power – is violence in one or another form. A crucial point to keep in mind is that these ideologies are often intertwined, and that even individuals who are not powerful can support them in their everyday actions, including using violence or coercion to do so. About racist, capitalist, patriarchal power and its relationship to violence, bell hooks has offered this insight:

> The social hierarchy in white supremacist, capitalist patriarchy is one in which theoretically men are the powerful, women the powerless; adults the powerful, children the powerless; white people the powerful, black people and other non-white peoples the powerless. In a given situation, whichever party is in power is likely to use coercive authority to maintain that power if it is challenged or threatened.[7]

Anthropocentrism, capitalism, racism and patriarchy are in no way all of the powerfully structuring sets of ideas in our society. We can also mention heterosexualism, nationalism, Eurocentrism and disablism. And then there is militarisation – the extension of the ideological discourse of using violence to take and maintain power. There is also the war-like thinking adopted from the military in many spheres of life that have little to do with actual war – about which I would like to say a little more. It is not difficult to see why I consider militarisation a reason for my pessimism that violence will *end* and patriarchy be *eradicated* in our society.

A common example of militarisation talk is the 'war on drugs', which you may have come across. The most curious thing is that militaristic processes are often adopted as a response to violence. In other words, state-legitimated violence is used against violence between civilians. As a response to violence, militarisation has not proven effective and may lead to more violence against men, women and children.[8] Consider these examples. In 2009, in Klipfontein View Extension 2, north-east of Johannesburg, the police killed three-year-old Atlegang Phalane with a shot to the chest because they mistook a pipe the boy was carrying in his hand for a gun.[9] In 2011, 33-year-old Andries Tatane was beaten with batons and shot dead by police officers during a service delivery protest in Ficksburg. The incident showing the police brutality was caught on video.[10] In the year 2012, when 34 miners were shot dead and 78 left injured on 16 August at Lonmin mine in North West Province, the police opened fire on mine workers who were protesting for higher wages.[11] There are many incidents that, in my reading, are indicative of a militarised mentality, with the police being used to *fight* civilians, resulting in the loss of many innocent lives. But this last example may be regarded as an egregious high point in the use of violence by the post-apartheid government. The Lonmin mine killings are known as the Marikana massacre.[12]

The list of incidents of police violence is long, and has continued to grow during the coronavirus pandemic. In April 2020, a month after Ramaphosa first announced the national lockdown, the police and soldiers reportedly killed nearly ten people, all of them black, for violating the regulations. Among the victims was 40-year-old Collins Khoza from Alexandra, killed for the supposed offence of drinking alcohol in his own yard.[13] Given the mindset of militarisation, trusting the police to offer protection against gender-based violence and femicide is folly. The use of excessive violence, which is normal for a militarised police force, to prevent violence is nothing if not ridiculous.[14] The police have not been able to do so in the past and there is no reason for confidence that they will be able to do so in the future. The problem is not only ineptitude, and lack of skills and capacity. It is also the war mentality underpinning a belief that intimate violence can be stopped through military-style action, by a police force to whom is given the right to perpetrate violence. It is, frankly, a mind-boggling idea. It arises from the framing that seeks to persuade us that there is a war in the country, as opposed to different forms of inequality (economic, racial, sexual and gender inequality being the most obvious), or poverty, or unaddressed historical and contemporary social trauma. It is the conviction that men and women in the police force, sometimes with the assistance of men and women in the army, must be tough, and that guns are the weapon of choice in the war against abusive and homicidal men. There is no space in this war discourse to teach new, alternative, peaceful, emotionally aware and loving masculinities. The ideology and structures of militarisation presume a violent world. The driving assumption is that violence has to be used or threatened in order to control others. In the end, militarisation is set against a view of the world in which people are nurtured from an early age toward caring for each other. Can we eradicate violence while holding on to the belief in militaristic power, when violence is indeed constitutive of society?

The second reason we can adduce is corruption, a phenomenon that appears to have seeped into the fabric of the new democratic South Africa with such speed and braggadocio it has left many of us speechless. Corruption stands in the way of changing our society toward a new order. There are very few people who would not concur with the observation that, unfortunately, post-apartheid South Africa is as corrupt as apartheid South Africa was. Maybe there is less corruption after apartheid than there was under apartheid; maybe there is more. It does not matter one way or another. Corruption is rife in our society, as South Africans were made patently aware of from the media reports and hearings at the Judicial Commission of Inquiry to Inquire into Allegations of State Capture, Corruption and Fraud in the Public Sector Including Organs of the State (the Zondo Commission).[15] The reports on and hearings of the commission pointed to the moral and ethical impairment of this society. And a financially corrupt society is, in a sense, a morally degraded one.[16] Can we then stop physical violence, if we cannot stop moral violence?[17]

The third reason is that the mismanagement of state resources stands in the way of the efficient reduction of violence. There is much we can say about this. While corruption is a large, ugly stain on the post-apartheid social fabric, other barriers toward becoming a well-functioning society are lack of capacity, inefficiency and bad management. It has been shown repeatedly that many components of the post-apartheid state cannot even carry out the simplest tasks, and perform other tasks badly. Services in several government departments are inefficient and poor. Municipalities do not function because they are inefficient and wasteful. The police are generally terrible at preventing violence and solving criminal cases. Can we succeed in a complex endeavour like changing society if we cannot even do the simple things involved in managing a municipality?

The final reason may be the most difficult to swallow, given that *as a society* we seem to have managed to act against the interest of protecting ourselves in the face of the coronavirus pandemic. Even in the face of death, it seems difficult to change ourselves as a society. The problem seems to emerge from the fact that a critical number of people in our society may have normalised a distrust of rules and laws – and not always without cause. This generalised disinclination to follow rules became clearest in the face of the Covid-19 pandemic. The rules appeared simple. They amounted to the injunction, 'protect yourselves'. But as months passed and the cases of infection and the number of deaths mounted, it became clear that we did not or could not protect ourselves and each other. It may be because at some point we learned not to respect the law, because the law was cruel and unjust. We were encouraged, and encouraged each other, to be ungovernable. That seems to have become something that is hard to undo. When, after apartheid, we became aware of the extent of corruption, fraud, unethical behaviour and mismanagement the country had experienced, there was a new and good reason not to trust political and economic elites. The lack of respect for rules and laws learned before the new dispensation thus persists. It can be inferred, for instance, from our high rates of transport-related injury. It can be glimpsed in our high number of anti-government protests. Most strikingly, we were reminded of this during the country's second wave of the coronavirus pandemic. The president became tearful during a televised address to the nation. Apparently he could not believe people were becoming infected and dying in large numbers because they were not following the simple recommendations to protect themselves and others: wear a mask, observe social distancing, wash hands, sanitise, keep gatherings small.

There are no simple recommendations to offer when it comes to ending violence and eradicating patriarchy, then. Transforming society to be less patriarchal is like conquering the universe when compared to overcoming

217

the pandemic. Whereas the virus did not discriminate according to sex or gender, which means both men and women were at risk, femicide and men's violence against women are targeted at women. And if we could not work together as a society to protect each other against a common enemy, how will we work together as a society when some people in that society are the enemy of others?

Here is the point again. Although our society may not be able to eliminate patriarchy, it can become a country where we have 200 homicides annually instead of 20 000, a fraction of the number of sexual offences, and far fewer children killed. We can reduce violence. We can empower women and shift masculinities. I am not even asking for a society where men discernibly care for the well-being of women and children, which is the vision we should hold on to. I am appealing just for a society with a lower body count. Not an equal one, just one where there is not so much gratuitous and direct violence, and where there are more caring men and boys.

36 | When work gets in the way of emotional connections

The call to my friend I spoke of in chapter 9 reminded me of what we can lose when we neglect to talk with our friends. And what we in fact do lose when we do not share of ourselves. The thing is this: men tend to be masters of *not* nourishing their emotional relationships. We, the heterosexuals, are taught that tending relationships is the work of women and gays. We might experience the hunger for love I have referred to several times, carry it with us throughout our lives, but emotional development is not for us. Emotions are for weaklings. Soft men. Crybabies.

It is a lie, of course. Emotions are not just the invisible glue that holds a couple together; they also serve as the invisible motor of the self. If there is anything that needs emotional nurturing it is our interior life, our inner being. There is no way around it except to go through it. We cannot permanently avoid talking about feelings, or showing how we feel. Saying we are worried. We are angry. We want to be touched. We feel sad. We are happy.

Talking about things, especially our emotional lives, is something of whose necessity I only became more aware as I matured. It may seem like oversensitive language, too psychotherapeutic, but is it not revealing that we speak of *sharing* our feelings and thoughts?

But knowing the importance of sharing your inner life or what has been happening in your life does not mean you are always putting the lesson into practice. I blame the demands of daily life. Often enough, we seem to be wanting to get things done, go somewhere, complete a task that looks terribly important, and the imagined to-do list gets in the way of living fully. I mean by this being present in the moment: stopping to watch the butterfly, listening to a neighbour telling you of the kind of week she has had, or putting together something to eat for a few days for a man ringing your doorbell.

Ironically, it is earning a living that often takes us away from the simple acts of living. This is understandable – but only to a certain extent. It is neoliberal, patriarchal capitalism that sets down this life formula, whereby work is the most important thing in our adult lives. The dominance that paid work holds over the rest of life is even stronger in the case of adult males. Paid work is a defining element of adult manhood. The domination of work over life begins with the insecurity that capitalism creates in society, by having a significant number of unemployed or underemployed men and women. This has been the case in South Africa for quite some time.

At the end of 2010, the year South Africa hosted the FIFA World Cup, when we were all supposed to be ecstatic, and more than a year after the fourth national democratic elections that brought Jacob Zuma to power, the total unemployment rate was 24.0 per cent. The fourth-quarter unemployment rates of the male and female labour forces were 21.8 per cent and 26.6 per cent, respectively.[1] Seen through apartheid racial categories, the unemployment rate was highest among blacks at 28.1 per cent and coloured at 21.3 per cent, and lowest among whites (5.5 per cent) and Indians (7.9 per cent).[2]

In 2014, an election year, the total rate of unemployment was 24.3 per cent.[3] The female unemployment rate was 26.6 per cent and the male unemployment rate 22.4 per cent. Again, the rate of unemployment was highest among blacks (27.2 per cent), followed by the rates among coloureds and Indians. Unemployment was lowest among whites, at 7.7 per cent.

At the end of 2019, another national election year which came with renewed promises of employment, the official unemployment rate in South Africa was 29.1 per cent.[4] That amounted to more than 6.7 million unemployed people. The race and gender patterns of unemployment of prior years persisted. For instance, among blacks the unemployment rate was 32.4 per cent, compared to a rate of 7.6 per cent among whites, lowest among the races. The rate among women was 31.3 per cent and among men 27.2 per cent.

Remunerated work is regarded as a defining element of adult masculinity. This implies that while unemployment is consistently higher among women, being a man without a job carries with it an additional, not-so-hidden burden, over and above the poverty that unemployment causes: failed masculinity. The ideology of capitalist, patriarchal masculinity considers a successful man to be one who is able to provide adequately not just for himself but for a family. Providing for an extended family increases the value of a man. As such, men who are unemployed are double failures, for being jobless and for not fulfilling the demands of valued manhood. What men who are unemployed want most is not emotional growth and connection, but paid work, because then they will not be failures as men. They think they can live with failing at psychological connections with other people, but they cannot live with failing at what patriarchy says it means to be a man. Ironically, not being able to support themselves and others is what devitalises them psychologically.

Capitalist ideology affects employed men as well. For working men, a job as often as not generates psychological insecurity (among professional workers), is back-breaking (among, for instance, mine workers and construction workers), or provokes anxiety, when it is not filled with pointlessness. As David Graeber observes, many jobs, including the work I do as a professor, have a 'bullshit quotient'; among professors, this includes filling out reports that very few, if any, people ever read, or sitting in meeting after meeting with no readily evident point.[5] Having a job that takes up most of your time means having less time to nurture other parts of your life, like playing with your children, connecting with friends and spending time with your partner. Neoliberal, capitalist patriarchy naturalises the demands on men and women to work long hours and be away from their families. For men, this demand to give more attention to work than to family and relationships is coupled with the view that they have to provide for their families, even though many do not. As bell hooks puts it:

Men who make a lot of money in this society and who are not independently wealthy usually work long hours, spending much of their time away from the company of loved ones. This is one circumstance they share with men who do not make much money but who also work long hours. Work stands in the way of love for most men then because the long hours they work often drain their energies; there is little or no time left for emotional labor, for doing the work of love.[6]

It should be clear that making a living is not the problem. The problem is work that disconnects men from life, which is to say from loving connectedness. The demand for men to spend long hours working, under threat of failing at work and as men, gets in the way of them having a rich emotional connection with their children and partners.

37 | Love cannot escape power

In August 1967, the African American civil rights leader Reverend Martin Luther King Jr delivered a talk to the 11th convention of the Southern Christian Leadership Conference, in Atlanta, Georgia, under the title 'Where Do We Go from Here?' The talk was subsequently published as 'Black Power' in the book *Where Do We Go from Here: Chaos or Community?* Something he said about love and power is of especial interest:

> What is needed is a realization that power without love is reckless and abusive and that love without power is sentimental and anemic. Power at its best is love implementing the demands of justice. Justice at its best is love correcting everything that stands against love.[1]

To consider masculinity is always to consider power: to examine what power allows us to do or not do, what it generates in us and others, and what it captures or disables. Paying critical attention to power leads us to recognise not only who has it, but who is at the receiving end of it, in what forms it comes and, above all, how it works and what it produces and hides. It seems, therefore, that we must understand power if we wish to understand men. It also seems important to be awake to the fact that power is not necessarily negative or oppressive. It can instead be seen as a form of love: power can be used to demand justice for others.

This suggests that, in concerning ourselves with masculinity, we cannot escape the matter of power, which is to say we cannot evade the question of the gendered pattern of power in a place. We are therefore always faced with the question of men and their relations to other men, women, non-conforming individuals, children, other species and the environment. Of course, power is not uniformly distributed among men; some men obviously have more power than others. It appears to me that in a society that privileges men just because they are men, it is for all aware men to invite other men to reflect on what having gender power implies, which is to say what the individual might do with the limited or immense power he may possess as a man.

If masculinity is about power, and power is always in play, men's loves cannot be thought of outside of men's social power. To speak of social power is to speak of social justice or injustice, of who is served by structures of power and who is disadvantaged in society. Thus, to consider love without considering social justice, specifically social justice among genders, is to reinforce an impoverishing, individualist view of love, as if each of us on our own has invented love, as if we are completely free to love without moral, religious, social or legal restrictions.

I have said that whether men need love is a question that invites attention because it attracts other questions that go beyond a simple yes or no answer. Questions such as why, given the pervasiveness of men's violence, a woman would put herself in the path of violence by getting close to a man; what kind of love men need; and of course, most crucially, why men commit violence against their loved ones. The last question – why, if you need love, would you violate a person you claim to love? – elicits a profound ambivalence in us about opening up to the contradictions that characterise all our lives. Love, as I have argued, can never be eternally and absolutely unwound from violence. It would be good, then, to bring more attention to men's ways of loving, or talking about love, so that we can understand their use of violence, which implies their ideas about power. We need to try to comprehend men's loves, in order to harness these loves and cross over the violent terrain to reach a loving masculinity. In other words, we need to transform men so that they become open to their interior selves and relationships.

I have also asked whether women are more attracted toward men who are benevolent, non-violent yet still patriarchal, or toward men who support feminist struggles and believe in gender equality and all it entails. The question brings us back to a certain form of masculinity that is dominant in society. There are more and more projects all over the world that engage men and boys, and aim to change power relations and masculinity itself.[2] Changing masculinity is part of the more general work of engaging men and boys. Shifting the attitudes and practices of men and boys toward gender equality is an important topic. Working with them in order to turn them from violence toward non-violence is another. Attitudes toward sex and reproductive health behaviour began to attract significant attention at some point in the history of HIV/Aids research; attending to these attitudes remains critical. Fatherhood, too, attracts attention. I have been part of such projects and believe they are necessary.[3] The work intended to engage men regarding what it means to be men, and to alert them to the relations between the genders, in our time and in this place, is ultimately about the re-evaluation, reconstitution and reconfiguration of masculinity.

In a world where power is held by the likes of Bashar al-Assad, Paul Biya, Jair Bolsonaro, Rodrigo Duterte, Xi Jinping, Paul Kagame, Alexander Lukashenko, Vladimir Putin, Donald Trump, Jacob Zuma and many others still living or dead, there are many of us who all too often no longer appear to know what it means to have the right (masculinity) stuff – if there ever was just one kind of right stuff.[4] Of course, there are many other prominent figures who embody forms of masculinity that contradict the values of truth, compassion, integrity, equality, justice and power sharing. They are found not only in politics but also in religious organisations (for example, Shepherd Bushiri and Alph Lukau), business (the Gupta brothers, Jeffrey Epstein), the arts (Harvey Weinstein, Bill Cosby, Sjava, Jub Jub) and other areas of life and work. It is precisely because of what these men represent – that is to say, recognisable performances of certain configurations of masculinity in power – that we are called to do this work of reflecting on what the dominant forms of masculinity are and can be, so that we can challenge them and invent a new hegemonic, non-oppressive masculinity. As Raewyn Connell observes, when we speak of masculinity we are referring to a configuration of gender practice; that is to say, masculinity is a gender project involving practices that come to form a pattern.[5] It is this pattern (of power) that needs to be unravelled. The domination of women by men will remain largely undisturbed unless we reach and transform the power patterns of men in the direction of loving masculinity and gender justice. Until we inject into a significant percentage of men and boys the desire to change the very things they hold dear, women's subordination will persist. Power over others is one of the things men are made to love by patriarchy. Vulnerability as a positive value, not so much. When power over others is resisted, some men resort to violence to reassert it. When we challenge power relations, then, perhaps in daily life, maybe in small, personal but cumulative actions, but also when we stand up against men's practices in large institutional, political and economic spheres, we are engaged in preventing violence. When we are open to the fact that love makes us vulnerable, but also connects us to others in deeply satisfying ways, when we learn to practise love in our everyday lives, in tiny yet sustaining ways, we are changing how we live with others and ourselves.

38 | What's up with all this attention given to boys?

I am walking on a street in Tshongweni section, Katlehong, the township where I grew up. It is the beginning of winter, June 2012. I do not have any specific destination in mind and probably am just taking in the sights of the old neighbourhood, seeing what has stayed the same and what has changed.

I have my camera on my shoulder. A puddle of rainwater has formed on the edge of the tarmac to the left of where I am walking. On my right are two cars, one white in colour and the other a bright yellow. Further away there is a big hauler without its carriage and another passenger car, this one dark blue. Between the two pairs of cars is a person – I think it is a woman – wearing pink pants and a light pink sweater. She has a parcel in her hands. She is walking in the direction of the soccer game being played by five boys in the middle of the street. She passes a man in blue jeans and a jacket with a hoodie who is walking in the opposite direction. Two men, both wearing yellow tops, are hanging around outside a house with a vibracrete wall, talking.

I stop and watch the game, camera at the ready. I shoot. In the picture I take, one of the boys, in a reddish sweater and yellow and green wool hat, is tackling another boy. A third boy, in faded jeans and a dark blue sweater with a check pattern on the front and a white T-shirt peeping from below the sweater, appears to have the ball, but it is out of view. He looks intent on dribbling past the tackler, or about to kick the ball.

I have included two girls in the picture I take. They are standing on the sidelines of the soccer game. One girl is wearing a brown top and sitting flat on the ground. The other is wearing jeans, boots and a colourful striped sweater. She is carrying what may be a doll on her back. But from the way it is wrapped, it might be a human baby.

I came back to this image (and others I have of boys and girls) while I was reflecting on a question an associate had thrown at me. 'What's up with all this attention and resources given to boys, men and masculinities?' the head of an NGO had asked. I do not recall how I responded. But the question stayed with me. I came to realise that it was not really a question. It might have been meant as a tease. Or maybe it was an accusation. Or it could have been an expression of concern. But I feel it carried a lot of affect, however I look at it. We went on to have some discussion, which in essence came down to the view of my interlocutor that there was too much attention, and too many resources, being given to boys, men and masculinities.

The rhetorical question was also inspired, I think, by the fact that I was at the time involved with a well-known NGO that was seen as a men's organisation, Sonke Gender Justice. (It was not a men's organisation. It was, and still is, a feminist human rights organisation that also has programmes on men. But it became known for its work on men.) One of the problems that my associate's complaint betrayed was some confusion between men's rights organisations and pro-feminist NGOs working with boys and men. They are different creatures, these two. There was and continues to be lit-tle confusion in my mind, however, about the significance of gender and sexuality as analytical categories in studying boys' and men's lives, and, of course, in trying to understand the societal subordination of girls and women. We have to dispel the confusion if we are going to nurture brighter lives and futures for girls and boys.

The person who asked me this, it is significant to note, was a sexuality and gender equality activist with a specific interest in children and youth rights. In my estimation, the fact that she was an activist on issues of chil-dren and youth rights implied she was a likely ally. It suggested to me that we would be of the same mind about the kind of attention we need to give to boys and girls. I was wrong.

I became aware over time that some people feel that a focus on boys and men means taking away attention and resources from girls and women. There may be funders, men's organisations, scholars and politicians who feel that women and girls have received more than enough resources and attention, and that it is the turn of men and boys. This view is not one to which I subscribe. It is a mistaken belief.

On the opposite side, there are grant-awarding bodies, women's organisations, researchers, policymakers and others like my associate, many of whom may not be as direct in expressing their views, who feel giving resources and attention to boys and men is not good for girls and women, that it is a bad idea and policy choice. I did not think this was rational thinking when I first became aware of it, and I still don't. It was short-sighted criticism. It was not going to help this country, and it seems that over time, unfortunately, I was proven right. What I thought was clear was that you cannot want or expect men to change unless you actually work to change them. We have to pay attention to boys before they start annoying girls and the rest of us, to put it mildly.

Worries and complaints about the funding and space given to the then 'fashionable topic' of boys, men and masculinities were nothing new to me in the late 1990s. I still encounter them today, more than two decades later. I still find them quite, well, disquieting. There is still support for the suspicion that caring for boys causes harm to girls.

The funding squeeze experienced by older feminist organisations and to which the activist was referring is something real and painful. Much of civil society, whose work remains imperative in contemporary South Africa, was facing a crisis of funding at that time. Now, as I return to what the person was asking me, NGOs as well as faith-based and community-based organisations are facing financial ruin yet again, because of what the coronavirus pandemic has wrought.

Over time I came to see that we have to keep trying to convince would-be allies – men, women, funders, legislators and government – that if we create environments in which boys are encouraged and nudged toward kinder, more egalitarian and more caring beliefs, attitudes and practices about girls' aspirations, that will make girls' lives safer, healthier, happier and richer. I mean the environments where they learn and play. There is something wrong, simply put, with observing boys playing soccer while girls stand on the side of the street watching them, or stand by with babies on their backs. At a simple level, every child needs play. It is important for their development. I do not know whether the boys invited the girls to play with them. I do not know if the girls were not interested in soccer.

But I would like to see both girls and boys playing, and even better, playing together, in Katlehong, in Gauteng, in the whole country, the whole of Africa, and surely the entire world. I would like to see boys and girls getting all the opportunities they need to live well, not like millionaires or superstars, but enjoying a quality life and making whatever contribution they wish to make to the world.

It is not just girls and boys who enjoy games. Every person, young and old, needs spaces of recreation. Love enjoys play. Life requires it. I am reminded of a long conversation I had about play with Pumla Dineo Gqola, to whom I have previously referred. I told her that I worry about the way some of the discourse about gender relations discourages play between men and women. She said she no longer wants to play with men. She then added, 'except maybe six men'. I know what she means. I think she knows what I mean.

To be sure, Gqola has written persuasively about how the notion of play can be twisted by masculinist heteronormativity. In her influential book *Rape: A South African Nightmare*, she says:

> The grip of violence is tightening around our collective necks. Those who pretend to be stunned by the statistics are lazily not making the connections between the various ways in which what is 'normal' heterosexual 'play' contain codes that inscribe feminine passivity and masculine aggression. We saw it in the twist of the arm as teenage girls, the assumption that girls 'play hard to get' and therefore should be pursued at all costs regardless of what they say, the bizarre and oppressive claims that women cannot say what they mean and mean what they say.[1]

Violence is not amusing. Patriarchal, heteronormative conceptions of play, which often conflate humiliation with pleasure, sexist jokes with fun, can belittle, scare and torment girls and women. Who needs play under such circumstances?

And yet, without creating opportunities for genuine, friendly play with each other, we lose more of what makes it possible to be free with one another. How can I understand you, where do I learn to say sorry if I inadvertently hurt you, how do I get you to accept my apology for the hurt I have caused you (in a sports game, for instance) because it was not intentional, if we cannot even play with one another? And if it is not possible to play artlessly with each other, tease each other, frolic together or chase one another around, surely we are inhibited from loving each other more freely?

To return to the activist, I appreciate why there is some reservation about studying and working with boys and men. However, I am convinced that the general argument against the (then) new focus on boys (and men) is misplaced. There is always cause to be worried about resources for social activism and government resources devoted to supporting women and girls. But to blame those doing critical, and sometimes even decolonial, work on masculinities is to misperceive the goal of working on masculinities.

It is also incorrect to think that there have been buckets of money specifically allocated to the quality education of impoverished boys for a productive, creative and meaningful life. Where some money has been given to support boys from deprived homes, there still is not the kind of close, loving attentiveness that is required to radically change the world around them.

It is not untrue that in many countries girls (and women) continue to confront violence and unjust discrimination daily, on the basis of age and gender. It is also not uncommon to find societies (with China being at one time the prime but not the only example) where there is a preference for sons over daughters.[2] Furthermore, in many families and societies around the world, girls and women still tend to enjoy less self-determination than boys and men. Unlike the latter, they cannot play as freely. For instance, all too often they get coerced into their first sexual experience by males. Forced marriage at an early age is not uncommon.[3] They are unable to take a walk without being harassed. Prohibited from leaving their homes unaccompanied by males, they might as well be under house arrest.

Yet it is ludicrous to believe that male children are in the same boat as older males. Boys are not men. They are developing beings. Rather than being punished for the sins of their fathers, or unfairly advantaged, they ought to be educated for an egalitarian and compassionate society. The failure to mould boys into supporters of equality falls on the shoulders of adults – of their parents and other adults in their society, of teachers, journalists, coaches, imams, priests, business leaders, chiefs and politicians.

Very few boys are born dictators. No boy runs the world. Usually it is a patriarchal social order, with the complicit support of the majority of men and women, that creates the rules and norms that subtly and overtly encourage boys to become men who enjoy dominating others. But while they may receive some benefit from being male, boys also suffer great consequences from the social order. Violence is often used against them by their parents and other older males and females. Like girls, boys in many countries face the ravages of social and economic inequalities. The patriarchal order is not geared toward making boys live happier, healthier and longer lives. In fact, being a boy, in particular a boy from a poor neighbourhood, sets one up on a path that features increased risk of premature death from accidents or violence.

Educating a girl for a feminist, educated, confident, happier and healthier life, without empowering a boy with progressive education to make him egalitarian, democratic, non-violent and able to live a healthy life, means we will be faced with the problem of pregnant children for the foreseeable future. It retards the general quality of life in our society. It would thus make girls' present and future lives better if we also gave boys the kind of education that made them more caring about girls' needs and aspirations. Naturally, to work with boys and men only, without due regard to the negative effects of the gender order on girls and women, is to tacitly support the status quo.

Therefore, instead of asking, 'What's up with all this attention given to boys?', we ought to be asking, 'What kind of attention shall we give to boys to make their own lives as well as girls' lives full of worth?' The kind of attention we need to give boys is attention that extends to all of their personhood, taking in their life of feeling as much as their behaviour toward others. That is, caring attention aimed at turning them, in their hearts and brains and behaviour, into people who believe in and support women's and girls' rights to their pleasure, dreams, bodies, feelings and voices. If we do not think boys deserve this kind of loving attention, we may continue not just to fail boys but also to discourage them from becoming different men, and thus also fail girls and women. The result is that sex discrimination will persist.

If boys grow up in a world that does not model the attention that shows them how to attend to the need for socio-emotional bonds in their lives, then we should not be surprised if they do not know what to do with their emotions and sense of disconnectedness. If we do not teach boys why and how to express their vulnerability, tender feelings, positive and negative thoughts, sadness and love, shame and gratitude, we, the adults, have to bear the responsibility if they cannot speak well of their feelings. If, as far as the life of feelings is concerned, we expect them to use a limited vocabulary to express and talk about their emotions, and do little to change their interior worlds, it is silly to be surprised when the only thing that makes sense to them when they suffer emotionally is to get mad.

39 | Without showing boys how to love, how will they become loving men?

Many children, boys and girls, suffer the hunger of absence of paternal love. This returns us to the first key proposition in these reflections: that men (who include fathers) in our society suffer from lovelessness, or an inconsistently gratified need for love. Lovelessness in this instance ensues from fatherlessness, the sense of paternal abandonment, a hunger for fatherly love that can perturb some men for years into their adulthood. That love hunger is, I have suggested, largely unacknowledged by most of us in our society.

There are no numbers as yet to directly support this proposition. How will I prove that I was unloved or inadequately loved by my father? Even harder will be the attempt to show how being unloved, or insufficiently loved, turned me into a violent or unloving man myself, which is my second key proposition. Love is not easy to measure. The pathway from lovelessness to violence is not a direct one. It will be hard, yet interesting, to pursue this line of study. But that is for the future. What I have done in these reflections is to advance the view that experiencing yourself as having been unloved in childhood, even unlovable, can be a hotbed for different kinds of physical and emotional violence against others and yourself. Of course, this does not mean people hurt others simply because they were unloved early in life. Sometimes a person hurts another because he or she feels demeaned at that moment. The person may wish the one who insulted him or her to hurt too. At other times, individuals hurt others simply because they want to assert power over them. Power, negative power, can never be overlooked when considering violence.

I have said love is hard to pin down, is related to our early life, appears in different forms and is socially determined. Love is always more and less than we can eloquently convey. For instance, while giving no gift or performing no special act of love at all on a birthday (because the loved one knows you love them) is upsetting, even the most expensive gift can be inadequate. Take the story of the Taj Mahal, built by Shah Jahan, who became the fifth emperor of the Mughal Empire, as a mausoleum for his wife Mumtaz Mahal, which I have twice gone to look at and marvel at – or simply because it is on the list of sights tourists should see. The mausoleum is in Agra, India, and a touching tale of love and loss is told about the structure. Costing what in today's terms would be billions of rands, the awe-inspiring white marble building on the bank of the Yamuna River is one of the wonders of the world. This is how far a man will go to prove his love and memorialise his loss.

Impressive indeed, and a touching story: but is the Taj Mahal too little, too much or just the perfect embodiment of love? I do not think we can ever fully grasp what people feel for others, know what love means to them, or completely know love itself. And if we cannot know what love means to others, but also must remain somewhat uncertain about the meaning of love *qua* love, we cannot fully know what it means to be without love, to feel that nobody cares.

Money is only one of the many factors that influence how we think, and do, love. That already tells you that love is always mediated, always connected to other economic, political, social, cultural and psychological concerns. For instance, religion, geographical proximity, language, shared interests, attractiveness and our early attachments are among a range of other variables that have an effect on who and how a person loves.

In a society like ours, with its history of structural hatred and coloniality, race hierarchies and racism are also not to be minimised. And racist ideology is truly an interesting issue to me. To know love in a racist context, to be free enough to see beyond the prejudice that pervades society, is infinitely intricate. Our politico-legal history redefined love on the basis of colonial and racist ideology. That is, racial hatred was institutionalised. Thus, it became easy to conflate racial belonging with love, or racial difference with the enemy, the Other, the unlovable. Generations of South Africans believed they could or could not be loved simply because they were Asian/Indian, black, coloured or white – colour-coded love and love-lessness. That meant we were miseducated into believing that some people do not deserve to be loved. A cruel history, characterised by systemic racist and sexist violence, not just segregated race groups and residential areas, affected interpersonal relations and formed the inner lives of us all. In the long aftermath of this history of racist hatred, we came to violate those who were not part of us, but also those in our intimate spaces. How could we avoid learning to be violent toward others when the seeds of warped love were planted in us? Hence, we have come to see deliberate physical and psychological violence in the same relationships where there is supposed to be affection and support.

What does having a caring father have do with learning to love within a society shaped by a history of racist hatred and violence? Although it is difficult to prove beyond any doubt that the lack of a father's support for his child indicates lack of love, it is not unreasonable to regard father absence as a key aspect of lack of father love. Let it be clear that by father absence I mean not just physical absence, but lack of consistent economic support and psychological care. And it is emotional absence that is of especial significance. I have already suggested that it is not quite true that only when the need for safety from violence is satisfied does the need for love demand our attention. One might say the lack of emotional nurturance is to the soul what lack of nutritious food is to the body. And so, with the fact of emotional absence in mind, I wish to posit that a deficit of fatherly love is a factor underlying why some adult men feel hurt and hurt others. In a society with a history of racist division, of institutionalised violence, of the warping of love needs, the hunger for father love can be huge. It is a love that must stand between the child and the world. It is a love that must buffer the hatred that surrounds the parent and child.

Many children live without their biological fathers. That is a fact. While being without a biological father in the household does not necessarily imply being unloved by one's biological father, having a caring father close by is beneficial when it comes to becoming a person. There are numbers to show this. Admitting the problems of doing so, I cautiously infer the deficiency of father love from the fact of physically absent fathers. According to the 2018 General Household Survey (GHS) produced by Statistics South Africa, the majority of children (43.1 per cent) lived with their mothers only, 19.8 per cent of children lived with neither of their biological parents, 33.8 per cent lived with both parents, and 3.3 per cent of children lived with their biological fathers only.[1] Similarly, in 2019 the GHS indicated that 42 per cent of children lived only with their mothers, 21.3 per cent of children did not live with their biological parents, 32.7 per cent lived with both parents, and 4 per cent lived only with their fathers.[2]

Taking an orphan as a child whose mother, father or both biological parents are deceased, the 2018 GHS also found that approximately 11.7 per cent of children were orphaned, with 2 per cent having lost both parents, 2.4 per cent their mothers and 7.4 per cent their fathers.[3] The 2019 GHS showed an increase in orphanhood, with 14.4 per cent of children classified as orphans. The percentage of children who had lost both biological parents was 2.4 per cent, those who had lost mothers 3.1 per cent, and those who had lost fathers 9 per cent.[4]

According to the Children's Institute at the University of Cape Town (drawing from and reanalysing the GHS data, which gives different percentages), the total number of orphans in 2018 was actually higher than the GHS figure, at 2.7 million or 14 per cent of all children.[5] Paternal orphans numbered more than 1.6 million, constituting 63 per cent of the population of orphans.

All this indicates that many more children grow up without father love than without mother love. No doubt, physical presence does not necessarily indicate love. It is not only orphans and children with absent fathers who suffer from a deficit of father love. A father can be emotionally 'out of it' even when he is in the house. Some men can only relate to the child and mother through emotional abuse, by withholding economic support where they have an income, or by inflicting overt violence.

The two main reasons for the father hunger that so many children experience are death and abandonment. These reasons are connected to each other. Both arise out of and contribute toward an unhealthy, patriarchal form of masculinity, one which often resorts to violence to assert its dominance.

Both the death of men and their absence from their children's lives are connected to a third reason: the uncommonness of models of how to raise caring boys to become caring men. Boys need love to become loving men. Both fatherlessness due to desertion and that due to death are about different forms of violence that men do to others and themselves.

If it is true that men's violence can be traced back to the love they did not receive or to conditional love they received from their own families when they were young, the real antithesis of violence is consistent, unconditional loving care. A weak criminal justice system, or lack of government violence-prevention programmes, will exacerbate men's violence. Surely, in such conditions violence will not be prevented or reduced. But loving care coming from fathers (alongside mothers, the extended family, and societal institutions around the person), especially in childhood, will keep boys connected to others and, presumably, prevent them from turning into violent men. Instead of more policing, harsher sentences, larger prisons and higher, electrified security fences and walls, it is likely that low levels of violence will be achieved, and will stay low, as a result of increased caring for each other, of our loving attachments.

The death of a father, it could be said, is a preferable reason to be fatherless – that is, if a choice is to be made between losing him to death or through desertion. Perhaps it makes a difference to a child who needs to be cared for each passing day by a present father and mother; perhaps not. But have you ever heard a three-year-old ask: why is Dad not coming back? Why did he die? It seems that most children who grow up without a father around have to be helped to deal with this absence in their lives.

'No one hungers for male love more than the little girl or boy,' writes bell hooks.[6] I understand that to mean that all children yearn to be loved, forever, by their fathers, not just by their mothers. It implies that prior to knowing how to love others as adults, children need to be shown non-controlling, non-abusive love by adult males as well as females. All children know that the hunger for adult male love is constant, daily, hourly.

Our mothers, to be sure, are our first loves. Ironically, precisely because they love us so well we often end up taking their love for granted, and mothers cannot always compete with the hunger for father love. Why? Because demonstrative father love is scarce in our society. Because this society, as a consequence of our history and current inequalities, desperately needs many more men who privilege nurturing others over controlling them. Because, in contrast to mother love, which comes in many forms, starting with feeding the child from her own body, father love is a rare commodity, often sporadic, unreliable even.

Though research evidence is mostly indirect, we are able to infer some support for what we can now label the father-love deficit hypothesis.[7] By father-love deficit I mean the lack of engaged male involvement in children's lives. In conjunction with other structural and subjective factors that feed men's aggression against others and their own ill health and death, lack of paternal love must be considered one of the major contributors to men's violence against others and inner-directed violence.

To say father love is scarce does not mean most fathers are distant and merely good-time dads. However, it does suggest that, in the majority of cases, mothers' affection is so close up as to be nearly unobservable. It points to the fact that, whereas men's involvement with their children is often discontinuous, the love of a mother comes through in constant, daily ways – in taking the children to the clinic for their shots, wiping snot, catching vomit in the hand, wiping buttocks, preparing food, doing the washing, taking them to school, remembering birthdays, and all kinds of uncelebrated acts that make us into social beings.

Michael Chabon writes that in contrast to the low standards we expect from fathers, 'good mothering is not measurable in a discrete instant, in an hour of rubbing a baby's gassy belly, in the braiding of a tangled mass of morning hair'.[8] And yet many of us fail to meet even these low standards. The collective gendered failure of men to nurture others, and themselves, means that children are more likely to lose fathers than mothers. It means adult men are much more often than women likely to ditch their offspring.

We have been concerned with biological fathers in this reflection on paternal love, of course. However, some men – brothers, uncles, grandfathers, stepfathers, teachers, coaches and other social fathers – have stepped into the breach left by biological fathers and taken up fathering responsibilities. These men fill some of the father love deficit, sating some of the emotional hunger of the child. Their role cannot be exaggerated. Their acts of practical and psychological care attest to the fact that many adult males have abandoned their children, or are inadequately involved with them.

The effect of disengaged biological fathers on girls is as important as it is on boys. The presence of an involved father in the life of his daughters is a critical element in their overall development, including their socio-emotional life.[9] In other words, to state a self-evident truth, daughters need good fathers. The fact that businesses, the government, NGOs, community-based organisations, sports clubs and individuals are doing something to support girls to become independent women must be appreciated, even though their support does not address the hunger for paternal affection in some girls.

Like girls, boys need engaged fathers. Beyond that simple fact, the presence or absence of a father in a boy's life is also crucial insofar as the latter's development of masculinity is concerned. As far as I know, there are not many interventions in the country to support boys who have been abandoned by their fathers to develop caring forms of boyhood and manhood. If equality between the genders is an important societal goal, there is an obvious need for programmes aimed at taking boys by the hand and leading them toward healthy, loving masculinity (and, later, toward compassionate, involved fatherhood, if they want to be fathers).

It seems to me easy to understand that empowering girls and women with education and skills is absolutely vital for their own well-being, and for the development of their families and society as a whole. However, perhaps girls' and women's education, skills, happiness and freedom are not so readily perceived as a social good by everyone. A society of highly educated girls and independent women may not be so wanted by others. Free girls and women may be too threatening to male power. Maybe some men's sense of powerlessness is heightened by the perception of women's and girls' power. Men's feelings notwithstanding, however, the value of girls' and women's emancipation in order to enjoy independent and flourishing lives is a principle to which I subscribe, and one that I actively support in my work and life.

But there seems to be a different relationship between a girl and her father to the one that a boy has with his father. Identification is a significant factor in this relationship between fathers and their sons. You may recall the words of Sigmund Freud that I quoted in chapter 5: 'the boy deals with his father by identifying himself with him'.[10] The father is an object with which the boy identifies (or disidentifies); that is, the boy must work out his ambivalent love for the father. And therefore, in addition to the care both girls and boys need from their parents, boys need the presence of a close male figure that they can use to grapple with their own identity as masculine subjects. Without the father, the boy cannot easily work though his early childhood ambivalence and hostility. He needs adult men in his life to 'weigh himself' against. He needs a father close by when he thinks about the kind of man he wants to be; he needs to be able to assess different models of manhood (even if he may end up rejecting his own father as a model of manhood).

Abandoning boys *to father themselves* is not advisable, then. In thinking of why men hurt others, we must open ourselves to thoughts about the kind of love we show to boys after a certain age. Too often, we hide our love for boys as they get older. Often, we show them very little love at all. Many times, we leave them to their own devices, to grow up, or 'man up'. Without showing them love and how to love, because we want to toughen them up, we hope they will still become loving men. But this is really strange. Leaving boys to find their own way toward caring adult masculinity seems to me to be implicated in the kinds of men they become – including feeling that they do not need others, even when they desperately do.

In 2013, South Africa and the rest of the world saw another instance of cruelty by men. What made this one stand out was that it was cruelty by the police, recorded on video. The video showed eight policemen dragging Mozambican taxi driver Mido Macia behind their police van.[11] I can only speculate about what provoked this act, but such brutality could stem not just from the fact that the use of violence is not exceptional in our society. It may also have to do with some of us being raised in environments where the idea of all human beings having a natural right to care was insufficiently nurtured. The same argument holds in instances where we have witnessed unbelievable acts of rape and murder, as was evident in the case of Anene Booysen.[12] Of course, the violence does not have to become so gruesome before we are moved to feel that we have a problem. We might not have foreseen that turning away from boys and expecting them to take care of themselves would generate the forms, severity and levels of men's violence against women and other men that we have witnessed over the years. Lack of care may not be the determining factor in why men hurt women, but a lack of empathy for others surely is implicated in some of the acts of violence that we observe in this country. Therefore, continuing to neglect boys' and young men's socio-emotional lives does not appear to be the best strategy to cultivate nurturing relationships between the sexes and among males, or to make sensitive adult men. Boys and young men will find it hard to be nurturing if there are few adults who show them how to do it. It is very hard for a person to learn how to be caring toward others and themselves if they are not taught how to care.

It is not unreasonable to think that a man who has abandoned his biological child has done so because he does not care. What, though, of those of us who do take responsibility for our children? How do we square our concern for the next generation in our families and our lack of concern for children who come begging at the gate? In what kind of world are our well-fed, well-looked-after and well-adjusted children going to live, where most of their contemporaries have grown up without being cared for? Let's take a guess.

I predict that it will be a world even less caring than the one we live in now. A world where the fences in the middle-class neighbourhoods will be much higher still. A world in which there are more social problems: more drugged people, more alcoholism, more depression and suicide, and more inventive ways of hurting each other.

Is that too pessimistic? Perhaps. The numbers of fatherless children do not create an overly optimistic picture though, do they?

Still, there is time to restore hope and to push back the dystopian male future. We, men, have some models in the men and women who tend to the barricades, who are working against the bleakness.

It seems to me that what is needed from us is clear. We must nurture boys as much as we are empowering girls. We must teach adult men how to father their children for this time, in this society.

In my view, teaching children to care for each other is the most important force against violence. It is up to us, us men, to turn up, and to take on this work.

40 | Inheriting and passing down a loving masculinity

A while back I read an article by the journalist Percy Zvomuya in a weekly newspaper.[1] Something he wrote, evocative yet mistaken, stuck in my memory. It may have been that the article was about Mario Balotelli, the Italian footballer who at the time had crossed to England and joined Manchester City. Of Ghanaian descent and adopted by Italian parents, the footballer could have been one the greatest stars of his generation. Who knows why he didn't realise his potential?

What has stayed with me from the article is a misleading belief that I suspect is quite widely held when thinking about identity, specifically cultural identity. It jumped out at me because I was at the time researching, reading and writing about the subject of traditions. And what is tradition but the beliefs, practices and views passed down from one generation to the next? This transmission of non-genetic inheritance is the principal manner in which a group, from families to nations, manages to reproduce itself.

Because I felt moved to respond to the article, if only to myself, I wrote down some of the things the journalist said. 'Ghanaianness isn't part of anyone's make-up, you don't pass on Ghanaian DNA to your children', was one of the things he claimed.

Zvomuya is right about the DNA – because he seems to restrict the idea of Ghanaianness to DNA, and DNA is genetic transmission. But he is wrong about what parents pass on to their children. Ghanaianness *is* passed on from parents to children – it is the parents' *cultural* DNA, to coin a phrase. This idea, of cultural transmission of national or cultural identity, which seems to be what Zvomuya is challenging, is in fact supported when he argues that Italianness was passed down to Mario from his Italian parents.[2]

What is true for Ghanaianness and Italianness holds true for Americanness and Nigerianness, Chineseness and South Africanness. No one is genetically South African. Being South African is not part of the biological make-up of any of us, but as a national identity it is part of who we are. To counter the suggestion that biology is more important than culture in our make-up, we can argue that whereas genes may be important in particular situations such as when proving paternity, at other times, most obviously when crossing territorial borders, being Ghanaian or South African is in fact the most important aspect of our identity at the passport control point.

Let me reiterate the point, then: parents actively or unconsciously (desire to) pass on to their children their stock of values, norms and beliefs about what it means to be a member of such-and-such a family. The same holds for cultures and corporations, football clubs and nations, schools and race groups: each of these entities uses several modes and strategies to inculcate what being a member of the in-group entails.

What are some of the things parents pass on to their children that are not genetic? Two prime examples of non-biological inheritance are language and wealth. All that needs saying about these is how consequential they are for life. We should therefore dispense with the notion that it is only genetic material that parents pass on to their children, and perhaps more significantly, that genes are always the most important substance offspring inherit from their progenitors. Parents pass on many other things to their progeny. (And it must be noted that genes need a conducive environment to express themselves, which is to say that a child who is a potential genius but does not receive adequate tutelage may never realise their potential; the social environment in which they grow up can be as influential as the genes they inherit.) Ghanaian parents therefore transmit to their offspring not only their genes but also their Ghanaianness – their culture, language and ways of seeing.

Due to the kind of society we live in, something else we pass on to our children is race *ideas*. Skin colour has genetic markers. But the *meanings* that get allocated to skin colour are not genetic. While there is nothing genetic about racial categorisation, generations of people in our society came to live as if being white, along with accepting the idea of whiteness as superior to other categories, was a natural thing. In fact, the meanings of whiteness were defined by law. Adults then passed on to their children not only the colour of their skin, where parents had similar skin colour, but also the social meanings and beliefs they held about skin colour in a racist society. These meanings and beliefs about the idea of colour as part of a person's identity continue to shape how we relate to one another.

The direction in which I am headed must be obvious by now. Something else that parents pass on to their children that is not in their DNA is what they believe about gender norms, beliefs, attitudes, relations and power. Parents are a source from which as children we learn, among many other things, masculinity and femininity, what being a boy or a girl means, and from which we derive our beliefs about what men and women can and cannot do.

If I am right that children inherit much more than DNA from the parents – and the literature on tradition supports this position – they can also inherit a loving form of masculinity, if the parental generation makes this model part of their culture.[3] Just as parents already do pass on traditional gender ideas, they can pass on ideas about democratic masculinity to their sons. Like any other tradition, new traditions of masculinity are transmissible.

Perhaps the most significant claim to be made is that one of the roles of parents as cultural subjects is precisely that of handing down to their offspring the beliefs, values, customs and worldviews of the previous generation. Every generation acts as a relay node for tradition. It is somewhat redundant to even state this; however, I should indicate that the tradition that fathers and mothers pass on to their young ones is normally considered a *cultural* tradition. Yet the beliefs that parents pass on to the next generation are inextricably linked to gender. Gender is a cultural (re)production. Beliefs about what it means to be a man or a woman (and indirectly, what it means to be non-conforming) are passed down with other beliefs such as how to treat the elderly and what it means to be human (that is, *motho* in Sesotho). Therefore, one of the roles parents perform is to transmit *gender* beliefs (we may also say gender traditions) to their children, whether they do this consciously or unconsciously. These gender traditions may be embedded within or envelop the cultural traditions that are transmitted to the next generation. That means that you are subjected to (or more appropriately, subjectified by) the gender order at the same time as you are made into a cultural subject by the cultural order. For example, you learn what it means to be a man at the same time as you learn what it is to be *mosotho* (a member of the Basotho culture); the two are nested in each other.

What this implies is not that parents pass on *everything* that the culture constructs about masculinity and femininity. That is not possible, simply because individual parents cannot know all of what it means to be a man or a woman in their own culture, let alone in other cultures (a point to underscore in a multicultural society like ours). Let us say you are an Afrikaner man. It is impossible to know everything about what Afrikaner manhood means. There is also the fact that like other manhoods, Afrikaner manhood does not come in one shape. As with any particular subject, individuals are only aware of *some* things about their own culture, this being the slice to which they are exposed. In addition, the meanings of cultural mores, customs and rituals are always contested, sometimes overtly, on other occasions surreptitiously. There is never a one hundred per cent consensus about what culture itself means, or how to express it. Ultimately, what this suggests is that parents tend to have certain relatively idiosyncratic interpretations, and support certain gender ideas and practices and not others; what they support is what gets communicated to their children (and even then not all of it), mostly indirectly but sometimes directly.

Furthermore, in more multicultural or multilingual societies like South Africa and Tanzania, the number of ideas to which people are exposed is potentially far greater than in more monocultural or monolingual countries like Japan and Greece. The more diverse the ideas about masculinity and femininity evident in a society, the less likely it is that the gender ideas transmitted to the next generation will be a closed set, and the less likely that parents can hand down every 'traditional' gender idea from their generation to the next.

At the same time, this does not mean we can pass on everything we know or do in our own lives. One reason is simply that there is never an opportunity to present a full course on all we know to our children, besides the fact that it would be weirdly cultish to do so. Raising children is unlike teaching them at school. Parents usually do not follow a syllabus. They cannot sit their children down and tell them everything, and then test them on whether they have memorised the lessons. Even if a child could achieve an A on a test of traditions, if there were such a thing, parents would never know where and how the lessons are put into practice.

There are many reasons why such a course of action is ill-advised, maybe even a waste of time. One such reason is that parents can never know all of the situations that their children will face in their own lives. Another is that children are likely to live in different circumstances to those in which their parents lived. Both reasons suggest that whatever ideas we try to and do impart to children as parents will have to change as the children grow up, and indeed may have to be adapted by the children if they are going to be of practical use in their own lives.

The claim I am trying so hard to make, about parents raising children for a different future yet transmitting some of the past to them, is a particularly significant one for the future of masculinity in our country. It is one many parents will be aware of and have experienced. An example of the desire of parents for a different, better, future for their children is where children go on to become the first in the family to go to university and onward to enjoy a thriving life. An even more poignant example is where children are born free, while their parents lived much of their lives under an oppressive system. For a significant number of parents, especially those whom apartheid corralled into 'non-white areas' and rural, ethnically defined 'Bantu homelands', the lives they were forced to endure and those their children can and sometimes do have can be rather different from each other.

I have said it is impossible for parents to transmit *everything* that the culture constructs about masculinity and femininity. This is hopeful news, actually; it holds out a hope which, if you look closely, is complex yet has far-reaching consequences, if it becomes reality.

Let me conclude, then, by repeating that in order to extirpate the violence deposited by history in our lives, we have to address the hunger for love in boys and men. We have to nurture love-filled cultural expressions of masculinity. One generation can turn things in a different direction – whether this is the older or younger generation. I am not sure where the cultural change will spring from. What I know is that it needs to be change in the direction of nurturing love in men and boys, and transforming masculinity toward more caring forms of expression.

It will never be plain sailing, though. If it is correct that parents transmit traditions along with their genes, we can expect whatever new, egalitarian, caring masculinity beliefs we pass on to our children to be challenged, and not just by the old, authoritarian, violent beliefs about masculinity. Beliefs about what it means to be a man are always being contested. Practices are continually questioned. Attitudes are challenged all the time. When a person claims that 'men do this', whatever this is, there is likely to be dissension, sometimes loudly and at other times muted. And so, even the caring masculinity boys may be taught at home will be challenged when they step outside the home – when they get to school, proceed to university, find employment in workplaces, and encounter ideas about masculinity in the media. They may start to question the wisdom of showing care to others. They may even resist the very ideas and beliefs that might make their lives more fulfilling.

All that being the case, the fact that masculinity is always in the process of becoming, being challenged, influenced, worked on or shifted, means that many opportunities exist for individuals to change their gender beliefs and practices. What we can hope for, and must grasp, is that along with whatever gender beliefs we inherit and transmit, we also inherit and transmit the idea that masculinity is subject to change. We can change.

Acknowledgements

I am not certain why Carmine agreed to talk with me about love. Our conversations, which go on all the time, and which I can never fully relay in a relatively short, single reflection in a book, have made these meditations immeasurably precious to me, and hopefully of worth to other women who may love men in a world where some men pose a constant danger to women. She might not agree with me if I liken her to romantic historical female characters in Korean television series or Spanish dramas, but it is no secret that she cries at certain moments of romantic comedies as much as she detests injustice. There is much about how to love that I continue to learn from her blend of earthiness, friendship, thoughtfulness, practicality, calm and care.

Mathabiso Gloria Lion, my mother, and I had a conversation about love. It was also a conversation about my father, men, her life and women. We recorded it. In our language. It was open. Informative. Full of twists and turns. With many laughs in between. Sadness too. I decided to leave our conversation out of the book. You should know that my mother does not just believe in the content of dreams, she can talk for days when she is in the mood. Often she will say to me, 'Wena o motho wa hao', which is best left untranslated, but it means a great deal. Or she might ask me, 'O motho a jwang wena mara?' The idea of botho is never too far off, then. She tells me she learns from me, my mother. I am aware that there was a time when I learned everything about how to be human from her. I can never repay you for that, mme. As for what I learned in our recorded conversation on love, in a word: there is always something I can learn from talking with my mother, if I manage to keep the child inside me out of the way. I also learn that I do not know my mother – but who does know their

249

mother? – though that is a fine thing to have realised at some point because, just as she asks me what kind of person I am, I am always learning about her unknown life. Some of these notes are for her life that made mine possible, and many other things besides.

I had several conversations over WhatsApp and Zoom with the editor and writer Carli Coetzee. Some of them about the book. Others about children, hearts and many things besides. I want to thank Carli for being the first reader of the full manuscript, for her editorial eye, for her generosity as a reader, and for her friendship.

Thank you to Daniel Radebe for his assistance with the bibliography.

I thank Ketso Ratele for teaching me how to be a father, every goddam day of the year, as he questions us, fights us, and I hope he will always remember the kindness he believes in. And to make a choice. And sleep. Play outside. Eat greens. Friends. Family. I am no longer as anxious as I was in the early years that he will get hurt, because I know he will, but I think it will be fine as long as he remembers the basic life stuff.

Finally, I extend my grateful acknowledgement to two anonymous reviewers of the manuscript for their time and generosity. I appreciate the abundance of questions and collegial spirit of their comments.

Notes

Chapter 1 Why do women love men?

1   Erik Erikson, *Childhood and Society* (New York: W.W. Norton, 1963), 263.

2   There are many definitions of the self, one of the most thoroughly researched, theorised and discussed topics in psychology. Some psychologists, for instance, see the self as the core of personality. Others regard it as some or all of the beliefs, abilities, values, attributes, thoughts, preferences, memories, feelings and attitudes a person and others hold about what that person is. And others still think the self is empty, filled with prevailing cultural constructions about what it means to be human. For example, see Philip Cushman, 'Why the Self Is Empty: Toward a Historically Situated Psychology', *American Psychologist* 45, no. 5 (1990): 599; Chie Kanagawa, Susan E. Cross and Hazel Rose Markus, '"Who Am I?" The Cultural Psychology of the Conceptual Self', *Personality and Social Psychology Bulletin* 27, no. 1 (2001): 90–103; Daphna Oyserman, 'Self-Concept and Identity', in *The Blackwell Handbook of Social Psychology*, ed. Abraham Tesser and Norbert Schwarz (Malden, MA: Blackwell, 2001), 499–517.

3   Known as *lobola* in isiZulu and isiXhosa, *mahadi* (Sesotho) is a custom whereby negotiators from the man's family and trusted friends arrange to visit the woman's family to ask for permission for him to marry her. The negotiation is conducted by men, revealing the patriarchal undercurrent of the custom. Traditionally, the negotiations included the transfer of cattle; however, money has now replaced cattle as the currency of love, if not the lifeblood of a good marriage.

4   Jimmy (Mzwanele) Manyi was a prominent government spokesperson who came under fire for saying on television that there was an 'over-concentration of coloureds in Western Cape' and that it 'is not working for them'. SAPA (South African Press Association), 'Manyi Criticised', *SowetanLive*, 5 February 2011, https://mg.co.za/article/2011-02-24-coloureds-overconcentrated-in-wcape-says-manyi/.

5   Philippi, around 18 kilometres from Pinelands, where we live, is a poor, large, semi-urban area in Cape Town's Cape Flats region.

Chapter 2 A double movement outward toward others and inward into the self

1 In March 2022, during the Academy Awards ceremony, actor Will Smith went up to the stage and slapped and then went on to curse the comedian Chris Rock during the live televised show. Rock had made a joke about Smith's partner Jada Pinkett Smith's hair that Smith found objectionable. A little later during the show, Smith was awarded the 2022 Best Actor award for his role as Richard Williams, the father of tennis stars Serena and Venus Williams. In his tearful acceptance speech, Smith said, 'Love will make you do crazy things,' which seems to have been a reference to the things Richard Williams did for his daughters and/or the violence the world had witnessed earlier. See Brian Lowry, '"CODA" Wins the Oscar in a Streaming Breakthrough, but Will Smith Steals the Show', *CNN*, 29 March 2022, https://edition.cnn.com/2022/03/27/entertainment/academy-awards-2022/index.html.

2 Karla Elliott, 'Caring Masculinities: Theorizing an Emerging Concept', *Men and Masculinities* 19, no. 3 (2016): 240–259; Sarah C. Hunter, Damien W. Riggs and Martha Augoustinos, 'Constructions of Primary Caregiving Fathers in Popular Parenting Texts', *Men and Masculinities* 23, no. 1 (2020): 150–169, accessed 20 January 2022, https://journals.sagepub.com/doi/10.1177/1097184X17730593; Pholoho Morojele and Ncamsile D. Motsa, 'Vulnerable Masculinities: Implications of Gender Socialisation in Three Rural Swazi Primary Schools', *South African Journal of Childhood Education* 9, no. 1 (2019): a580, accessed 20 January 2022, https://sajce.co.za/index.php/sajce/article/view/580.

3 bell hooks, *The Will to Change: Men, Masculinity and Love* (New York: Washington Square Press, 2004).

Chapter 3 Love needs

1 Abraham H. Maslow, 'Preface to Motivation Theory', *Psychosomatic Medicine* 5 (1943): 85–92, https://doi.org/10.1097/00006842-194301000-00012; Abraham H. Maslow, 'A Theory of Human Motivation', *Psychological Review* 50, no. 4 (1943): 370–396.

2 For example, Seymour Adler, 'Maslow's Need Hierarchy and the Adjustment of Immigrants', *International Migration Review* 11, no. 4 (1977): 444–451; Allan R. Buss, 'Humanistic Psychology as Liberal Ideology: The Socio-Historical Roots of Maslow's Theory of Self-Actualization', *Journal of Humanistic Psychology* 19, no. 3 (1979): 43–55; Seyed Hadi Mousavi and Hossein Dargahi, 'Ethnic Differences and Motivation Based on Maslow's Theory on Iranian Employees', *Iranian Journal of Public Health* 42, no. 5 (2013): 516–521.

3 See Kopano Ratele, *The World Looks Like This from Here: Thoughts on African Psychology* (Johannesburg: Wits University Press, 2019).

4 Maslow, along with people such as the Chicago-born Carl Rogers, belongs to a tradition within psychology known as the humanistic psychology movement. The driving impulse of humanistic psychology was to counter the view of

humans found in psychoanalytic psychology, and even more so in behaviourist psychology, which had come to dominate explanations of behaviour. The former, founded by the Austrian Sigmund Freud, had been a dominant theorical explanation in the early twentieth century, while the latter, among whose leading exponents were the Russian Ivan Pavlov as well as the Americans John B. Watson and Burrhus Frederic Skinner, dominated psychology from approximately the 1920s to the middle of the century.

5   Maslow, 'A Theory', 370.

6   Maslow, 'A Theory', 370.

7   Abraham H. Maslow, 'Deficiency Motivation and Growth Motivation', *General Semantics Bulletin* 18–19 (1956): 33–42.

8   Maslow, 'A Theory', 380–381.

9   This need was hauntingly on display during the coronavirus pandemic when people in different countries were dying because of inadequate supplies of medical oxygen at hospitals. For example, see Jason Beaubien, 'Africa Is Running Out of Oxygen', *NPR*, 24 June 2021, https://www.npr.org/sections/goatsandsoda/2021/06/24/1009475339/africa-is-running-out-of-oxygen; Linda Geddes, 'Why Indian Hospitals Are Running Out of Medical Oxygen and How to Fix It', Gavi: The Vaccine Alliance, 9 May 2021, https://www.gavi.org/vaccineswork/why-indian-hospitals-are-running-out-medical-oxygen-and-how-fix-it.

10   For example, see Institute for Economics and Peace, *Global Peace Index 2020: Measuring Peace in a Complex World*, June 2020, https://www.visionofhumanity.org/wp-content/uploads/2020/10/GPI_2020_web.pdf; Institute for Security Studies, *Crime Hub*, n.d., accessed 20 January 2022, https://issafrica.org/crimehub/facts-and-figures/national-crime; Statistics South Africa, *Statistical Release P0341: Victims of Crime: Governance, Public Safety, and Justice Survey* (Pretoria: Statistics South Africa, 2020).

11   Kopano Ratele, Shahnaaz Suffla, Lu-Anne Swart and Nick Malherbe, 'Historical Trauma and Structure in Violence Against and by Young Men', in *Youth in South Africa: Agency, (In)Visibility and National Development*, ed. Ariane De Lannoy, Malose Langa and Heidi Brooks (Johannesburg: MISTRA, 2021), 353–380; South African Police Service, *Crime Statistics: Crime Situation in Republic of South Africa (April to March 2019–20)*, accessed 28 March 2022, https://www.saps.gov.za/services/april_to_march_2019_20_presentation.pdf.

12   For example, see International Monetary Fund, *IMF Country Focus: Six Charts Explain South Africa's Inequality*, 30 January 2020, https://www.imf.org/en/News/Articles/2020/01/29/na012820six-charts-on-south-africas-persistent-and-multi-faceted-inequality; Lameez Omarjee, 'SA's Unemployment Rate Hits Record 34.4%', *Fin24*, 24 August 2021, https://www.news24.com/fin24/economy/sas-unemployment-rate-hits-record-344-20210824; Statistics South Africa, *Inequality Trends in South Africa: A Multidimensional Diagnostic of Inequality*, Report No. 03-10-19 (Pretoria: Statistics South Africa, 2019).

13   Feminist phenomenologists are interested in the gender/sex aspects of being-in-the-world.

14 Elmien Lesch and Alberta S. van der Watt, 'Living Single: A Phenomenological Study of a Group of South African Single Women', *Feminism & Psychology* 28, no. 3 (2018): 400.

15 Raewyn Connell, *The Men and the Boys* (Oxford: Polity Press, 2000), 25.

16 See Chelsea Pickens and Virginia Braun, '"Stroppy Bitches Who Just Need to Learn How to Settle"? Young Single Women and Norms of Femininity and Heterosexuality', *Sex Roles* 79, no. 7 (2018): 431–448, https://doi.org/10.1007/s11199-017-0881-5.

17 Anthony Giddens, *The Transformation of Intimacy: Sexuality, Love and Eroticism in Modern Societies* (Redwood City, CA: Stanford University Press, 1992), 131.

18 Sigmund Freud, 'Short Account of Psycho-Analysis', in *The Standard Edition of the Complete Psychological Works of Sigmund Freud, Vol. 19 (1923–1925): The Ego and the Id and Other Works* (London: Vintage, 2001), 189–209.

19 Jørgen Lorentzen, 'Love and Intimacy in Men's Lives', *NORA: Nordic Journal of Women's Studies* 15, no. 2–3 (2007): 190.

20 Lorentzen, 'Love and Intimacy', 190.

21 Martha Nussbaum, *Political Emotions: Why Love Matters for Justice* (Cambridge, MA: Belknap Press, 2013).

22 Regarding men's discrepant affective needs, see, for example, Susan M. Allen, 'Gender Differences in Spousal Caregiving and Unmet Need for Care', *Journal of Gerontology* 49, no. 4 (1994): S187–S195; Aliraza Javaid, 'Male Rape, Stereotypes, and Unmet Needs: Hindering Recovery, Perpetuating Silence', *Violence and Gender* 3, no. 1 (2016): 7–13; Roland F. Levant, 'Toward the Reconstruction of Masculinity', *Journal of Family Psychology* 5, no. 3–4 (1992): 379–402.

23 Maslow, 'Deficiency Motivation', 40.

Chapter 4 We can change how we love, but not without changing how we fight

1 Thich Nhat Hanh, *How to Fight* (London: Rider, 2017), 95.

2 *Whoonga* is a highly addictive drug concoction typically comprising low-grade heroin, marijuana and other substances, smoked or intravenously injected as a recreational drug in parts of South Africa.

3 Sigmund Freud, 'A Special Type of Choice of Object Made by Men: Contribution to the Psychology of Love – 1', in *The Standard Edition of the Complete Psychological Works of Sigmund Freud, Vol. 11 (1910): Five Lectures on Psycho-Analysis, Leonardo da Vinci and Other Works* (London: Vintage, 2001), 168–169.

4 Alan Soble, ed., *Eros, Agape and Philia: Readings in the Philosophy of Love* (New York: Paragon House, 1989).

5 Robert J. Sternberg, 'A Triangular Theory of Love', *Psychological Review* 93, no. 2 (1986): 119.

6 Kenneth R. Ginsburg, 'The Importance of Play in Promoting Healthy Child Development and Maintaining Strong Parent–Child Bonds', *Pediatrics* 119, no. 1 (2007): 182–191; Jaipaul L. Roopnarine and Kimberly L. Davidson, 'Parent–Child

Play Across Cultures: Advancing Play Research', *American Journal of Play* 7, no. 2 (2015): 228–252; Catherine S. Tamis-LeMonda, Ina Č. Užgiris and Marc H. Bornstein, 'Play in Parent–Child Interactions', in *Handbook of Parenting, Vol. 5: Practical Issues in Parenting*, ed. Marc H. Bornstein (Hillsdale, NJ: Lawrence Erlbaum Associates, 2002), 221–241.

7   See Mandisa Malinga and Kopano Ratele, '"It Has Changed Me from the Person that I Was Before": Love and the Construction of Young Black Masculinities', in *Doing Gender, Doing Love: Interdisciplinary Voices*, ed. Serena Petrella (Oxford: Inter-Disciplinary Press, 2014), 73–101.

8   However, see, for example, Kopano Ratele, 'Apartheid, Anti-Apartheid and Post-Apartheid Sexualities', in *The Prize and the Price: Shaping Sexualities in South Africa*, ed. Melissa Steyn and Mikki van Zyl (Cape Town: HSRC Press, 2009), 290–305; Kopano Ratele and Tamara Shefer, 'Desire, Fear and Entitlement: Sexualising Race and Racialising Sexuality in (Re)membering Apartheid', in *Race, Memory and the Apartheid Archive: Towards a Transformative Psychosocial Praxis*, ed. Garth Stevens, Norman Duncan and Derek Hook (London: Palgrave, 2013), 188–207.

9   National Department of Health (NDoH), Statistics South Africa (Stats SA), South African Medical Research Council (SAMRC) and ICF, *South Africa Demographic and Health Survey 2016* (Pretoria and Rockville, MD: NDoH, Stats SA, SAMRC and ICF, 2019), 329.

Chapter 5   Love hunger shows itself in many acts, and violence may be one of them

1   For example, Malinga and Ratele, '"It Has Changed Me"'.

2   Candice Rule-Groenewald, '"Just Knowing You Found the Person that You're Ready to Spend Your Life With": Love, Romance and Intimate Relationships', *Agenda* 27, no. 2 (2013): 30–37.

3   Malinga and Ratele, '"It Has Changed Me"'.

4   Rebecca Helman and Kopano Ratele, 'Everyday (In)Equality at Home: Complex Constructions of Gender in South African Families', *Global Health Action* 9, no. 1 (2016), https://doi.org/10.3402/gha.v9.31122.

5   Cathexis means investing sexual objects with psychical energy.

6   Sigmund Freud, 'The Ego and the Id', in *The Standard Edition of the Complete Psychological Works of Sigmund Freud, Vol. 19 (1923–1925): The Ego and the Id and Other Works* (London: Vintage, 2001), 31–32. Something else of interest to us that Freud said about boys in the same text is that a boy's relation to his father is inherently ambivalent, and that only by giving up his mother as a love object and intensifying his identification with his father can his masculinity be consolidated.

7   But see, for example, Lamar L. Johnson, Nathaniel Bryan and Gloria Boutte, 'Show Us the Love: Revolutionary Teaching in (Un)Critical Times', *Urban Review* 51, no. 1 (2019): 46–64; Maija Lanas and Michalinos Zembylas, 'Towards a Transformational Political Concept of Love in Critical Education', *Studies in*

Philosophy and Education 34, no. 1 (2015): 31–44; Eduard Spranger, 'The Role of Love in Education', *Universitas* 2, no. 3 (1958): 536–547.

8 Daniel Liston, 'Love and Despair in Teaching', *Educational Theory* 50, no. 1 (2000): 81.

9 Mosibudi Mangena, *We Can Fix Ourselves: Building a Better South Africa Through Black Consciousness* (Cape Town: Kwela Books, 2021), 10.

10 Freud, 'Short Account', 203. Having cited Freud several times, I should again make it clear that I am not advocating for psychoanalytic explanations of love. Therefore, I am not to be heard saying that Freud's theory is correct, simply that he is someone who had something to say about love that is worth considering.

Chapter 6   Why there is no love in the *Plan*

1 Instead of the words women/woman, contemporary intersectional feminist activists and scholars increasingly use 'womxn' to indicate inclusivity and to avoid the sexist language suggested by the inclusion of man/men in woman/ women. I restrict my use of the word 'womxn' to instances when I am referring to #TotalShutDown, or directly quoting a source.

2 Staff Reporter, '#THETOTALSHUTDOWN: Memorandum of Demands', *Mail & Guardian*, 2 August 2018, https://mg.co.za/article/2018-08-02-the totalshutdown-memorandum-of-demands/.

3 Interim Steering Committee on Gender-Based Violence and Femicide (ISCGBVF), *Emergency Response Action Plan on Gender-Based Violence and Femicide*, 30 April 2020, accessed 28 December 2020, http://www.thepresidency.gov.za/ documents.

4 Republic of South Africa, *National Strategic Plan on Gender-Based Violence and Femicide: Human Dignity and Healing, Safety, Freedom & Equality in Our Lifetime* (Pretoria: Republic of South Africa, 2020), accessed 28 December 2020, https:// www.justice.gov.za/vg/gbv/NSP-GBVF-FINAL-DOC-04-05.pdf.

5 See, for example, Deevia Bhana and Rob Pattman, 'Girls Want Money, Boys Want Virgins: The Materiality of Love Amongst South African Township Youth in the Context of HIV and AIDS', *Culture, Health & Sexuality* 13, no. 8 (2011): 961–972; Lisa Bowleg, 'Love, Sex, and Masculinity in Sociocultural Context: HIV Concerns and Condom Use Among African American Men in Heterosexual Relationships', *Men and Masculinities* 7, no. 2 (2004): 166–186; Peter Redman, 'The Discipline of Love: Negotiation and Regulation in Boys' Performance of a Romance-Based Heterosexual Masculinity', *Men and Masculinities* 4, no. 2 (2001): 186–200.

6 Steve Biko, *I Write What I Like* (Johannesburg: Picador Africa, 2004).

7 See the programme's website, accessed 22 October 2021, http://www.lovenothate. org.za/.

8 Republic of South Africa, *National Strategic Plan*, 18.

9 Republic of South Africa, *National Strategic Plan*, 28.

10 A Thuthuzela Care Centre is a one-stop forensic and medical service available to rape and abuse victims.

11 Republic of South Africa, *National Strategic Plan*, 31, 51.

12 Michael Billig, *Freudian Repression: Conversation Creating the Unconscious* (Cambridge: Cambridge University Press, 1999); Michael Billig, 'Studying Repression in a Changing World', *European Journal of School Psychology* 1, no. 1 (2003): 39.

13 Sarah C. Hunter, Damien W. Riggs and Martha Augoustinos, 'Hegemonic Masculinity Versus a Caring Masculinity: Implications for Understanding Primary Caregiving Fathers', *Social and Personality Psychology Compass* 11, no. 3 (2017): e12307; Sofia José Santos, *MenCare in Latin America: Challenging Harmful Masculine Norms and Promoting Positive Changes in Men's Caregiving: EMERGE Case Study 5* (Promundo-US, Sonke Gender Justice and the Institute of Development Studies, 2015); Joyce Y. Lee and Shawna J. Lee, 'Caring Is Masculine: Stay-at-Home Fathers and Masculine Identity', *Psychology of Men & Masculinity* 19, no. 1 (2018): 47–58.

Chapter 7 I love you, but I wish to hurt you

1 For example, Ola W. Barnett and Alyce D. LaViolette, *It Could Happen to Anyone: Why Battered Women Stay* (New Delhi: Sage Publications, 1993); Claudia Garcia-Moreno, Henrica A.F.M. Jansen, Mary Ellsberg, Lori Heise and Charlotte H. Watts, 'Prevalence of Intimate Partner Violence: Findings from the WHO Multi-Country Study on Women's Health and Domestic Violence', *The Lancet* 368, no. 9543 (2006): 1260–1269; Rachel Jewkes, 'Intimate Partner Violence: Causes and Prevention', *The Lancet* 359, no. 9315 (2002): 1423–1429.

2 For example, Virginia Goldner, Peggy Penn, Marcia Sheinberg and Gillian Walker, 'Love and Violence: Gender Paradoxes in Volatile Attachments', *Family Process* 29, no. 4 (1990): 343–364; June Henton, Rodney Cate, James Koval, Sally Lloyd and Scott Christopher, 'Romance and Violence in Dating Relationships', *Journal of Family Issues* 4, no. 3 (1983): 467–482; Julia T. Wood, 'The Normalization of Violence in Heterosexual Romantic Relationships: Women's Narratives of Love and Violence', *Journal of Social and Personal Relationships* 18, no. 2 (2001): 239–261.

3 Saferspaces, 'Toxic Masculinity and Violence in South Africa', n.d., accessed 21 October 2021, https://www.saferspaces.org.za/understand/entry/toxic-masculinity-and-violence-in-south-africa; Leballo Tjemolane, 'We Need a Lockdown on Toxic Masculinities', *IOL*, 9 April 2020, https://www.news24.com/news24/columnists/guestcolumn/opinion-a-lockdown-on-toxic-and-outdated-masculinities-needed-more-than-ever-20200409; Andile Zulu, 'The Heavy Price of Pushing Masculinity', *Mail & Guardian*, 18 February 2021, https://mg.co.za/opinion/2021-02-18-the-heavy-price-of-pushing-masculinity/.

4 Robert Morrell, 'Fathers, Fatherhood and Masculinity in South Africa', in *Baba: Men and Fatherhood in South Africa*, ed. Linda Richter and Robert Morrell (Cape Town: HSRC Press, 2006), 21.

5 For interested readers, although it has nothing to say about female masculinity in our cultures, Judith Halberstam's book *Female Masculinity* (Durham, NC: Duke University Press, 2019) is a good read.

6 Karla Elliott, 'Challenging Toxic Masculinity in Schools and Society', *On the Horizon* 26, no. 1 (2018): 17–22.
7 Carol Harrington, 'What Is "Toxic Masculinity" and Why Does it Matter?', *Men and Masculinities* 24, no. 2 (2021): 345–352. The mythopoetic men's movement is a movement of men revolving around wilderness retreats and therapeutic workshops, with a heavy reliance on myths, rituals, fairy tales, legends, poetry and ancient stories. Not to be confused with the pro-feminist men's movement, which aligns itself with the goal of gender justice, the major aim of the mythopoetic movement is to help recover men's deep, spiritual, mature masculinity, this being distinguished from toxic, either hyper-masculine or soft, immature masculinity.
8 Andrea Waling, 'Problematising "Toxic" and "Healthy" Masculinity for Addressing Gender Inequalities', *Australian Feminist Studies* 34, no. 101 (2019): 366.
9 Harrington, 'What Is "Toxic Masculinity"', 346.
10 See, for example, Veronica Beechey, 'On Patriarchy', *Feminist Review* 3, no. 1 (1979): 66–82; Deniz Kandiyoti, 'Bargaining with Patriarchy', *Gender & Society* 2, no. 3 (1988): 274–290; Sylvia Walby, 'Theorising Patriarchy', *Sociology* 23, no. 2 (1989): 213–234.

Chapter 8 To love is to receive and to give

1 Chimamanda Ngozi Adichie, *Dear Ijeawele, or a Feminist Manifesto in Fifteen Suggestions* (London: Fourth Estate, 2017), 54.
2 Wessel van den Berg and Tawanda Makusha, eds., *State of South Africa's Fathers 2018* (Cape Town: Sonke Gender Justice and Human Sciences Research Council, 2018).
3 Kopano Ratele and Mzikazi Nduna, 'An Overview of Fatherhood in South Africa', in *State of South Africa's Fathers 2018*, ed. Wessel van den Berg and Tawanda Makusha (Cape Town: Sonke Gender Justice and Human Sciences Research Council, 2018), 32.
4 Adichie, *Dear Ijeawele*, 55.

Chapter 9 Talking matters

1 For example, see Lillian Comas-Díaz, 'Cultural Variation in the Therapeutic Relationship', in *Evidence-Based Psychotherapy: Where Practice and Research Meet*, ed. Carol D. Goodheart, Alan E. Kazdin and Robert J. Sternberg (Washington, DC: American Psychological Association, 2006), 81–105; Elsa Marziali and Leslie Alexander, 'The Power of the Therapeutic Relationship', *American Journal of Orthopsychiatry* 61, no. 3 (1991): 383–391; Carl R. Rogers, 'The Therapeutic Relationship: Recent Theory and Research', *Australian Journal of Psychology* 17, no. 2 (1965): 95–108.
2 For example, see Sheila McNamee, 'Radical Presence: Alternatives to the Therapeutic State', *European Journal of Psychotherapy & Counselling* 17, no. 4 (2015): 373–383; Ian Parker, *Psy-Complex in Question: Critical Review in Psychology,*

Psychoanalysis and Social Theory (Winchester: Zero Books, 2018); Nikolas Rose, *The Psychological Complex: Psychology, Politics and Society in England 1869–1939* (London: Routledge, 1985).

3 Carl R. Rogers, 'Empathic: An Unappreciated Way of Being', *Counselling Psychologist* 5, no. 2 (1975): 2.

4 Lorentzen, 'Love and Intimacy'.

5 I use the term 'hold' in the way the famed psychoanalyst Donald Winnicott described holding, to speak of the parent–child environment or space; however I extend it to the situation of two adults, where one relates with empathy to the other. Winnicott wrote: 'The term "holding" is used here to denote not only the actual physical holding of the infant, but also the total environmental provision prior to the concept of living with.' Donald W. Winnicott, *The Maturational Processes and the Facilitating Environment: Studies in the Theory of Emotional Development* (London: Routledge, 2018), 41.

6 Erikson, *Childhood and Society*.

Chapter 10 Listening carefully is an articulate act of love in action

1 *Roosterbroodjies* are bread rolls cooked on a coal fire.

Chapter 11 Why does love hurt?

1 Nazareth, performer, 'Love Hurts', written by Felice and Boudleaux Bryant, accessed 8 January 2022, https://www.youtube.com/watch?v=soDZBW-1P04.

2 William H. Masters, Virginia E. Johnson and Robert C. Kolodny, *Masters and Johnson on Sex and Human Loving*, 2nd ed. (Boston: Little, Brown and Company, 1985), 216.

3 James S. Nairne, *Psychology: The Adaptive Mind* (Pacific Grove, CA: Brooks/Cole, 1996), 483.

4 World Health Organization, *Understanding and Addressing Violence Against Women: Intimate Partner Violence*, Document No. WHO/RHR/12.36 (Geneva: World Health Organization, 2012).

5 Dalit Yassour Borochowitz and Zvi Eisikovits, 'To Love Violently: Strategies for Reconciling Love and Violence', *Violence Against Women* 8, no. 4 (2002): 476–494.

6 Halimah DeShong, 'Gender Discourses of Romantic Loving and Violence', in *Doing Gender, Doing Love: Interdisciplinary Voices*, ed. Serena Petrella (Oxford: Inter-Disciplinary Press, 2014), 112.

7 Under apartheid, black women who worked as domestic help for white women and men were sometimes referred to as 'kitchen girls' (although it was more common to refer to them as 'girls' or *'meisies'*).

Chapter 13 Producing and embodying the loving images we want of ourselves

1 Mama Hope, 'African Men. Hollywood Stereotypes', YouTube video, 25 April 2012, https://www.youtube.com/watch?v=qSElmEmEjb4&feature=emb_title.

2 Mama Hope, 'Media on a Mission', accessed 22 October 2021, https://www. mamahope.org/media/.

Chapter 15 'I am more scared of them'
1 See MultiChoice, 'MultiChoice Partners with Government and Civil Society Organizations for GBV Initiative', 6 August 2020, https://www.multichoice.com/ media/news/multichoice-partners-with-government-and-civil-society-organi-zations-for-gbv-initiative.

Chapter 16 Men who speak with fists
1 Pearlie Joubert, 'Men Who Speak with Fists', *Mail & Guardian*, 19 November 2007, https://mg.co.za/article/2007-11-19-men-who-speak-with-fists/.
2 Nhat Hanh, *How to Fight*.
3 Joubert, 'Men Who Speak with Fists'.

Chapter 17 Violence wears many faces
1 Lesley Brown, ed., *The New Shorter Oxford English Dictionary on Historical Principles* (Oxford: Clarendon Press, 1993), 3583.
2 Etienne G. Krug, James A. Mercy, Linda L. Dahlberg and Anthony B. Zwi, eds., *World Report on Violence and Health* (Geneva: World Health Organization, 2002), 5.
3 Johan Galtung, 'Violence, Peace, and Peace Research', *Journal of Peace Research* 6, no. 3 (1969): 168.
4 Galtung, 'Peace Research', 169.
5 Krug et al., *World Report on Violence*, 3.
6 Martin Luther King Jr, 'Letter from Birmingham Jail', *UC Davis Law Review* 26, no. 4 (1993): 836.

Chapter 18 'Brothers, check yourselves!'
1 Azania House was the name the students of the #RhodesMustFall movement gave to the building they had occupied, whose official name is Bremner House; see Wikipedia, *Rhodes Must Fall*, accessed 20 January 2022, https://en.wikipedia. org/wiki/RhodesMustFall; Wikipedia, *FeesMustFall*, accessed 20 January 2022, https://en.wikipedia.org/wiki/FeesMustFall). I have written about this inci-dent in Kopano Ratele, 'Engaging Young Male University Students: Towards a Situated, Social-Psychological Pro-Feminist Praxis', in *Engaging Youth in Activism, Research and Pedagogical Praxis: Transnational and Intersectional Perspectives on Gender, Sex and Race*, ed. Tamara Shefer, Jeff Hearn, Kopano Ratele and Floretta Boonzaier (New York: Routledge, 2018), 93–109.
2 The #RhodesMustFall movement began in early 2015 as a movement of students at the University of Cape Town against racist and colonial symbols and educa-tion. The students were supported by some faculty and non-academic staff. The

broad aim of the movement was to transform the university, but it began with the specific goal of bringing down the statue of the super-rich colonialist Cecil John Rhodes.

3 The thinking informing what has come to be referred to as intersectional feminism has a long history among African American women. See Angela Davis, *Women, Race and Class* (London: Women's Press, 1982); Gloria T. Hull, Patricia Bell Scott and Barbara Smith, eds., *All the Women Are White, All the Blacks Are Men, But Some of Us Are Brave: Black Women's Studies* (London: Feminist Press, 1982). Kimberlé Crenshaw is credited with coining the term 'intersectionality'. She states that 'neither Black liberationist politics nor feminist theory can ignore the intersectional experiences of those whom the movements claimed as their respective constituents'. Kimberlé Crenshaw, 'Demarginalizing the Intersections of Race and Sex: A Black Feminist Critique of Antidiscrimination Doctrine, Feminist Theory and Antiracist Politics', *University of Chicago Legal Forum* 1 (1989): 166; see also Kimberlé Crenshaw, 'Mapping the Margins: Intersectionality, Identity Politics, and Violence Against Women of Color', *Stanford Law Review* 43, no. 6 (1991): 1243–1244.

4 Ashley van Niekerk, Susanne Tonsing, Mohamed Seedat, Roxanne Jacobs, Kopano Ratele and Rod McClure, 'The Invisibility of Men in South African Violence Prevention Policy: National Prioritization, Male Vulnerability, and Framing Prevention', *Global Health Action* 8, no. 1 (2015): 1–10, https://doi.org/10.3402/gha.v8.27649.

5 Lindsay Clowes, 'The Limits of Discourse: Masculinity as Vulnerability', *Agenda* 27, no. 1 (2013): 14.

6 Samuel Adu-Poku, 'Envisioning (Black) Male Feminism: A Cross-Cultural Perspective', *Journal of Gender Studies* 10, no. 2 (2001): 157.

7 David Ikard and Mark Anthony Neal, 'Introduction: Transforming Black Men in Feminism', *Palimpsest: A Journal on Women, Gender, and the Black International* 1, no. 2 (2012): vii.

8 hooks, *Will to Change*, xiv.

9 hooks, *Will to Change*, xiii.

Chapter 20 Why is there violence where we expect to find love?

1 Lynn Jamieson, *Intimacy: Personal Relationships in Modern Societies* (Cambridge: Polity Press, 1998), 1.

Chapter 21 Really nice guys

1 Eva Trobisch, dir., *Alles ist gut*, distributed by Netflix, 2018.

2 For some writing on diversity and refugees in Germany, see Chiponda Chimbelu, 'What's Life Really Like for Black People in Germany?' *DW*, 25 April 2020, https://www.dw.com/en/whats-life-really-like-for-black-people-in-germany/a-53159443; Sekou Keita and Helen Dempster, 'Five Years Later, One Million Refugees Are Thriving in Germany', Center for Global Development,

4 December 2020, https://www.cgdev.org/blog/five-years-later-one-million-refugees-are-thriving-germany; David Meyer, 'Corporate Germany Has a Race Problem – and a Lack of Data Is Not Helping', *Fortune*, 19 June 2020, https://fortune.com/2020/06/19/corporate-germany-race-diversity-data/.

3 On New Year's Eve in 2015 in Cologne, it was reported that more than 1 000 men seemingly set out to sexually attack women. The incident ignited widespread debate and received wide coverage in Germany and around the world. A discourse conveyed in the reports was that what caused the men to harass the women (and in two cases women were raped) was that they were immigrants, refugees and asylum seekers. For examples of the coverage, see Gaby Hinsliff, 'Let's Not Shy Away from Asking Hard Questions About the Cologne Attacks', *The Guardian*, 8 January 2016, https://www.theguardian.com/commentisfree/2016/jan/08/cologne-attacks-hard-questions-new-years-eve; Damien McGuinness, 'Germany Shocked by Cologne New Year Gang Assaults on Women', *BBC News*, 5 January 2016, https://www.bbc.com/news/world-europe-35231046; Antony Smale, 'As Germany Welcomes Migrants, Sexual Attacks in Cologne Point to a New Reality', *New York Times*, 14 January 2016, https://www.nytimes.com/2016/01/15/world/europe/as-germany-welcomes-migrantssexual-attacks-in-cologne-point-to-a-new-reality.html.

4 Pumla Dineo Gqola, *Rape: A South African Nightmare* (Johannesburg: MF Books Joburg, 2015), 38.

5 Among several insights about unrapability, Gqola writes: 'Not only were slave women objects and legally incapable of being raped, they were constructed as hypersexual and therefore would not have been rapable even when free.' Gqola, *Rape*, 43.

6 Tracy Going, *Brutal Legacy: A Memoir* (Johannesburg: MF Books Joburg, 2018).

7 Going, *Brutal Legacy*; Lou-Maré Kruger, *Of Motherhood and Melancholia: Notebook of a Psycho-Ethnographer* (Pietermaritzburg: University of KwaZulu-Natal Press, 2020).

Chapter 22 'There was nothing suspicious about him'

1 Republic of South Africa, 'Proclamation No. 3 of 2018 by the President of the Republic of South Africa: Judicial Commission of Inquiry to Inquire into Allegations of State Capture, Corruption and Fraud in the Public Sector Including Organs of the State', *Government Gazette* 631, no. 41403 (2018).

2 See South African Police Service, 'SAPS Crimestats', accessed 27 October 2021, https://www.saps.gov.za/services/older_crimestats.php.

3 Taggart Frost, David V. Stimpson and Micol R.C. Maughan, 'Some Correlates of Trust', *Journal of Psychology* 99, no. 1 (1978): 104, https://doi.org/10.1080/00223980.1978.9921447.

4 Jeffry A. Simpson, 'Foundations of Interpersonal Trust', in *Social Psychology: Handbook of Basic Principles*, ed. Arie W. Kruglanski and E. Tory Higgins (New York: Guildford Press, 2007), 589.

5 Francis Fukuyama, *Trust: Social Virtues and the Creation of Prosperity* (New York: Simon and Schuster, 1996), 26.

6 Erikson, *Childhood and Society*, 249.
7 Erikson, *Childhood and Society*, 249.
8 Erikson, *Childhood and Society*, 249.
9 Simpson, 'Foundations of Interpersonal Trust', 587.
10 Michele Williams, 'In Whom We Trust: Group Membership as an Affective Context for Trust Development', *Academy of Management Review* 26, no. 3 (2001): 377–396.
11 Des Erasmus, 'KwaZulu-Natal Residents Living in the Shadow of a Serial Killer', *City Press*, 6 September 2020, https://www.news24.com/citypress/news/kwazulu-natal-residents-living-in-the-shadow-of-a-serial-killer-20200906.
12 Erasmus, 'Serial Killer'.
13 Erasmus, 'Serial Killer'.
14 Sometimes, not trusting people is advisable, surely. For example, at another time, I received a call that my room at a conference in Australia, where I was to be one of the keynote panel speakers, had been subsidised. The caller gave me the names of the organisers and other details of the conference; the call made sense. All I needed to do was give them my credit card details to make sure that I would pitch up. But my suspicions kicked in, and I told the male voice over the phone he would need to call back after a while. When he did call back, I asked why he was trying to scam me. He did not deny that it was a scam but instead said, 'Sorry', and dropped the call.
15 See South African Police Service, 'SAPS Crimestats'.

Chapter 23 They don't teach about sexual consent at university or at home

1 A #ConsentBox is tool for discussion about sexual consent. Participants write down their experiences, thoughts, feelings and ideas about consent and place them in a box, and these are critically interrogated.
2 Information about the House of Yes can be found at https://houseofyes.org/experience/.
3 House of Yes, 'About Yes', accessed 22 October 2021, https://houseofyes.org/experience/.
4 Slavoj Žižek, 'Apparently, Clubs Now Need to Hire Consent Guardians – Clearly We've Misunderstood Human Sexuality', *Independent*, 31 December 2018, https://www.independent.co.uk/voices/consent-sex-clubs-house-of-yes-con-senticorns-sadomasochism-freud-capitalism-a8705551.html?fbclid=IwAR0U-Ao2TB-VwJMrk9Rw8jIDto3pKxJxayZFG6UhqnCwJV7O_d3J4FPEzQOA.
5 Catherine Del Monte, 'Beware the Violence of Intimacy: On Consent and Safe Spaces', *Daily Maverick*, 6 December 2020, https://www.dailymaverick.co.za/article/2020-12-06-beware-the-violence-of-intimacy-on-consent-and-safe-spaces/.
6 I added, after these responses to Del Monte's questions: 'See attached. This is part of the online work we have already begun to do, and it is focused on university students but also other groups. We post it via this page, https://www.facebook.com/masculinityandhealthresearchunit/.'

Chapter 24 Jeanne and Emmanuel

1 Alrick Brown, dir., *Kinyarwanda*, Independent Filmmaker Labs, premiered at Sundance Film Festival 2011. See https://africa.film/kinyarwanda-an-al-rick-brown-feature-film/, accessed 23 January 2022, for details of the film and its awards.
2 Brown, *Kinyarwanda*.
3 I first presented these reflections in Kigali, Rwanda, at a symposium on 'Historical Trauma and Memory: Living with the Haunting Power of the Past', organised by Pumla Gobodo-Madikizela at the Kigali Serena Hotel on 4–6 April 2018.
4 *Gacaca* courts were community courts driven by the idea of transitional, restorative justice and communal healing following the Rwandan genocide.
5 Archbishop Desmond Tutu, 'Forgiveness: "What Do You Do to Forgive Someone?"', Desmond Tutu Peace Foundation, accessed 14 February 2022, https://www.youtube.com/watch?v=uo2LGGqtjqM.
6 *eNCA*, 'Winnie, the Fearless', 2 April 2018, https://www.enca.com/south-africa/winnie-the-fearless.

Chapter 25 Is the lesbian an alibi for an untenable model of masculinity?

1 Sarah Allen and Nakamori Yasufumi, eds., *Zanele Muholi* (London: Tate Publishing, 2020).
2 Kopano Ratele, 'Hegemonic African Masculinities and Men's Heterosexual Lives: Some Uses for Homophobia', *African Studies Review* 57, no. 2 (2014): 115–130.

Chapter 26 Will we reduce rates of rape of women and children when we cannot face prison rape?

1 *Tsotsi* means a streetwise guy or street criminal. *Ditsotsi* is the plural form.
2 *Izigebengu* (anglicised to *'sgebengus*) means the same thing as *ditsotsi*. *Isigebengu* or *'sgebengu* is the singular form.
3 Azania Rising Productions and Just Detention International–South Africa, *Taking Off the Mask*, accessed 14 February 2022, https://www.youtube.com/watch?v=VBsLIEXQ0Fs.
4 I should say this: life can be so harsh outside prison for many young men that a boy, when he cannot catch a break from the struggle to survive, when he is hungry and does not know where his next meal will come from, and he learns that in prison they get a full meal, thinks that prison doesn't sound so bad. But then he gets told that he is likely to get raped. That instils the fear of hell in a person. It did in me. So, one exists in this liminal space between the hell of a wretched life outside and the fear of rape inside.
5 Rachel Jewkes, Kristin Dunkle, Mary P. Koss, Jonathan B. Levin, Mzikazi Nduna, Nwabisa Jama and Yandisa Sikweyiya, 'Rape Perpetration by Young, Rural South African Men: Prevalence, Patterns and Risk Factors', *Social Science & Medicine* 63, no. 11 (2006): 2949–2961; Lisa Vetten and Kopano Ratele, 'Men and Violence', *Agenda* 27, no. 1 (2013): 4–11, http://dx.doi.org/10.1080/10130950.2013.813769.

6 But see, for example, Matthew Jakupcak, Matthew T. Tull and Lizabeth Roemer, 'Masculinity, Shame, and Fear of Emotions as Predictors of Men's Expressions of Anger and Hostility', *Psychology of Men & Masculinity* 6, no. 4 (2005): 275–284; Michael S. Kimmel, 'Masculinity as Homophobia: Fear, Shame, and Silence in the Construction of Gender Identity', in *Theorizing Masculinities*, ed. Harry Brod and Michael Kaufman (New York: Routledge, 1994), 119–141.

Chapter 27 Trying to transform men is not a futile exercise, but it is slow and difficult work

1 Botho Molosankwe, 'Mom Tells of Lesbian's Horror Death', *IOL*, 30 December 2013, https://www.iol.co.za/news/mom-tells-of-lesbians-horror-death-1541081; *News24*, 'Duduzile Zozo Killer Sentenced to 30 Years in Prison', 26 November 2014, https://www.news24.com/News24/Duduzile-Zozo-killer-gets-30-years-in-prison-20150430; Chanel September, 'The Anene Booysen Story', *EWN*, 1 November 2013, https://ewn.co.za/2013/10/31/The-Anene-Booysen-Story. Even the United Nations was moved to condemn the gruesome murder of Anene Booysen – see United Nations Information Centre Pretoria, 'United Nations Strongly Condemns the Rape and Murder of Anene Booysen', *News & Media*, 13 February 2013, https://archive.is/20130416012306/http://pretoria.unic.org/news-a-media/1-latest/2074-united-nations-strongly-con-demns-the-rape-and-murder-of-anene-booysen-#selection-423.1-455.34.

2 Republic of South Africa, *National Strategic Plan*.

3 Republic of South Africa, *National Strategic Plan*, 45.

4 Patriarchal beliefs do inhere in women too, to be sure, and women who raise or educate boys also need anti-patriarchal education if they are to embrace vulner-ability as a positive character element in masculinity.

5 Brittany Everitt-Penhale and Kopano Ratele, 'Rethinking "Traditional Masculinity" as Constructed, Multiple, and ≠ Hegemonic Masculinity', *South African Review of Sociology* 46, no. 2 (2015): 4–22; Kopano Ratele, 'Masculinities Without Tradition', *Politikon* 40, no. 1 (2013): 133–156.

6 hooks, *Will to Change*, 114.

7 hooks, *Will to Change*, 114.

8 Biko, *I Write What I Like*.

9 We should also ask why some women love women who hurt them, and why some men love women or men who hurt them.

10 Jacqueline Rainers, 'What If Your Boyfriend Is a Rapist?', *City Press*, 7 March 2021, accessed 22 October 2021, https://www.news24.com/citypress/voices/what-if-your-boyfriend-is-a-rapist-20210307.

11 For example, Ismael Loinaz, Isabel Marzabal and Antonio Andrés-Pueyo, 'Risk Factors of Female Intimate Partner and Non-Intimate Partner Homicides', *European Journal of Psychology Applied to Legal Context* 10, no. 2 (2018): 49–55, https://doi.org/10.5093/ejpalc2018a4; Sanyukta Mathur et al., 'High Rates of Sexual Violence by Both Intimate and Nonintimate Partners Experienced by Adolescent Girls and Young Women in Kenya and Zambia: Findings Around

Violence and Other Negative Health Outcomes', *PLoS ONE* 13, no. 9 (2018): e0203929; World Health Organization, *Global and Regional Estimates of Violence Against Women: Prevalence and Health Effects of Intimate Partner Violence and Non-Partner Sexual Violence* (Geneva: World Health Organization, 2013).

12 Kopano Ratele, Rebecca Helman and Pascal Richardson, 'Attitudes on Gender Equality and Inequality among Parents in South Africa', in *State of South Africa's Fathers 2021*, ed. Wessel van den Berg, Tawanda Makusha and Kopano Ratele (Cape Town and Stellenbosch: Sonke Gender Justice, Human Sciences Research Council and Stellenbosch University, 2021), 134–137.

13 World Bank, 'The World Bank in South Africa: Overview', 2019, accessed 22 October 2021, https://www.worldbank.org/en/country/southafrica/overview#:~:text=South%20Africa%20remains%20a%20dual,increased%20from%20 0.61%20in%201996.

14 World Bank, 'World Bank in South Africa'.

Chapter 28 A few key ideas to consider when thinking about men and changing masculinity

1 Samuel Paul Veissière, 'The Real Problem with "Toxic Masculinity": Why Our Culture Needs Strong and Nuanced Gender Archetypes', *Psychology Today*, 16 February 2018, https://www.psychologytoday.com/us/blog/culture-mind-and-brain/201802/the-real-problem-toxic-masculinity.

2 Sam de Boise, 'Editorial: Is Masculinity Toxic?' *NORMA: International Journal for Masculinity Studies* 14, no. 3 (2019): 147–151, https://doi.org./10.1080/1890213 8.2019.1654742.

3 Mark Follman, 'Armed and Misogynist: How Toxic Masculinity Fuels Mass Shootings', *Mother Jones*, May/June 2019, https://www.motherjones.com/crime-justice/2019/06/domestic-violence-misogyny-incels-mass-shootings/; Phillip Reese, 'When Masculinity Turns "Toxic": A Gender Profile of Mass Shootings', *Los Angeles Times*, 7 October 2019, https://www.latimes.com/science/story/2019-10-07/mass-shootings-toxic-masculinity.

4 Miriam J. Abelson, *Men in Place: Trans Masculinity, Race, and Sexuality in America* (Minneapolis: University of Minnesota Press, 2019); Robin Bauer, 'Desiring Masculinities while Desiring to Question Masculinity? How Embodied Masculinities Are Renegotiated in Les-Bi-Trans-Queer BDSM Practices', *NORMA: International Journal for Masculinity Studies* 11, no. 4 (2019): 237–254; Esethu Monakali and Dennis A. Francis, '"I Get Fire Inside Me That Tells Me I'm Going to Defy": The Discursive Construction of Trans Masculinity in Cape Town, South Africa', *Men and Masculinities*, 29 December 2020, https://doi.org/1 0.1177%2F1097184X20982025.

5 Serena Owusua Dankwa, '"The One Who First Says I Love You": Same-Sex Love and Female Masculinity in Postcolonial Ghana', *Ghana Studies* 14, no. 1 (2011): 223–264; Halberstam, *Female Masculinity*; Yu-Ying Hu, 'Mainstreaming Female Masculinity, Signifying Lesbian Visibility: The Rise of the *Zhongxing*

Phenomenon in Transnational Taiwan', *Sexualities* 22, no. 1–2 (2019): 182–202, https://journals.sagepub.com/doi/full/10.1177/1363460717701690.

6   Sandy Lazarus, Susanne Tonsing, Kopano Ratele and Ashley van Niekerk, 'Masculinity as a Key Risk and Protective Factor to Male Interpersonal Violence: An Exploratory and Critical Review', *African Safety Promotion: A Journal of Injury and Violence Prevention* 9, no. 1 (2011): 23–50.

7   Raymond M. Bergner, 'What Is Behavior? And So What?' *New Ideas in Psychology* 29, no. 2 (2011): 154.

8   Brown, *Oxford English Dictionary*, 476.

9   Tim Carrigan, Bob Connell and John Lee, 'Toward a New Sociology of Masculinity', *Theory and Society* 14, no. 5 (1985): 551–604; Raewyn Connell and James W. Messerschmidt, 'Hegemonic Masculinity: Rethinking the Concept', *Gender & Society* 19, no. 6 (2005): 836.

10 Ratele, 'Hegemonic African Masculinities'.

11 Raewyn Connell, *Masculinities* (Berkeley: University of California Press, 2005).

Chapter 29   The politician told students you can't ask for money from somebody who raped you

1   Esther Lewis and Andisiwe Makinana, 'Accuser "Enjoyed Sex with Zuma"', *IOL*, 23 January 2009, accessed 16 January 2022, https://www.iol.co.za/news/politics/accuser-enjoyed-sex-with-zuma-432215; Sonke Gender Justice, 'Khwezi Enjoyed It – the Words that Haunt Malema', 9 August 2016, accessed 16 January 2022, https://genderjustice.org.za/news-item/khwezi-enjoyed-words-haunt-malema/.

2   Julia R. Schwendinger and Herman Schwendinger, 'Rape Myths: In Legal, Theoretical, and Everyday Practice', *Crime and Social Justice* 1 (Spring/Summer 1974): 18–26.

3   Martha R. Burt, 'Cultural Myths and Supports for Rape', *Journal of Personality and Social Psychology* 38, no. 2 (1980): 217.

4   Kimberly A. Lonsway and Louise F. Fitzgerald, 'Rape Myths', *Psychology of Women Quarterly* 18, no. 2 (1994): 134 (emphasis in the original).

5   Susan Brownmiller, *Against Our Will: Men, Women and Rape* (New York: Ballantine Books, 1975).

6   Brownmiller, *Against Our Will*, 311–312.

7   *News24*, 'Malema: I'm Very Sorry About Remarks', *IOL*, 23 June 2011, https://www.news24.com/News24/Malema-Im-very-sorry-about-remarks-20110623; SAPA (South African Press Association), 'Malema Says Sorry for Sexist Remarks', *TimesLive*, 23 June 2011, https://www.timeslive.co.za/news/south-africa/2011-06-23-malema-says-sorry-for-sexist-remarks/; David Smith, 'South African Court Finds ANC's Julius Malema Guilty of Hate Speech', *The Guardian*, 15 March 2010, https://www.theguardian.com/world/2010/mar/15/anc-julius-malema-guilty-hate-speech.

8   Brownmiller, *Against Our Will*, 312–313.

9   Rebecca Helman, 'Reattributing Shame as an Act of Social Justice', *Mail & Guardian Thought Leader*, 9 April 2019, https://thoughtleader.co.za/reattributing-shame-as-an-act-of-social-justice/.

Chapter 30 'Dad, look at me'

1   Sigmund Freud, 'Three Essays on the Theory of Sexuality', in *The Standard Edition of the Complete Psychological Works of Sigmund Freud, Vol. 7 (1901–1905): A Case of Hysteria, Three Essays on Sexuality and Other Works* (London: Vintage, 2001), 156–157.

2   Frantz Fanon, *Black Skin, White Masks*, trans. Charles Lam Markmann (New York: Grove Press, 1967[1952]), 84. 'Negro' (alongside boy, son, Ratele, *kwedini*, man, *monna*) is one of the many words of endearment I use toward Ketso, my child.

Chapter 31 'I have never hit a woman' gets you no loving man award

1   Kruger, *Of Motherhood and Melancholia*, 105 (my emphasis).

2   Iavan Pijoos, '"I Know You Don't Want This Child But I Can't Abort Again": Tshegofatso Pule to Shoba', *TimesLive*, 22 April 2021, https://www.timeslive. co.za/news/south-africa/2021-04-22-i-know-you-dont-want-this-child-but-i-cant-abort-again-tshegofatso-pule-to-shoba/.

3   Kgomotso Modise, 'Ntuthuko Shoba Found Guilty of Killing Tshegofatso Pule', *EWN*, 25 March 2022, https://ewn.co.za/2022/03/25/shoba-found-guilty-of-killing-tshegofatso-pule.

Chapter 32 Before death, before conception, in the many in-between moments, then repeat

1   The first iteration of this piece was published in *TimesLive* in September 2012 after the publication of that year's crime statistics. For the original version, see Kopano Ratele, 'What the Latest Police Statistics Don't Tell You About Murder', *TimesLive*, 25 September 2012, https://www.timeslive.co.za/ideas/2012-09-25-what-the-latest-police-statistics-dont-tell-you-about-murder-ilive/. This reflection is a major revision.

2   South African Police Service, 'Analysis of the National Crime Statistics: Addendum to the Annual Report 2011–2012', compiled by SAPS Strategic Management (Pretoria: South African Police Service, 2012), https://www.saps. gov.za/about/stratframework/annual_report/2011_2012/saps_crime_stats_report_%202011-12.pdf.

3   South African Police Service, 'SAPS Crimestats'.

4   Marie Rosenkrantz Lindegaard, 'Homicide in South Africa', in *The Handbook of Homicide*, ed. Fiona Brookman, Edward R. Maguire and Mike Maguire (Chichester: John Wiley & Sons, 2017), 499–514; Mohamed Seedat, Ashley van Niekerk, Rachel Jewkes, Shahnaaz Suffla and Kopano Ratele, 'Violence and Injuries in South Africa: Prioritising an Agenda for Prevention', *The Lancet* 374, no. 9694 (2009): 1011–1022; Lu-Anne Swart, Sherianne Kramer, Kopano Ratele and Mohamed Seedat, 'Non-Experimental Research Designs: Investigating the Spatial Distribution and Social Ecology of Male Homicide', in *Transforming*

Research Methods in the Social Sciences, ed. Sumaya Laher, Angelo Fynn and Sherianne Kramer (Johannesburg: Wits University Press, 2019), 19–35.
5   *BBC News*, 'Four Minnesota Police Officers Fired after Death of Unarmed Black Man', 27 May 2020, https://www.bbc.com/news/world-us-canada-52806572.

Chapter 33   Baldwin was a full man

1   Teju Cole, 'Black Body: Rereading James Baldwin's "Stranger in the Village"', *New Yorker*, 19 August 2014, https://www.newyorker.com/books/page-turner/black-body-re-reading-james-baldwins-stranger-village.
2   James Baldwin, 'My Dungeon Shook: Letter to My Nephew on the One Hundredth Anniversary of the Emancipation', in *The Fire Next Time* (London: Penguin, 1964), 11–18.
3   C.L.R. James, *The Black Jacobins: Toussaint L'Ouverture and the San Domingo Revolution* (New York: Vintage, 1989 [1938]), 290.

Chapter 34   The masculinity of a man who is a boy

1   As far as I understand it, *botho* urges respect for people who are older than one-self, not merely because they are older, but because, usually, within the contexts in which people lived in the past, they had survived, accumulated experience, supported younger ones, treated others with dignity, developed wisdom and so earned respect.
2   Thando Mgqolozana, *A Man Who Is Not a Man* (Cape Town: Abantu Publishing, 2018).
3   See Yanga Sibembe, 'Apartheid Museum Debate Investigates the Black Body as a Site of Oppression', *Daily Maverick*, 22 March 2019, https://www.dailymaverick.co.za/article/2019-03-22-apartheid-museum-debate-investigates-the-black-body-as-a-site-of-oppression/.
4   Earlier I spoke about women who are 'unrapable'. Uninjurability and unrapability are part of the same fabric, if not two instances of the same phenomenon: how the harm other people experience is conceived.
5   Sophie Trawalter, Kelly M. Hoffman and Adam Waytz, 'Racial Bias in Perceptions of Others' Pain', *PLoS ONE* 7, no. 11: e48546, https://doi.org/10.1371/journal.pone.0048546.
6   Phillip Atiba Goff, Jennifer L. Eberhardt, Melissa J. Williams and Matthew Christian Jackson, 'Not Yet Human: Implicit Knowledge, Historical Dehumanization, and Contemporary Consequences', *Journal of Personality and Social Psychology* 94, no. 2 (2008): 292–306.
7   Susan Opotow, 'Moral Exclusion and Injustice: An Introduction', *Journal of Social Issues* 46, no. 1 (1990): 1–20.

Chapter 35   Mr President, end patriarchy?

1   Republic of South Africa, *National Strategic Plan*, 2.
2   Republic of South Africa, *National Strategic Plan*.

3 Cyril Ramaphosa, 'Political Overview by President Cyril Ramaphosa', ANC National Executive Committee Meeting, 7 December 2020, 8 (emphasis mine), https://cisp.cachefly.net/assets/articles/attachments/84207_201206_nec_political_overview_final.pdf.

4 For example, Patrick Dintwa, 'A North West ANC Councillor Accused of Rape Suspended', *SABC News*, 31 July 2021, https://www.sabcnews.com/sabcnews/a-north-west-anc-councillor-accused-of-rape-suspended/; *Health-e News*, 'Reinstatement of ANC Member Accused of Raping 8-Year-Old Daughters Shocks Country', 25 November 2020, https://health-e.org.za/2020/11/25/anc-mpumalanga-rape-case/; Ntebatse Masipa, 'ANC Official Accused of Rape', *Daily Sun*, 4 January 2021, https://www.dailysun.co.za/News/anc-official-accused-of-rape-20210104.

5 For example, Lebogang Seale, 'SA Not Ready for Female President – ANCWL', *IOL*, 9 October 2013, https://www.iol.co.za/news/politics/sa-not-ready-for-female-president-ancwl-1589121; Staff Reporter, 'ANCWL Reiterates Support for Zuma', *Mail & Guardian*, 13 April 2016, https://mg.co.za/article/2016-04-13-ancwl-reiterates-support-for-president-zuma/.

6 National Planning Commission, *National Development Plan 2030: Our Future – Make It Work* (Pretoria: The Presidency, 2011).

7 bell hooks, *Feminist Theory: From Margin to Center* (London: Routledge, 2015), 118–119.

8 See Jodi Williams, 'Militarisation – Our New Response to Societal Issues', *Daily Maverick*, 15 November 2017, https://www.dailymaverick.co.za/article/2017-11-15-op-ed-militarisation-our-new-response-to-societal-issues/.

9 Pumza Fihlani, 'Are South African Police Trigger-happy?', *BBC News*, 12 November 2009, http://news.bbc.co.uk/2/hi/africa/8354961.stm.

10 *BBC News*, 'South Africa Police on Trial for Ficksburg Murder', 23 April 2012, https://www.bbc.com/news/world-africa-17814472; Beauregard Tromp, Angelique Serrao and SAPA (South African Press Association), 'Tatane Was "Shot Dead"', *IOL*, 18 April 2011, https://www.iol.co.za/capeargus/tatane-was-shot-dead-1058200.

11 *BBC News*, 'South Africa's Lonmin Marikana Mine Clashes Killed 34', 17 August 2012, https://www.bbc.com/news/world-africa-19292909; Mandy de Waal, 'Marikana: What Really Happened? We May Never Know', *Daily Maverick*, 23 August 2012, https://www.dailymaverick.co.za/article/2012-08-23-marikana-what-really-happened-we-may-never-know/.

12 South African History Online, 'Marikana Massacre: 16 August 2012', 16 August 2013, https://www.sahistory.org.za/article/marikana-massacre-16-august-2012#:~:text=On%2016%20August%202012%2C%20the,of%20the%20miners%20were%20arrested.

13 Piet Rampedi, Karabo Ngoepe and Manyane Manyane, 'SA Lockdown: Soldiers Accused of Beating Alexandra Man to Death with Sjambok', *IOL*, 12 April 2020, https://www.iol.co.za/sundayindependent/news/

sa-lockdown-soldiers-accused-of-beating-alexandra-man-to-death-with-sjambok-46619454.

14   Gareth Newham, 'Arresting a Few Policemen Will Not Solve South Africa's Violent Policing Problem', *ISS Today*, 18 April 2011, https://issafrica.org/amp/iss-today/arresting-a-few-policemen-will-not-solve-south-africas-violent-policing-problem.

15   Republic of South Africa, 'Proclamation No. 3'.

16   Michael A. Diamond and Seth Allcorn, *Private Selves in Public Organizations* (New York: Palgrave Macmillan, 2009); Michael Eigen, 'Moral Violence: Space, Time, Causality, Definition', *Journal of Melanie Klein and Object Relations* 13, no. 1 (1995): 37–45.

17   Michael P. Johnson, 'Patriarchal Terrorism and Common Couple Violence: Two Forms of Violence Against Women', *Journal of Marriage and the Family* 57 (May 1995): 283–294.

Chapter 36 When work gets in the way of emotional connections

1   Statistics South Africa, *Statistical Release P0211: Quarterly Labour Force Survey Quarter 4: 2010* (Pretoria: Statistics South Africa, 2011).

2   Statistics South Africa, *Quarterly Labour Force Survey Quarter 4: 2010.*

3   Statistics South Africa, *Statistical Release P0211: Quarterly Labour Force Survey Quarter 4: 2014* (Pretoria: Statistics South Africa, 2015).

4   Statistics South Africa, *Statistical Release P0211: Quarterly Labour Force Survey Quarter 4: 2019* (Pretoria: Statistics South Africa, 2020).

5   See David Graeber, 'On the Phenomenon of Bullshit Jobs: A Workplace Rant', *Strike* 3 (August 2013), https://www.strike.coop/bullshit-jobs/; David Graeber, *Bullshit Jobs* (New York: Simon & Schuster, 2018).

6   hooks, *Will to Change*, 94.

Chapter 37 Love cannot escape power

1   Martin Luther King Jr, 'Black Power', in *Where Do We Go from Here: Chaos or Community?* (Boston: Beacon Press, 1968), 38.

2   For example, see Gary Barker, Cristine Ricardo, Marcos Nascimento and World Health Organization, *Engaging Men and Boys in Changing Gender-Based Inequity in Health: Evidence from Programme Interventions* (Geneva: World Health Organization, 2007); Michael Flood and Richard Howson, eds., *Engaging Men in Building Gender Equality* (Newcastle upon Tyne: Cambridge Scholars Publishing, 2015); Dean Peacock and Gary Barker, 'Working with Men and Boys to Prevent Gender-Based Violence: Principles, Lessons Learned, and Ways Forward', *Men and Masculinities* 17, no. 5 (2014): 578–599; World Health Organization, *Policy Approaches to Engaging Men and Boys in Achieving Gender Equality and Health Equity* (Geneva: World Health Organization, 2010).

3   Kopano Ratele, 'Working Through Resistance in Engaging Boys and Men Towards Gender Equality and Progressive Masculinities', *Culture, Health &*

Sexuality 17, suppl. no. 2 (2015): 144–158; Kopano Ratele, Ravi Verma, Salvador Cruz and Anisur Rahman Khan, 'Engaging Men to Support Women in Science, Medicine, and Global Health', *The Lancet* 393, no. 10171 (2019): 609–610; Tamara Shefer, Jeff Hearn, Kopano Ratele and Floretta Boonzaier, eds., *Engaging Youth in Activism, Research and Pedagogical Praxis: Transnational and Intersectional Perspectives on Gender, Sex and Race* (New York: Routledge, 2018).

4   The right (masculinity) stuff references *The Right Stuff*, an American film directed by Philip Kaufman, based on the book of the same title by Tom Wolfe, that tells the story of the US military pilots who were involved in aeronautical research and the first human flights into space. Philip Kaufman, dir., *The Right Stuff* (distributed by Warner Brothers, 1983); Tom Wolfe, *The Right Stuff* (New York: Farrar, Straus and Giroux, 1979).

5   Connell, *The Men and the Boys*.

Chapter 38   What's up with all this attention given to boys?

1   Gqola, *Rape*, 66.

2   Tania Branigan, 'China's Great Gender Crisis', *The Guardian*, 2 November 2011, https://www.theguardian.com/world/2011/nov/02/chinas-great-gender-crisis; Sundari Ravindran, 'Health Implications of Sex Discrimination in Childhood: A Review Paper and an Annotated Bibliography' (Geneva: World Health Organization and United Nations Children's Fund, 1986).

3   For example, I never understood *for myself* why the practice called *ukuthwala* – kidnapping a woman to be married without her consent – practised in certain cultures in our country might have been instituted; that is to say, until I realised that there is nothing to be understood about the practice, as it is simply patriarchal entitlement by men over women's bodies, as well as over their reproductive and unpaid economic labour.

Chapter 39   Without showing boys how to love, how will they become loving men?

1   Statistics South Africa, *General Household Survey, 2018: Statistical Release P0318* (Pretoria: Statistics South Africa, 2019).

2   Statistics South Africa, *General Household Survey, 2019: Statistical Release P0318* (Pretoria: Statistics South Africa, 2020).

3   Statistics South Africa, *General Household Survey, 2018*.

4   Statistics South Africa, *General Household Survey, 2019*.

5   Katherine Hall, 'Demography of South Africa's Children', in *South African Child Gauge 2019*, ed. Maylene Shung-King, Lori Lake, David Sanders and Michael Hendricks (Cape Town: Children's Institute, University of Cape Town, 2019), 216–220.

6   hooks, *Will to Change*, 2.

7   For example, Katherine Hall, 'Demography of South Africa's Children', in *South African Child Gauge 2020*, ed. Julian May, Chantell Witten and Lori Lake (Cape

Town: Children's Institute, University of Cape Town, 2020), 156–158; Statistics
South Africa, *General Household Survey, 2019*; Van den Berg and Makusha, *State of
South Africa's Fathers 2018*.

8   Michael Chabon, *Manhood for Amateurs* (London: Fourth Estate, 2009), 12.

9   See, for example, Shauna M. Cooper, 'Associations between Father–Daughter
Relationship Quality and the Academic Engagement of African American
Adolescent Girls: Self-Esteem as a Mediator?' *Journal of Black Psychology* 35, no. 4
(2009): 495–516; Franklin B. Krohn and Zoe Bogan, 'The Effects Absent Fathers
Have on Female Development and College Attendance', *College Student Journal*
35, no. 4 (2001): 598–609; Linda Nielsen, 'College Daughters' Relationships with
their Fathers: A 15 Year Study', *College Student Journal* 41, no. 1 (2007): 112–122.

10   Freud, 'The Ego and the Id', 31.

11   Agence France-Presse, 'Eight South African Policemen Guilty of Murdering
Taxi Driver', *The Guardian*, 25 August 2015, https://www.theguard-
ian.com/world/2015/aug/25/eight-south-african-policemen-guilty-
of-murdering-taxi-driver; Faranaaz Parker, 'Cops Drag Man to His
Death – for Stopping Traffic', *Mail & Guardian*, 1 March 2013, https://mg.co.za/
article/2013-03-01-00-cops-drag-man-to-his-death-for-stopping-traffic/.

12   September, 'The Anene Booysen Story'.

Chapter 40 Inheriting and passing down a loving masculinity

1   Percy Zvomuya, 'Mad, Bad, Breathtaking Balotelli', *Mail & Guardian*, 9–14 December 2011, https://mg.co.za/article/2011-12-09-mad-bad-breathtaking-
balotelli/.

2   There are many examples that highlight the contribution of genetics and the environment as they relate to identity. Most of these involve adopted children who
go on to live ordinary lives in the countries of their adoptive parents. Some of
these examples, like Balotelli and Mo Farah, are more famous than others. When
Farah was running in the Olympics in the United Kingdom, his story was told
as a 'British' success story; see, for example, *BBC Sport*, 'Mo Farah Seals Second
Olympic Gold with 5,000m Win', 11 August 2012, https://www.bbc.com/sport/av/
olympics/19228975. (I thank Carli Coetzee for reminding me of Farah's story.)

3   On the inheritance of traditions, see Mona DeKoven Fishbane, '"Honor Your
Father and Your Mother": Intergenerational Values and Jewish Tradition', in
Spiritual Resources in Family Therapy, ed. Froma Walsh (New York: Guilford
Press, 2009), 174–193; Stephen G. Gilles, 'On Educating Children: A Parentalist
Manifesto', *University of Chicago Law Review* 63, no. 3 (1996): 937–1034; Yen Le
Espiritu, '"We Don't Sleep Around Like White Girls Do": Family, Culture, and
Gender in Filipina American Lives', *Signs: Journal of Women in Culture and Society*
26, no. 2 (2001): 415–440; Ratele, 'Masculinities Without Tradition'.

Bibliography

Abelson, Miriam J. *Men in Place: Trans Masculinity, Race, and Sexuality in America.* Minneapolis: University of Minnesota Press, 2019.

Adichie, Chimamanda Ngozi. *Dear Ijeawele, or a Feminist Manifesto in Fifteen Suggestions.* London: Fourth Estate, 2017.

Adler, Seymour. 'Maslow's Need Hierarchy and the Adjustment of Immigrants'. *International Migration Review* 11, no. 4 (1977): 444–451.

Adu-Poku, Samuel. 'Envisioning (Black) Male Feminism: A Cross-Cultural Perspective'. *Journal of Gender Studies* 10, no. 2 (2001): 157–167.

Agence France-Presse. 'Eight South African Policemen Guilty of Murdering Taxi Driver'. *The Guardian*, 25 August 2015. https://www.theguardian.com/world/2015/aug/25/eight-south-african-policemen-guilty-of-murdering-taxi-driver.

Allen, Sarah and Nakamori Yasufumi, eds. *Zanele Muholi.* London: Tate Publishing, 2020.

Allen, Susan M. 'Gender Differences in Spousal Caregiving and Unmet Need for Care'. *Journal of Gerontology* 49, no. 4 (1994): S187–S195.

Azania Rising Productions and Just Detention International–South Africa. *Taking Off the Mask.* Accessed 14 February 2022. https://www.youtube.com/watch?v=VBsLIEXQOFs.

Baldwin, James. 'My Dungeon Shook: Letter to My Nephew on the One Hundredth Anniversary of the Emancipation'. In *The Fire Next Time*, 11–18. London: Penguin, 1964.

Barker, Gary, Cristine Ricardo, Marcos Nascimento and World Health Organization. *Engaging Men and Boys in Changing Gender-Based Inequity in Health: Evidence from Programme Interventions.* Geneva: World Health Organization, 2007.

Barnett, Ola W. and Alyce D. LaViolette. *It Could Happen to Anyone: Why Battered Women Stay.* New Delhi: Sage Publications, 1993.

Bauer, Robin. 'Desiring Masculinities while Desiring to Question Masculinity? How Embodied Masculinities Are Renegotiated in Les-Bi-Trans-Queer BDSM Practices'. *NORMA: International Journal for Masculinity Studies* 11, no. 4 (2019): 237–254.

BBC News. 'Four Minnesota Police Officers Fired after Death of Unarmed Black Man', 27 May 2020. https://www.bbc.com/news/world-us-canada-52806572.

BBC News. 'South Africa Police on Trial for Ficksburg Murder', 23 April 2012. https://www.bbc.com/news/world-africa-17814472.

BBC News. 'South Africa's Lonmin Marikana Mine Clashes Killed 34', 17 August 2012. https://www.bbc.com/news/world-africa-19292909.

BBC Sport. 'Mo Farah Seals Second Olympic Gold with 5,000m Win', 11 August 2012. https://www.bbc.com/sport/av/olympics/19228975.

Beaubien, Jason. 'Africa Is Running Out of Oxygen'. NPR, 24 June 2021. https://www.npr.org/sections/goatsandsoda/2021/06/24/1009475339/africa-is-running-out-of-oxygen.

Beechey, Veronica. 'On Patriarchy'. *Feminist Review* 3, no. 1 (1979): 66–82.

Bergner, Raymond M. 'What Is Behavior? And So What?' *New Ideas in Psychology* 29, no. 2 (2011): 147–155.

Bhana, Deevia and Rob Pattman. 'Girls Want Money, Boys Want Virgins: The Materiality of Love Amongst South African Township Youth in the Context of HIV And AIDS'. *Culture, Health & Sexuality* 13, no. 8 (2011): 961–972.

Biko, Steve. *I Write What I Like*. Johannesburg: Picador Africa, 2004.

Billig, Michael. *Freudian Repression: Conversation Creating the Unconscious*. Cambridge: Cambridge University Press, 1999.

Billig, Michael. 'Studying Repression in a Changing World'. *European Journal of School Psychology* 1, no. 1 (2003): 37–42.

Borochowitz, Dalit Yassour and Zvi Eisikovits. 'To Love Violently: Strategies for Reconciling Love and Violence'. *Violence Against Women* 8, no. 4 (2002): 476–494.

Bowleg, Lisa. 'Love, Sex, and Masculinity in Sociocultural Context: HIV Concerns and Condom Use among African American Men in Heterosexual Relationships'. *Men and Masculinities* 7, no. 2 (2004): 166–186.

Branigan, Tania. 'China's Great Gender Crisis'. *The Guardian*, 2 November 2011. https://www.theguardian.com/world/2011/nov/02/chinas-great-gender-crisis.

Brown, Alrick, dir. *Kinyarwanda*. Independent Filmmaker Labs. Premiered at Sundance Film Festival 2011. Accessed 23 January 2022. https://africa.film/kinyarwanda-an-alrick-brown-feature-film/.

Brown, Lesley, ed. *The New Shorter Oxford English Dictionary on Historical Principles*. Oxford: Clarendon Press, 1993.

Brownmiller, Susan. *Against Our Will: Men, Women and Rape*. New York: Ballantine Books, 1975.

Burt, Martha R. 'Cultural Myths and Supports for Rape'. *Journal of Personality and Social Psychology* 38, no. 2 (1980): 217–230.

Buss, Allan R. 'Humanistic Psychology as Liberal Ideology: The Socio-Historical Roots of Maslow's Theory of Self-Actualization'. *Journal of Humanistic Psychology* 19, no. 3 (1979): 43–55.

Carrigan, Tim, Bob Connell and John Lee. 'Toward a New Sociology of Masculinity'. *Theory and Society* 14, no. 5 (1985): 551–604.

Chabon, Michael. *Manhood for Amateurs*. London: Fourth Estate, 2009.

Chimbelu, Chiponda. 'What's Life Really Like for Black People in Germany?' *DW*, 25 April 2020. https://www.dw.com/en/whats-life-really-like-for-black-people-in-germany/a-53159443.

Clowes, Lindsay. 'The Limits of Discourse: Masculinity as Vulnerability'. *Agenda* 27, no. 1 (2013): 12–19.

Cole, Teju. 'Black Body: Rereading James Baldwin's "Stranger in the Village"'. *New Yorker*, 19 August 2014. https://www.newyorker.com/books/page-turner/black-body-re-reading-james-baldwins-stranger-village.

Comas-Díaz, Lillian. 'Cultural Variation in the Therapeutic Relationship'. In *Evidence-Based Psychotherapy: Where Practice and Research Meet*, edited by Carol D. Goodheart, Alan E. Kazdin and Robert J. Sternberg, 81–105. Washington, DC: American Psychological Association, 2006.

Connell, Raewyn. *Masculinities*. Berkeley: University of California Press, 2005.

Connell, Raewyn. *The Men and the Boys*. Oxford: Polity Press, 2000.

Connell, Raewyn and James W. Messerschmidt. 'Hegemonic Masculinity: Rethinking the Concept'. *Gender & Society* 19, no. 6 (2005): 829–859.

Cooper, Shauna M. 'Associations between Father–Daughter Relationship Quality and the Academic Engagement of African American Adolescent Girls: Self-Esteem as a Mediator?' *Journal of Black Psychology* 35, no. 4 (2009): 495–516.

Crenshaw, Kimberlé. 'Demarginalizing the Intersections of Race and Sex: A Black Feminist Critique of Antidiscrimination Doctrine, Feminist Theory and Antiracist Politics'. *University of Chicago Legal Forum* 1 (1989): 139–167.

Crenshaw, Kimberlé. 'Mapping the Margins: Intersectionality, Identity Politics, and Violence Against Women of Color'. *Stanford Law Review* 43, no. 6 (1991): 1241–1299.

Cushman, Philip. 'Why the Self Is Empty: Toward a Historically Situated Psychology'. *American Psychologist* 45, no. 5 (1990): 599–611.

Daintith, John, Elizabeth Martin, Fran Alexander and John Wright, eds. *Bloomsbury Thesaurus*. London: Bloomsbury Publishing, 1993.

Dankwa, Serena Owusua. '"The One Who First Says I Love You": Same-Sex Love and Female Masculinity in Postcolonial Ghana'. *Ghana Studies* 14, no. 1 (2011): 223–264.

Davis, Angela. *Women, Race and Class*. London: Women's Press, 1982.

De Boise, Sam. 'Editorial: Is Masculinity Toxic?' *NORMA: International Journal for Masculinity Studies* 14, no. 3 (2019): 147–151. https://doi.org/10.1080/18902138.2019.1654742.

DeLamater, John D. and Daniel J. Myers. *Social Psychology*. Belmont, CA: Wadsworth Cengage Learning, 2010.

Del Monte, Catherine. 'Beware the Violence of Intimacy: On Consent and Safe Spaces'. *Daily Maverick*, 6 December 2020. https://www.dailymaverick.co.za/article/2020-12-06-beware-the-violence-of-intimacy-on-consent-and-safe-spaces/.

DeShong, Halimah. 'Gender Discourses of Romantic Loving and Violence'. In *Doing Gender, Doing Love: Interdisciplinary Voices*, edited by Serena Petrella, 103–122. Oxford: Inter-Disciplinary Press, 2014.

De Waal, Mandy. 'Marikana: What Really Happened? We May Never Know'. *Daily Maverick*, 23 August 2012. https://www.dailymaverick.co.za/article/2012-08-23-marikana-what-really-happened-we-may-never-know/.

Diamond, Michael A. and Seth Allcorn. *Private Selves in Public Organizations*. New York: Palgrave Macmillan, 2009.

Dintwa, Patrick. 'A North West ANC Councillor Accused of Rape Suspended'. *SABC News*, 31 July 2021. https://www.sabcnews.com/sabcnews/a-north-west-anc-councillor-accused-of-rape-suspended/.

Eigen, Michael. 'Moral Violence: Space, Time, Causality, Definition'. *Journal of Melanie Klein and Object Relations* 13, no. 1 (1995): 37–45.

Elliott, Karla. 'Caring Masculinities: Theorizing an Emerging Concept'. *Men and Masculinities* 19, no. 3 (2016): 240–259.

Elliott, Karla. 'Challenging Toxic Masculinity in Schools and Society'. *On the Horizon* 26, no. 1 (2018): 17–22.

eNCA. 'Winnie, the Fearless', 2 April 2018. https://www.enca.com/south-africa/winnie-the-fearless.

Erasmus, Des. 'KwaZulu-Natal Residents Living in the Shadow of a Serial Killer'. *City Press*, 6 September, 2020. https://www.news24.com/citypress/news/kwazulu-natal-residents-living-in-the-shadow-of-a-serial-killer-20200906.

Erikson, Erik. *Childhood and Society*. New York: W.W. Norton, 1963.

Everitt-Penhale, Brittany and Kopano Ratele. 'Rethinking "Traditional Masculinity" as Constructed, Multiple, and ≠ Hegemonic Masculinity'. *South African Review of Sociology* 46, no. 2 (2015): 4–22.

Fanon, Frantz. *Black Skin, White Masks*, translated by Charles Lam Markmann. New York: Grove Press, 1967 [1952].

Fihlani, Pumza. 'Are South African Police Trigger-happy?' *BBC News*, 12 November 2009. http://news.bbc.co.uk/2/hi/africa/8354961.stm.

Fishbane, Mona DeKoven. '"Honor Your Father and Your Mother": Intergenerational Values and Jewish Tradition'. In *Spiritual Resources in Family Therapy*, edited by Froma Walsh, 174–193. New York: Guilford Press, 2009.

Flood, Michael and Richard Howson, eds. *Engaging Men in Building Gender Equality*. Newcastle upon Tyne: Cambridge Scholars Publishing, 2015.

Follman, Mark. 'Armed and Misogynist: How Toxic Masculinity Fuels Mass Shootings'. *Mother Jones*, May/June 2019. https://www.motherjones.com/crime-justice/2019/06/domestic-violence-misogyny-incels-mass-shootings/.

Freud, Sigmund. 'The Ego and the Id'. In *The Standard Edition of the Complete Psychological Works of Sigmund Freud, Vol. 19 (1923–1925): The Ego and the Id and Other Works*, 1–66. London: Vintage, 2001.

Freud, Sigmund. 'Short Account of Psycho-Analysis'. In *The Standard Edition of the Complete Psychological Works of Sigmund Freud, Vol. 19 (1923–1925): The Ego and the Id and Other Works*, 189–209. London: Vintage, 2001.

Freud, Sigmund. 'A Special Type of Choice of Object Made by Men: Contribution to the Psychology of Love – 1'. In *The Standard Edition of the Complete Psychological Works of Sigmund Freud, Vol. 11 (1910): Five Lectures on Psycho-Analysis, Leonardo da Vinci and Other Works*, 163–175. London: Vintage, 2001.

Freud, Sigmund. 'Three Essays on the Theory of Sexuality'. In *The Standard Edition of the Complete Psychological Works of Sigmund Freud, Vol. 7 (1901–1905): A Case of Hysteria, Three Essays on Sexuality and Other Works*, 123–245. London: Vintage, 2001.

Frost, Taggart, David V. Stimpson and Micol R.C. Maughan. 'Some Correlates of Trust'. *Journal of Psychology* 99, no. 1 (1978): 103–108. https://doi.org/10.1080/0 0223980.1978.9921447.

Fukuyama, Francis. *Trust: Social Virtues and the Creation of Prosperity*. New York: Simon & Schuster, 1996.

Galtung, Johan. 'Violence, Peace, and Peace Research'. *Journal of Peace Research* 6, no. 3 (1969): 167–191.

Garcia-Moreno, Claudia, Henrica A.F.M. Jansen, Mary Ellsberg, Lori Heise and Charlotte H. Watts. 'Prevalence of Intimate Partner Violence: Findings from the WHO Multi-Country Study on Women's Health and Domestic Violence'. *The Lancet* 368, no. 9543 (2006): 1260–1269.

Geddes, Linda. 'Why Indian Hospitals Are Running Out of Medical Oxygen and How to Fix It'. Gavi: The Vaccine Alliance, 9 May 2021. https://www.gavi.org/vaccineswork/why-indian-hospitals-are-running-out-medical-oxygen-and-how-fix-it.

Giddens, Anthony. *The Transformation of Intimacy: Sexuality, Love and Eroticism in Modern Societies*. Redwood City, CA: Stanford University Press, 1992.

Gilles, Stephen G. 'On Educating Children: A Parentalist Manifesto'. *University of Chicago Law Review* 63, no. 3 (1996): 937–1034.

Ginsburg, Kenneth R. 'The Importance of Play in Promoting Healthy Child Development and Maintaining Strong Parent–Child Bonds'. *Pediatrics* 119, no. 1 (2007): 182–191.

Goff, Phillip Atiba, Jennifer L. Eberhardt, Melissa J. Williams and Matthew Christian Jackson. 'Not Yet Human: Implicit Knowledge, Historical Dehumanization, and Contemporary Consequences'. *Journal of Personality and Social Psychology* 94, no. 2 (2008): 292–306.

Going, Tracy. *Brutal Legacy: A Memoir*. Johannesburg: MF Books Joburg, 2018.

Goldner, Virginia, Peggy Penn, Marcia Sheinberg and Gillian Walker. 'Love and Violence: Gender Paradoxes in Volatile Attachments'. *Family Process* 29, no. 4 (1990): 343–364.

Gqola, Pumla Dineo. *Rape: A South African Nightmare*. Johannesburg: MF Books Joburg, 2015.

Graeber, David. *Bullshit Jobs*. New York: Simon & Schuster, 2018.

Graeber, David. 'On the Phenomenon of Bullshit Jobs: A Work Rant'. *Strike* 3 (August 2013). https://www.strike.coop/bullshit-jobs/.

Halberstam, Judith. *Female Masculinity*. Durham, NC: Duke University Press, 2019.

Hall, Katherine. 'Demography of South Africa's Children'. In *South African Child Gauge 2019*, edited by Maylene Shung-King, Lori Lake, David Sanders and Michael Hendricks, 216–220. Cape Town: Children's Institute, University of Cape Town, 2019.

Hall, Katherine. 'Demography of South Africa's Children'. In *South African Child Gauge 2020*, edited by Julian May, Chantell Witten and Lori Lake, 156–158. Cape Town: Children's Institute, University of Cape Town, 2020.

Harrington, Carol. 'What Is "Toxic Masculinity" and Why Does It Matter?' *Men and Masculinities* 24, no. 2 (2021): 345–352.

Health-e News. 'Reinstatement of ANC Member Accused of Raping 8-Year-Old Daughters Shocks Country', 25 November 2020. https://health-e.org.za/2020/11/25/anc-mpumalanga-rape-case/.

Helman, Rebecca. 'Reattributing Shame as an Act of Social Justice'. *Mail & Guardian Thought Leader*, 9 April 2019. https://thoughtleader.co.za/reattributing-shame-as-an-act-of-social-justice/.

Helman, Rebecca and Kopano Ratele. 'Everyday (In)Equality at Home: Complex Constructions of Gender in South African Families'. *Global Health Action* 9, no. 1 (2016). https://doi.org/10.3402/gha.v9.31122.

Henton, June, Rodney Cate, James Koval, Sally Lloyd and Scott Christopher. 'Romance and Violence in Dating Relationships'. *Journal of Family Issues* 4, no. 3 (1983): 467–482.

Hinsliff, Gaby. 'Let's Not Shy Away from Asking Hard Questions About the Cologne Attacks'. *The Guardian*, 8 January 2016. https://www.theguardian.com/commentisfree/2016/jan/08/cologne-attacks-hard-questions-new-years-eve.

hooks, bell. *Feminist Theory: From Margin to Center*. London: Routledge, 2015.

hooks, bell. *The Will to Change: Men, Masculinity and Love*. New York: Washington Square Press, 2004.

House of Yes. 'About Yes'. Accessed 22 October 2021. https://houseofyes.org/experience./.

Hu, Yu-Ying. 'Mainstreaming Female Masculinity, Signifying Lesbian Visibility: The Rise of the *Zhongxing* Phenomenon in Transnational Taiwan'. *Sexualities* 22, no. 1–2 (2019): 182–202. https://journals.sagepub.com/doi/full/10.1177/1363460717701690.

Hull, Gloria T., Patricia Bell Scott and Barbara Smith, eds. *All the Women Are White, All the Blacks Are Men, But Some of Us Are Brave: Black Women's Studies*. London: Feminist Press, 1982.

Hunter, Sarah C., Damien W. Riggs and Martha Augoustinos. 'Constructions of Primary Caregiving Fathers in Popular Parenting Texts'. *Men and Masculinities* 23, no. 1 (2020): 150–169. https://journals.sagepub.com/doi/10.1177/1097184X17730593.

Hunter, Sarah C., Damien W. Riggs and Martha Augoustinos. 'Hegemonic Masculinity Versus a Caring Masculinity: Implications for Understanding Primary Caregiving Fathers'. *Social and Personality Psychology Compass* 11, no. 3 (2017): e12307. https://onlinelibrary.wiley.com/doi/10.1111/spc3.12307.

Ikard, David and Mark Anthony Neal. 'Introduction: Transforming Black Men in Feminism'. *Palimpsest: A Journal on Women, Gender, and the Black International* 1, no. 2 (2012): vi–ix.

Institute for Economics and Peace. *Global Peace Index 2020: Measuring Peace in a Complex World*. June 2020. https://www.visionofhumanity.org/wp-content/uploads/2020/10/GPI_2020_web.pdf.

Institute for Security Studies. *Crime Hub*. Accessed 20 January 2022. https://issafrica.org/crimehub/facts-and-figures/national-crime.

Interim Steering Committee on Gender-Based Violence and Femicide (ISCGBVF). *Emergency Response Action Plan on Gender-Based Violence and Femicide*. 30 April 2020. http://www.thepresidency.gov.za/documents.

International Monetary Fund. *IMF Country Focus: Six Charts Explain South Africa's Inequality*. 30 January 2020. https://www.imf.org/en/News/Articles/2020/01/29/na012820six-charts-on-south-africas-persistent-and-multi-faceted-inequality.

Jakupcak, Matthew, Matthew T. Tull and Lizabeth Roemer. 'Masculinity, Shame, and Fear of Emotions as Predictors of Men's Expressions of Anger and Hostility'. *Psychology of Men & Masculinity* 6, no. 4 (2005): 275–284.

James, Cyril Lionel Robert (C.L.R.). *The Black Jacobins: Toussaint L'Ouverture and the San Domingo Revolution*. New York: Vintage, 1989 [1938].

Jamieson, Lynn. *Intimacy: Personal Relationships in Modern Societies*. Cambridge: Polity Press, 1998.

Javaid, Aliraza. 'Male Rape, Stereotypes, and Unmet Needs: Hindering Recovery, Perpetuating Silence'. *Violence and Gender* 3, no. 1 (2016): 7–13.

Jewkes, Rachel. 'Intimate Partner Violence: Causes and Prevention'. *The Lancet* 359, no. 9315 (2002): 1423–1429.

Jewkes, Rachel, Kristin Dunkle, Mary P. Koss, Jonathan B. Levin, Mzikazi Nduna, Nwabisa Jama and Yandisa Sikweyiya. 'Rape Perpetration by Young, Rural South African Men: Prevalence, Patterns and Risk Factors'. *Social Science & Medicine* 63, no. 11 (2006): 2949–2961.

Johnson, Lamar L., Nathaniel Bryan and Gloria Boutte. 'Show Us the Love: Revolutionary Teaching in (Un)Critical Times'. *Urban Review* 51, no. 1 (2019): 46–64.

Johnson, Michael P. 'Patriarchal Terrorism and Common Couple Violence: Two Forms of Violence Against Women'. *Journal of Marriage and the Family* 57 (May 1995): 283–294.

José Santos, Sofia. *MenCare in Latin America: Challenging Harmful Masculine Norms and Promoting Positive Changes in Men's Caregiving: EMERGE Case Study 5.* Promundo-US, Sonke Gender Justice and Institute of Development Studies, 2015.

Joubert, Pearlie. 'Men Who Speak with Fists'. *Mail & Guardian*, 19 November 2007. https://mg.co.za/article/2007-11-19-men-who-speak-with-fists/.

Kanagawa, Chie, Susan E. Cross and Hazel Rose Markus. '"Who Am I?" The Cultural Psychology of the Conceptual Self'. *Personality and Social Psychology Bulletin 27*, no. 1 (2001): 90–103.

Kandiyoti, Deniz. 'Bargaining with Patriarchy'. *Gender & Society 2*, no. 3 (1988): 274–290.

Kaufman, Philip, dir. *The Right Stuff.* Distributed by Warner Brothers, 1983.

Keita, Sekou and Helen Dempster. 'Five Years Later, One Million Refugees Are Thriving in Germany'. Center for Global Development, 4 December 2020. https://www.cgdev.org/blog/five-years-later-one-million-refugees-are-thriving-germany.

Kimmel, Michael S. 'Masculinity as Homophobia: Fear, Shame, and Silence in the Construction of Gender Identity'. In *Theorizing Masculinities*, edited by Harry Brod and Michael Kaufman, 119–141. New York: Routledge, 1994.

King Jr, Martin Luther. 'Black Power'. In *Where Do We Go from Here: Chaos or Community?* 23–69. Boston: Beacon Press, 1968.

King Jr, Martin Luther. 'Letter from Birmingham Jail'. *UC Davis Law Review 26*, no. 4 (1993): 835–851.

Krohn, Franklin B. and Zoe Bogan. 'The Effects Absent Fathers Have on Female Development and College Attendance'. *College Student Journal 35*, no. 4 (2001): 598–609.

Krug, Etienne G., James A. Mercy, Linda L. Dahlberg and Anthony B. Zwi, eds. *World Report on Violence and Health.* Geneva: World Health Organization, 2002.

Kruger, Lou-Maré. *Of Motherhood and Melancholia: Notebook of a Psycho-Ethnographer.* Pietermaritzburg: University of KwaZulu-Natal Press, 2020.

Lanas, Maija and Michalinos Zembylas. 'Towards a Transformational Political Concept of Love in Critical Education'. *Studies in Philosophy and Education 34*, no. 1 (2015): 31–44.

Lazarus, Sandy, Susanne Tonsing, Kopano Ratele and Ashley van Niekerk. 'Masculinity as a Key Risk and Protective Factor to Male Interpersonal Violence: An Exploratory and Critical Review'. *African Safety Promotion: A Journal of Injury and Violence Prevention 9*, no. 1 (2011): 23–50.

Lee, Joyce Y. and Shawna J. Lee. 'Caring Is Masculine: Stay-at-Home Fathers and Masculine Identity'. *Psychology of Men & Masculinity 19*, no. 1 (2018): 47–58.

Le Espiritu, Yen. '"We Don't Sleep Around Like White Girls Do": Family, Culture, and Gender in Filipina American Lives'. *Signs: Journal of Women in Culture and Society 26*, no. 2 (2001): 415–440.

Lesch, Elmien and Alberta S. van der Watt. 'Living Single: A Phenomenological Study of a Group of South African Single Women'. *Feminism & Psychology* 28, no. 3 (2018): 390–408.

Levant, Roland F. 'Toward the Reconstruction of Masculinity'. *Journal of Family Psychology* 5, no. 3–4 (1992): 379–402.

Lewis, Esther and Andisiwe Makinana. 'Accuser "Enjoyed Sex with Zuma"'. *IOL*, 23 January 2009. https://www.iol.co.za/news/politics/accuser-enjoyed-sex-with-zuma-432215.

Lindegaard, Marie Rosenkrantz. 'Homicide in South Africa'. In *The Handbook of Homicide*, edited by Fiona Brookman, Edward R. Maguire and Mike Maguire, 499–514. Chichester: John Wiley & Sons, 2017.

Liston, Daniel. 'Love and Despair in Teaching'. *Educational Theory* 50, no. 1 (2000): 81–102.

Loinaz, Ismael, Isabel Marzabal and Antonio Andrés-Pueyo. 'Risk Factors of Female Intimate Partner and Non-Intimate Partner Homicides'. *European Journal of Psychology Applied to Legal Context* 10, no. 2 (2018): 49–55. https://doi.org/10.5093/ejpalc2018a4.

Lonsway, Kimberly A. and Louise F. Fitzgerald. 'Rape Myths'. *Psychology of Women Quarterly* 18, no. 2 (1994): 133–164.

Lorentzen, Jørgen. 'Love and Intimacy in Men's Lives'. *NORA: Nordic Journal of Women's Studies* 15, no. 2–3 (2007): 190–198.

Lowry, Brian. '"CODA" Wins the Oscar in a Streaming Breakthrough, but Will Smith Steals the Show'. *CNN*, 29 March 2022. https//edition.cnn.com/2022/03/27/entertainment/academy-awards-2022/index.html.

Malinga, Mandisa and Kopano Ratele. '"It Has Changed Me from the Person that I Was Before": Love and the Construction of Young Black Masculinities'. In *Doing Gender, Doing Love: Interdisciplinary Voices*, edited by Serena Petrella, 73–101. Oxford: Inter-Disciplinary Press, 2014.

Mama Hope. 'African Men. Hollywood Stereotypes'. YouTube video, 25 April 2012. https://www.youtube.com/watch?v=qSElmEmEjb4&feature=emb_title.

Mama Hope. 'Media on a Mission'. Accessed 22 October 2021. https://www.mama-hope.org/media/.

Mangena, Mosibudi. *We Can Fix Ourselves: Building a Better South Africa Through Black Consciousness*. Cape Town: Kwela Books, 2021.

Marziali, Elsa and Leslie Alexander. 'The Power of the Therapeutic Relationship'. *American Journal of Orthopsychiatry* 61, no. 3 (1991): 383–391.

Masipa, Ntebatse. 'ANC Official Accused of Rape'. *Daily Sun*, 4 January 2021. https://www.dailysun.co.za/News/anc-official-accused-of-rape-20210104.

Maslow, Abraham H. 'Deficiency Motivation and Growth Motivation'. *General Semantics Bulletin* 18–19 (1956): 33–42.

Maslow, Abraham H. 'Preface to Motivation Theory'. *Psychosomatic Medicine* 5 (1943): 85–92. https://doi.org/10.1097/00006842-194301000-00012.

Maslow, Abraham H. 'A Theory of Human Motivation'. *Psychological Review* 50, no. 4 (1943): 370–396.

Masters, William H., Virginia E. Johnson and Robert C. Kolodny. *Masters and Johnson on Sex and Human Loving*. 2nd edition. Boston: Little, Brown and Company, 1985.

Mathur, Sanyukta, Jerry Okal, Maurice Musheke, Nanlesta Pilgrim, Sangram Kishor Patel, Ruchira Bhattacharya et al. 'High Rates of Sexual Violence by Both Intimate and Nonintimate Partners Experienced by Adolescent Girls and Young Women in Kenya and Zambia: Findings Around Violence and Other Negative Health Outcomes'. *PLoS ONE* 13, no. 9 (2018): e0203929.

McGuinness, Damien. 'Germany Shocked by Cologne New Year Gang Assaults on Women'. *BBC News*, 5 January 2016. https://www.bbc.com/news/world-europe-35231046.

McNamee, Sheila. 'Radical Presence: Alternatives to the Therapeutic State'. *European Journal of Psychotherapy & Counselling* 17, no. 4 (2015): 373–383.

Meyer, David. 'Corporate Germany Has a Race Problem – and a Lack of Data Is Not Helping'. *Fortune*, 19 June 2020. https://fortune.com/2020/06/19/corporate-germany-race-diversity-data/.

Mgqolozana, Thando. *A Man Who Is Not a Man*. Cape Town: Abantu Publishing, 2018.

Modise, Kgomotso. 'Ntuthuko Shoba Found Guilty of Killing Tshegofatso Pule'. *EWN*, 25 March 2022. https://ewn.co.za/2022/03/25/shoba-found-guilty-of-killing-tshegofatso-pule.

Molosankwe, Botho. 'Mom Tells of Lesbian's Horror Death'. *IOL*, 30 December 2013. https://www.iol.co.za/news/mom-tells-of-lesbians-horror-death-1541081.

Monakali, Esethu and Dennis A. Francis. '"I Get Fire Inside Me that Tells Me I'm Going to Defy": The Discursive Construction of Trans Masculinity in Cape Town, South Africa'. *Men and Masculinities*, 29 December 2020. https://doi.org/10/1177/109 7184X20982025.

Morojele, Pholoho and Ncamsile D. Motsa. 'Vulnerable Masculinities: Implications of Gender Socialisation in Three Rural Swazi Primary Schools'. *South African Journal of Childhood Education* 9, no. 1 (2019): a580. https://sajce.co.za/index.php/sajce/article/view/580.

Morrell, Robert. 'Fathers, Fatherhood and Masculinity in South Africa'. In *Baba: Men and Fatherhood in South Africa*, edited by Linda Richter and Robert Morrell, 13–25. Cape Town: HSRC Press, 2006.

Mousavi, Seyed Hadi and Hossein Dargahi. 'Ethnic Differences and Motivation Based on Maslow's Theory on Iranian Employees'. *Iranian Journal of Public Health* 42, no. 5 (2013): 516–521.

MultiChoice. 'MultiChoice Partners with Government and Civil Society Organizations for GBV Initiative', 6 August 2020. https://www.multichoice.com/media/news/multichoice-partners-with-government-and-civil-society-organizations-for-gbv-initiative.

Nairne, James S. *Psychology: The Adaptive Mind*. Pacific Grove, CA: Brooks/Cole, 1996.

National Department of Health (NDoH), Statistics South Africa (Stats SA), South African Medical Research Council (SAMRC) and ICF. *South Africa Demographic and Health Survey 2016*. Pretoria and Rockville, MD: NDoH, Stats SA, SAMRC and ICF, 2019.

National Planning Commission. *National Development Plan 2030: Our Future – Make It Work*. Pretoria: The Presidency, 2011.

Nazareth, performer. 'Love Hurts'. Written by Felice and Boudleaux Bryant. Accessed 8 January 2022. https://www.youtube.com/watch?v=soDZBW-1P04.

Newham, Gareth. 'Arresting a Few Policemen Will Not Solve South Africa's Violent Policing Problem'. *ISS Today*, 18 April 2011. https://issafrica.org/amp/iss-today/arresting-a-few-policemen-will-not-solve-south-africas-violent-policing-problem.

News24. 'Duduzile Zozo Killer Sentenced to 30 Years in Prison', 26 November 2014. https://www.news24.com/News24/Duduzile-Zozo-killer-gets-30-years-in-prison-20150430.

News24. 'Malema: I'm Very Sorry About Remarks'. *IOL*, 23 June 2011. https://www.news24.com/News24/Malema-Im-very-sorry-about-remarks-20110623.

Nhat Hanh, Thich. *How to Fight*. London: Rider, 2017.

Nhat Hanh, Thich. *How to Love*. London: Rider, 2016.

Nielsen, Linda. 'College Daughters' Relationships with their Fathers: A 15 Year Study'. *College Student Journal* 41, no. 1 (2007): 112–122.

Nussbaum, Martha. *Political Emotions: Why Love Matters for Justice*. Cambridge, MA: Belknap Press, 2013.

Omarjee, Lameez. 'SA's Unemployment Rate Hits Record 34.4%'. *Fin24*, 24 August 2021. https://www.news24.com/fin24/economy/sas-unemployment-rate-hits-record-344-20210824.

Opotow, Susan. 'Moral Exclusion and Injustice: An Introduction'. *Journal of Social Issues* 46, no. 1 (1990): 1–20.

Oyserman, Daphna. 'Self-Concept and Identity'. In *The Blackwell Handbook of Social Psychology*, edited by Abraham Tesser and Norbert Schwarz, 499–517. Malden, MA: Blackwell, 2001.

Parker, Faranaaz. 'Cops Drag Man to His Death – for Stopping Traffic'. *Mail & Guardian*, 1 March 2013. https://mg.co.za/article/2013-03-01-00-cops-drag-man-to-his-death-for-stopping-traffic/.

Parker, Ian. *Psy-Complex in Question: Critical Review in Psychology, Psychoanalysis and Social Theory*. Winchester: Zero Books, 2018.

Peacock, Dean and Gary Barker. 'Working with Men and Boys to Prevent Gender-Based Violence: Principles, Lessons Learned, and Ways Forward'. *Men and Masculinities* 17, no. 5 (2014): 578–599.

Pickens, Chelsea and Virginia Braun. '"Stroppy Bitches Who Just Need to Learn How to Settle"? Young Single Women and Norms of Femininity and Heterosexuality'. *Sex Roles* 79, no. 7 (2018): 431–448. https://doi.org/10.1007/s11199-017-0881-5.

Pijoos, Iavan. '"I Know You Don't Want This Child But I Can't Abort Again": Tshegofatso Pule to Shoba'. *TimesLive*, 22 April 2021. https://www.timeslive.co.za/news/south-africa/2021-04-22-i-know-you-dont-want-this-child-but-i-cant-abort-again-tshegofatso-pule-to-shoba/.

Rainers, Jacqueline. 'What If Your Boyfriend Is a Rapist?' *City Press*, 7 March 2021. https://www.news24.com/citypress/voices/what-if-your-boyfriend-is-a-rapist-20210307.

Ramaphosa, Cyril. 'Political Overview by President Cyril Ramaphosa'. ANC National Executive Committee Meeting, 7 December 2020. https://cisp.cachefly.net/assets/articles/attachments/84207_201206_nec_political_overview_final.pdf.

Rampedi, Piet, Karabo Ngoepe and Manyane Manyane. 'SA Lockdown: Soldiers Accused of Beating Alexandra Man to Death with Sjambok'. *IOL*, 12 April 2020. https://www.iol.co.za/sundayindependent/news/sa-lockdown-soldiers-accused-of-beating-alexandra-man-to-death-with-sjambok-46619454.

Rashe-Matoti, Phumeza. 'Unbroken Silence'. Unpublished drama script. First performed at the Centre for Humanities Research, University of the Western Cape, 2017.

Ratele, Kopano. 'Apartheid, Anti-Apartheid and Post-Apartheid Sexualities'. In *The Prize and the Price: Shaping Sexualities in South Africa*, edited by Melissa Steyn and Mikki van Zyl, 290–305. Cape Town: HSRC Press, 2009.

Ratele, Kopano. 'Engaging Young Male University Students: Towards a Situated, Social-Psychological Pro-Feminist Praxis'. In *Engaging Youth in Activism, Research and Pedagogical Praxis: Transnational and Intersectional Perspectives on Gender, Sex and Race*, edited by Tammy Shefer, Jeff Hearn, Kopano Ratele and Floretta Boonzaier, 93–109. New York: Routledge, 2018.

Ratele, Kopano. 'Hegemonic African Masculinities and Men's Heterosexual Lives: Some Uses for Homophobia'. *African Studies Review* 57, no. 2 (2014): 115–130.

Ratele, Kopano. 'Masculinities Without Tradition'. *Politikon* 40, no. 1 (2013): 133–156.

Ratele, Kopano. 'What the Latest Police Statistics Don't Tell You About Murder'. *TimesLive*, 25 September 2012, https://www.timeslive.co.za/ideas/2012-09-25-what-the-latest-police-statistics-dont-tell-you-about-murder-ilive/.

Ratele, Kopano. 'Working Through Resistance in Engaging Boys and Men Towards Gender Equality and Progressive Masculinities'. *Culture, Health & Sexuality* 17, suppl. no. 2 (2015): 144–158.

Ratele, Kopano. *The World Looks Like This from Here: Thoughts on African Psychology*. Johannesburg: Wits University Press, 2019.

Ratele, Kopano, Rebecca Helman and Pascal Richardson. 'Attitudes on Gender Equality and Inequality among Parents in South Africa'. In *State of South Africa's Fathers 2021*, edited by Wessel van den Berg, Tawanda Makusha and Kopano Ratele, 134–137. Cape Town and Stellenbosch: Sonke Gender Justice, Human Sciences Research Council and Stellenbosch University, 2021.

Ratele, Kopano and Mzikazi Nduna. 'An Overview of Fatherhood in South Africa'. In *State of South Africa's Fathers 2018*, edited by Wessel van den Berg and Tawanda Makusha, 29–46. Cape Town: Sonke Gender Justice and Human Sciences Research Council, 2018.

Ratele, Kopano and Tamara Shefer. 'Desire, Fear and Entitlement: Sexualising Race and Racialising Sexuality in (Re)membering Apartheid'. In *Race, Memory and the Apartheid Archive: Towards a Transformative Psychosocial Praxis*, edited by Garth Stevens, Norman Duncan and Derek Hook, 188–207. London: Palgrave, 2013.

Kopano Ratele, Shahnaaz Suffla, Lu-Anne Swart and Nick Malherbe. 'Historical Trauma and Structure in Violence Against and by Young Men'. In *Youth in South Africa: Agency, (In)Visibility and National Development*, edited by Ariane De Lannoy, Malose Langa and Heidi Brooks, 353–380. Johannesburg: MISTRA, 2021.

Ratele, Kopano, Ravi Verma, Salvador Cruz and Anisur Rahman Khan. 'Engaging Men to Support Women in Science, Medicine, and Global Health'. *The Lancet* 393, no. 10171 (2019): 609–610.

Ravindran, Sundari. 'Health Implications of Sex Discrimination in Childhood: A Review Paper and an Annotated Bibliography'. Geneva: World Health Organization and United Nations Children's Fund, 1986.

Redman, Peter. 'The Discipline of Love: Negotiation and Regulation in Boys' Performance of a Romance-Based Heterosexual Masculinity'. *Men and Masculinities* 4, no. 2 (2001): 186–200.

Reese, Phillip. 'When Masculinity Turns "Toxic": A Gender Profile of Mass Shootings'. *Los Angeles Times*, 7 October 2019. https://www.latimes.com/science/story/2019-10-07/mass-shootings-toxic-masculinity.

Republic of South Africa. *National Strategic Plan on Gender-Based Violence and Femicide: Human Dignity and Healing, Safety, Freedom & Equality in Our Lifetime*. Pretoria: Republic of South Africa, 2020. https://www.justice.gov.za/vg/gbv/NSP-GBVF-FINAL-DOC-04-05.pdf.

Republic of South Africa. 'Proclamation No. 3 of 2018 by the President of the Republic of South Africa: Judicial Commission of Inquiry to Inquire into Allegations of State Capture, Corruption and Fraud in the Public Sector Including Organs of the State'. *Government Gazette* 631, no. 41403 (2018).

Rogers, Carl R. 'Empathic: An Unappreciated Way of Being'. *Counselling Psychologist* 5, no. 2 (1975): 2–10.

Rogers, Carl R. 'The Therapeutic Relationship: Recent Theory and Research'. *Australian Journal of Psychology* 17, no. 2 (1965): 95–108.

Roopnarine, Jaipaul L. and Kimberly L. Davidson. 'Parent–Child Play Across Cultures: Advancing Play Research'. *American Journal of Play* 7, no. 2 (2015): 228–252.

Rose, Nikolas. *The Psychological Complex: Psychology, Politics and Society in England 1869–1939*. London: Routledge, 1985.

Rule-Groenewald, Candice. '"Just Knowing You Found the Person that You're Ready to Spend Your Life With": Love, Romance and Intimate Relationships'. *Agenda* 27, no. 2 (2013): 30–37.

Saferspaces. 'Toxic Masculinity and Violence in South Africa'. Accessed 21 October 2021. https://www.saferspaces.org.za/u/entry/toxic-masculinity-and-violence-in-south-africa.

SAPA (South African Press Association). 'Malema Says Sorry for Sexist Remarks'. *TimesLive*, 23 June 2011. https://www.timeslive.co.za/news/south-africa/2011-06-23-malema-says-sorry-for-sexist-remarks/.

SAPA (South African Press Association). 'Manyi Criticised'. *SowetanLive*, 5 February 2011. https://mg.co.za/article/2011-02-24-coloureds-overconcentrated-in-wcape-says-manyi/.

Schwendinger, Julia R. and Herman Schwendinger. 'Rape Myths: In Legal, Theoretical, and Everyday Practice'. *Crime and Social Justice* 1 (Spring/Summer 1974): 18–26.

Seale, Lebogang. 'SA Not Ready for Female President – ANCWL'. *IOL*, 9 October 2013. https://www.iol.co.za/news/politics/sa-not-ready-for-female-president-an-cwl-1589121.

Seedat, Mohamed, Ashley van Niekerk, Rachel Jewkes, Shahnaaz Suffla and Kopano Ratele. 'Violence and Injuries in South Africa: Prioritising an Agenda for Prevention'. *The Lancet* 374, no. 9694 (2009): 1011–1022.

September, Chanel. 'The Anene Booysen Story'. *EWN*, 1 November 2013. https://ewn.co.za/2013/10/31/The-Anene-Booysen-Story.

Shefer, Tamara, Jeff Hearn, Kopano Ratele and Floretta Boonzaier, eds. *Engaging Youth in Activism, Research and Pedagogical Praxis: Transnational and Intersectional Perspectives on Gender, Sex and Race*. New York: Routledge, 2018.

Sibembe, Yanga. 'Apartheid Museum Debate Investigates the Black Body as a Site of Oppression'. *Daily Maverick*, 22 March 2019. https://www.dailymaverick.co.za/article/2019-03-22-apartheid-museum-debate-investigates-the-black-body-as-a-site-of-oppression/.

Simpson, Jeffry A. 'Foundations of Interpersonal Trust'. In *Social Psychology: Handbook of Basic Principles*, edited by Arie W. Kruglanski and E. Tory Higgins, 587–607. New York: Guildford Press, 2007.

Smale, Antony. 'As Germany Welcomes Migrants, Sexual Attacks in Cologne Point to a New Reality'. *New York Times*, 14 January 2016. https://www.nytimes.com/2016/01/15/world/europe/as-germany-welcomes-migrantssexual-attacks-in-cologne-point-to-a-new-reality.html.

Smith, David. 'South African Court Finds ANC's Julius Malema Guilty of Hate Speech'. *The Guardian*, 15 March 2010. https://www.theguardian.com/world/2010/mar/15/anc-julius-malema-guilty-hate-speech.

Soble, Alan, ed. *Eros, Agape and Philia: Readings in the Philosophy of Love.* New York: Paragon House, 1989.

Sonke Gender Justice. 'Khwezi Enjoyed It – the Words that Haunt Malema', 9 August 2016. https://genderjustice.org.za/news-item/khwezi-enjoyed-words-haunt-malema/.

South African History Online. 'Marikana Massacre: 16 August 2012'. 16 August 2013. https://www.sahistory.org.za/article/marikana-massacre-16-august-2012#:~:-text=On%2016%20August%202012%2C%20the,of%20the%20miners%20were%20arrested.

South African Police Service. 'Analysis of the National Crime Statistics: Addendum to the Annual Report 2011–2012'. Compiled by SAPS Strategic Management. Pretoria: South African Police Service, 2012. https://www.saps.gov.za/about/stratframework/annualreport/2011_2012/saps_crime_stats_report_%202011-12.pdf.

South African Police Service. *Crime Statistics: Crime Situation in Republic of South Africa (April to March 2019–20).* Accessed 28 March 2022. https://www.saps.gov.za/services/april_to_march_2019_20_presentation/pdf.

South African Police Service. 'SAPS Crimestats'. Accessed 27 October 2021. https://www.saps.gov.za/services/older_crimestats.php.

Spranger, Eduard. 'The Role of Love in Education'. *Universitas* 2, no. 3 (1958): 536–547.

Staff Reporter. 'ANCWL Reiterates Support for Zuma'. *Mail & Guardian*, 13 April 2016. https://mg.co.za/article/2016-04-13-ancwl-reiterates-support-for-president-zuma/.

Staff Reporter. '#THETOTALSHUTDOWN: Memorandum of Demands'. *Mail & Guardian*, 2 August 2018. https://mg.co.za/article/2018-08-02-thetotalshutdown-memorandum-of-demands/.

Statistics South Africa. *General Household Survey, 2018. Statistical Release P0318.* Pretoria: Statistics South Africa, 2019.

Statistics South Africa. *General Household Survey, 2019. Statistical Release P0318.* Pretoria: Statistics South Africa, 2020.

Statistics South Africa. *Inequality Trends in South Africa: A Multidimensional Diagnostic of Inequality.* Report No. 03-10-19. Pretoria: Statistics South Africa, 2019.

Statistics South Africa. *Statistical Release P0211: Quarterly Labour Force Survey Quarter 4: 2010.* Pretoria: Statistics South Africa, 2011.

Statistics South Africa. *Statistical Release P0211: Quarterly Labour Force Survey Quarter 4: 2014.* Pretoria: Statistics South Africa, 2015.

Statistics South Africa. *Statistical Release P0211: Quarterly Labour Force Survey Quarter 4: 2019.* Pretoria: Statistics South Africa, 2020.

Statistics South Africa. *Statistical Release P0341: Victims of Crime: Governance, Public Safety, and Justice Survey*. Pretoria: Statistics South Africa, 2020.

Sternberg, Robert J. 'A Triangular Theory of Love'. *Psychological Review* 93, no. 2 (1986): 119–135.

Swart, Lu-Anne, Sherianne Kramer, Kopano Ratele and Mohamed Seedat. 'Non-Experimental Research Designs: Investigating the Spatial Distribution and Social Ecology of Male Homicide'. In *Transforming Research Methods in the Social Sciences*, edited by Sumaya Laher, Angelo Fynn and Sherianne Kramer, 19–35. Johannesburg: Wits University Press, 2019.

Tamis-LeMonda, Catherine S., Ina Č. Užgiris and Marc H. Bornstein. 'Play in Parent–Child Interactions'. In *Handbook of Parenting, Vol. 5: Practical Issues in Parenting*, edited by Marc H. Bornstein, 221–241. Hillsdale, NJ: Lawrence Erlbaum Associates, 2002.

Tjemolane, Leballo. 'We Need a Lockdown on Toxic Masculinities'. *IOL*, 9 April 2020. https://www.news24.com/news24/columnists/guestcolumn/opinion-a-lock-down-on-toxic-and-outdated-masculinities-needed-more-than-ever-20200409.

Trawalter, Sophie, Kelly M. Hoffman and Adam Waytz. 'Racial Bias in Perceptions of Others' Pain'. *PLoS ONE* 7, no. 11: e48546. https://doi.org/10.1371/journal.pone.0048546.

Trobisch, Eva, dir. *Alles ist gut*. Distributed by Netflix, 2018.

Tromp, Beauregard, Angelique Serrao and SAPA (South African Press Association). 'Tatane Was "Shot Dead"'. *IOL*, 18 April 2011. https://www.iol.co.za/capeargus/tatane-was-shot-dead-1058200.

Tutu, Desmond. 'Forgiveness: "What Do You Do to Forgive Someone?"' Desmond Tutu Peace Foundation. Accessed 14 February 2022. https://www.youtube.com/watch?v=uo2LGGqtjqM.

United Nations Information Centre Pretoria. 'United Nations Strongly Condemns the Rape and Murder of Anene Booysen'. *News & Media*, 13 February 2013. https://archive.is/20130416012306/http://pretoria.unic.org/news-a-media/1-lat-est/2074-united-nations-strongly-condemns-the-rape-and-murder-of-anene-booysen-#selection-423.1-455.34.

Van den Berg, Wessel and Tawanda Makusha, eds. *State of South Africa's Fathers 2018*. Cape Town: Sonke Gender Justice and Human Sciences Research Council, 2018.

Van Niekerk, Ashley, Susanne Tonsing, Mohamed Seedat, Roxanne Jacobs, Kopano Ratele and Rod McClure. 'The Invisibility of Men in South African Violence Prevention Policy: National Prioritization, Male Vulnerability, and Framing Prevention'. *Global Health Action* 8, no. 1 (2015): 1–10. https://doi.org/10.3402/gha.v8.27649.

Veissière, Samuel Paul. 'The Real Problem with "Toxic Masculinity": Why Our Culture Needs Strong and Nuanced Gender Archetypes'. *Psychology Today*, 16 February 2018. https://www.psychologytoday.com/us/blog/culture-mind-and-brain/201802/the-real-problem-toxic-masculinity.

Vetten, Lisa and Kopano Ratele. 'Men and Violence'. *Agenda* 27, no. 1 (2013): 4–11. http://dx.doi.org/10.1080/10130950.2013.813769.

Walby, Sylvia. 'Theorising Patriarchy'. *Sociology* 23, no. 2 (1989): 213–234.

Waling, Andrea. 'Problematising "Toxic" and "Healthy" Masculinity for Addressing Gender Inequalities'. *Australian Feminist Studies* 34, no. 101 (2019): 362–375.

Wikipedia. *FeesMustFall*. Accessed 20 January 2022. https://en.wikipedia.org/wiki/FeesMustFall.

Wikipedia. *Rhodes Must Fall*. Accessed 20 January 2022. https://en.wikipedia.org/wiki/Rhodes_Must_Fall.

Williams, Jodi. 'Militarisation – Our New Response to Societal Issues'. *Daily Maverick*, 15 November 2017. https://www.dailymaverick.co.za/article/2017-11-15-op-ed-militarisation-our-new-response-to-societal-issues/.

Williams, Michele. 'In Whom We Trust: Group Membership as an Affective Context for Trust Development'. *Academy of Management Review* 26, no. 3 (2001): 377–396.

Winnicott, Donald. *The Maturational Processes and the Facilitating Environment: Studies in the Theory of Emotional Development*. London: Routledge, 2018.

Wolfe, Tom. *The Right Stuff*. New York: Farrar, Straus and Giroux, 1979.

Wood, Julia T. 'The Normalization of Violence in Heterosexual Romantic Relationships: Women's Narratives of Love and Violence'. *Journal of Social and Personal Relationships* 18, no. 2 (2001): 239–261.

World Bank. 'The World Bank in South Africa: Overview'. 2019. https://www.worldbank.org/en/country/southafrica/overview#:~:text=South%20Africa%20remains%20a%20dual,increased%20from%200.61%20in%201996.

World Health Organization. *Global and Regional Estimates of Violence Against Women: Prevalence and Health Effects of Intimate Partner Violence and Non-Partner Sexual Violence*. Geneva: World Health Organization, 2013.

World Health Organization. *Policy Approaches to Engaging Men and Boys in Achieving Gender Equality and Health Equity*. Geneva: World Health Organization, 2010.

World Health Organization. *Understanding and Addressing Violence Against Women: Intimate Partner Violence* (Document No. WHO/RHR/12.36). Geneva: World Health Organization, 2012.

Žižek, Slavoj. 'Apparently, Clubs Now Need to Hire Consent Guardians – Clearly We've Misunderstood Human Sexuality'. *Independent*, 31 December 2018. https://www.independent.co.uk/voices/consent-sex-clubs-house-of-yes-consenti-corns-sadomasochism-freud-capitalism-a8705551.html?fbclid=IwAR0U-Ao2TB-VwJMrk9Rw8jIDto3pKxJxayZFG6UhqnCwJV7O_d3J4FPEzQOA.

Zulu, Andile. 'The Heavy Price of Pushing Masculinity'. *Mail & Guardian*, 18 February 2021. https://mg.co.za/opinion/2021-02-18-the-heavy-price-of-pushing-masculinity/.

Zvomuya, Percy. 'Mad, Bad, Breathtaking Balotelli'. *Mail & Guardian*, 9–14 December 2011. https://mg.co.za/article/2011-12-09-mad-bad-breathtaking-balotelli/.

Index

power
    domination and 29–30, 32
    love and 58, 223–226
    masculinity and 183–184, 223–226
    money and 121
    needs and 37
    rape and 104, 189, 194–195
    rights and 116
    sexuality and 158
    violence and 32, 69, 104, 214, 226, 234
practical support 43
premarital sex 5
Presidential Summit on Gender-Based
    Violence and Femicide (GBVF) 56
preventionists, of sexual violence 147
prisons 159–165, 264n4
privacy 61, 70
private property, damage to 103
pro-feminist practice 109–116, 258n7
prominent figures 180, 225
property, damage to 103
protector role of men 194–195
protests 56–57, 70, 97, 108–111, 115, 179,
    260n1, 260n2
psychiatrists 78
psychoanalytic psychology 31, 252n4
psychological violence 26, 83–86, 106,
    205–208
psychologists 75–76, 78
psychosocial death 37
psychosocial development 4, 132–133,
    135–136
'psy-complex' 75
Pule, Tshegofatso 195–196
punishment 34, 46, 160
    see also discipline

Q
quality of relationship 6

R
race 7–9, 12–14, 50, 172–173, 200
race ideas 244–245
racialisation 27, 115–116, 129, 244–245
racism 33–35, 125, 129–130, 172–173, 183,
    203–204, 214, 235–236
racist ideology 235–236
racist masculinity 180

racist patriarchy 90, 129–130
rage and anger 54–55, 101–102, 152–156
Rainers, Jacqueline 174
Ramaphosa, Cyril 56, 210–213
rape
    achievement, to never rape is no 118,
        194–196
    blaming of victims 189
    gender and 26, 115
    myths 125, 185–190
    power and 104, 189, 194–195
    prisons 161–165, 264n4
    silence and 127–131
    stranger rape 69, 174–175
    unrapability 262n5, 269n4
    see also sexual assault
Rape: A South African Nightmare 230
Rashe-Matoti, Phumeza 63, 64–65
reciprocity in relationships 72
recognition 192
recreation *see* play
rejection 20, 47
relationships 75, 77–78, 175, 219–222
religion 34–35, 58, 78, 184, 225
remuneration 105–106
responsibility 48
restrictiveness 203–204
revenge 149–156
revolutionary love 53
#RhodesMustFall movement 108–111,
    260n1, 260n2
Rhodes University 141–144
Richardson, Pascal 145
right (masculinity) stuff 225, 272n4
rights 105, 116
Right Stuff, The (film) 272n4
risk 138–140
Rock, Chris 252n1
Rogers, Carl 77
romantic love *see* sexual love
Rule-Groenewald, Candice 50
rules 217–218
Rwandan genocide 148–152

S
Sapozhnikova, Anya 144–147
science, trust in 135
security companies 134

Printed and bound by CPI Group (UK) Ltd, Croydon, CR0 4YY

09/06/2025

14685795-0001